Inne

Teachings
of the
Golden Dawn

Inner Order
Teachings
of the
Golden Dawn

Pat Zalewski

THOTH PUBLICATIONS
Loughborough, Leicestershire

Cover design by Tabatha Cicero
Additional diagrams by Tommy Westlund.

Printed and bound in Great Britain

Published by
Thoth Publications
64 Leopold Street, Loughborough, LE11 5DN

ISBN 978-1-870450-48-5
web address: www.thoth.co.uk
email: enquiries@thoth.co.uk

Contents

Introduction

The resurrection of the Golden Dawn from moribund esoteric curiosity to the living and working esoteric orders we see today, has been the result of the work of very few people. That such a few can have a key impact on the development of the spiritual lives of thousands is a testament to their work, and the genius behind the Golden Dawn tradition itself.

One of the main players behind this resurrection is Pat Zalewski, who was one the first to show to the public that the Golden Dawn is a complete system of magical training.

Unlike many who have come to the Golden Dawn system through the books of Israel Regardie or Aleister Crowley, Pat trained under some important magicians from the New Zealand Golden Dawn temple Whare Ra. Not only did this Golden Dawn temple remain vibrant after all the others collapsed, it offered its students some of the best esoteric training ever seen. When it did finally die, in the late 1970's some of its senior members went on to train others in the tradition. Pat trained under Jack Taylor who was one of the most experienced ritual magicians that Whare Ra produced.

Fortunately, I was able to see some of these Whare Ra magicians in action, when I joined its side order, the Order of the Table Round. Then, most of the ritual officers were ex-Whare Ra members who applied their knowledge of initiation techniques to this different ritual. While I have been a member of many different groups and experienced many different initiations, I am yet to find a group that could duplicate all that team of officers could do in a single rite. That teaching I found when I read Pat's books for the first time and it has been extremely useful for me in working my own Golden Dawn group.

One thing that people should be aware of, the former adepts of Whare Ra were not a loose lipped bunch. They took their oaths extremely seriously and would not tell anyone anything unless the person asked the right question or showed that they knew what they were talking about. As a result, getting information out of some of them was like getting blood out of a stone. The fact that Pat managed to work with these people and gained their trust is an indication of his stature.

Unfortunately a lot of these old Whare Ra adepts are dead now and much of what Whare Ra has taught has been lost. In the case of Whare Ra, much material was actually burnt by the chiefs when the Order shut its doors. Fortunately, an esoteric order that stands for 70 years leaves bits of paper everywhere, no matter how good its esoteric security.

Pat was able to combine these, with the oral training he received from the Whare Ra members, to make these teachings more than just intellectual chewing gum.

When Pat started to write about the Golden Dawn system, there were few who would have thought that they would see working temples of the tradition. People sniffily said that now that the Golden Dawn had all its rituals and papers published, its contacts had withdrawn and its rites were meaningless.

Pat proved them wrong by setting up his own group in New Zealand and, more to the point, it started to produce adepts. Pat's work was mirrored by those in the US, including Chic and Tabatha Cicero and the results were the same. Now there are countless Golden Dawn temples working throughout the world, with more members than the original founders could even dream of.

For many of the groups that started to work practically, it is Pat's books that became 'must have' manuals.

However, as these groups evolved and their members started attaining the higher grades, there appeared a slight problem that many people were unaware of. What most people considered as being Golden Dawn was actually only the outer order. The rites that started at 0=0 and ended at 4=7 were only preparing the candidate for more important work in the Rosicrucian based 'inner order' which was called the Roseae Rubeae Et Aureae Crucis. Since the largest amount of documentation about this order came from one of its former members, Israel Regardie, we are limited about what we know about this material, by what he knew or was prepared to publish. Regardie only obtained the 5=6 grade and there was much more work above that.

This has led some Golden Dawn groups to either create their own material for an inner order, or look to other groups to provide it with a ritual and teaching structure for the higher grades.

While the Regardie inner order material was not small, it is only the tip of the iceberg for what was available. When a person joined Whare Ra's inner order they were given a mountain of papers and work to get on with. They were given a lot more information in later grades.

However, Whare Ra was not just a paper based order. There was a lot of oral and practical teaching that accompanied that material. This not only unlocked the secrets of the Golden Dawn system, it also provided the magician with a life time of esoteric work.

In this book, Pat has provided both the unpublished paperwork and the oral teachings that reflect, not only his lifetime's work in the Golden Dawn, but the combined experience of Whare Ra's best ritual magicians.

Studying this book will give many Golden Dawn groups a hint of what it is like to be a working GD temple and, more importantly, help evolve the deeper aspects of the tradition.

In releasing this material, Pat will no doubt attract the attention of the Internet-based would-be Grand Magi of the Golden Dawn, who, to justify their own lack of importance in the grand scheme of things, will call him oath breaker or otherwise question his right to publish such teachings. Over the years watching these types attempting to make themselves gods with their vacuous pontifications before their ephemeral and transient students, I can only say that it is just as well that the tradition has some level headed, straight talking people like Pat around to inspire it with proper teaching materials. This book is exactly what you need if you are practically working within the Golden Dawn tradition.

Nick Farrell
Sofia, Bulgaria
August 2005

Preface

When I was first initiated into the Golden Dawn, Jack Taylor, a former Hierophant of Whare Ra temple in New Zealand, told me that he felt that the 5=6 level, as used by Whare Ra and the Stella Matutina was barely adequate for further advancement. Many of the teachings of the grades of 6=5 and 7=4 at Whare Ra were deficient. Minor lectures were handed out with virtually no teaching other than on the mechanics and inner mechanisms of ritual. While this was no small thing in itself it was lacking some of the finer points.

In the Golden Dawn there were two levels of the 5=6. These were the Zelator Adeptus Minor and the Theoricus Adeptus Minor grades. Lectures for these were drawn up by Mathers and Westcott and circulated to the Adepti. When the split in the Golden Dawn occurred, then the Alpha et Omega temples continued with the Mathers system of the sub-grades. The framework or structure of them was simple. Zelator Adeptus Minor grades related to the Neophyte Ritual. The Theoricus Adeptus Minor rank related to the 1=10 Ritual and so on. The 4=7 ritual related to the Philosophus Adeptus Minor Rank. The 6=5 grade studied the Portal and the 7=4 studied the 5=6 Ritual.

The basis for all the Mathers papers in this instance were lectures on the Elemental grades, like the Z1 and Z3, only explaining the mechanics of each of the elemental rituals instead of the 0=0. At Whare Ra, they decided to give this out in the form of an 'Allocution' and this was attached to the Elemental grade rituals. What Felkin gave out, was just as informative as that done by Mathers. At Whare Ra they had more information about the elemental grades than that which those in the Golden Dawn did by the time they got to 5=6. When I reached the Inner Order, Taylor told me to go over the rituals and especially the diagrams and to re-introduce the sub grades of the 5=6. My basic thesis for that was in my previous book *Golden Dawn Ritual and Commentaries*.

I have always been of the opinion that what happens in any else's temple is their business, including their study curriculum. I have had more than one temple head ask me about the teaching of the 6=5 and 7=4 ranks. One claimed he was a 7=4 and then in the same breath was asked if I had any 7=4 papers - as he was never given any. Some temples went up to the 5=6 level with the grades above that being given mainly though for Ego inflation. In the end, the Whare Ra Temple in New Zealand ended up like that, although they did some terrific ritual work. I have worked with people from Whare Ra who got up to 6=5 level and though they were short on scholarship they were big in ritual ability. I realised that everything came back to the practical mechanics of ritual, and what they taught at Whare Ra was right, but it was not good enough. The intellectual aspect had to be understood as well. Taylor knew this and pushed me into this area relentlessly.

People like to know the 'why' of things, and that is one of the reasons I progressed and extrapolated the Mathers concept of grade requirements, using his Theoricus Adeptus Minor level (and other papers I have been privy to) as a template for higher ones. The grades requirement for the 5=6 should be as full as possible, and the study of the sub grades I think is a step in the right direction. That requires going back into the Elemental rituals and looking at them in more thorough context than previously anticipated. When you look at the work of the God forms and the subtle anatomy and how it is utilised in ritual one can only wonder at what more there is left to discover with the Golden Dawn system.

In *Secret Inner Order Rituals of the Golden Dawn* there is outlined the course structure I used between 1982-83 (though the book was published in 1988) on sub grades of the 5=6. This was inferior and was intended merely to take the Theoricus Adeptus Minor teaching and spread them out over the 5=6 level. It was experimental, something I did not use long and it was changed by the time the book was published. Later I decided to go the way Mathers intended and experimented a little, now I have taken it back to the original Mathers/Westcott formulae.

Included in this book are most of the previous unpublished teachings of Mathers for the Theoricus Adeptus Minor grade of the old Golden Dawn. The one manuscript that has been published, though it is hard to get, is a paper that Mathers used called 'Homer's

Golden Chain'. Although I have a full copy of it, the version that was passed around for the Adepti was what I have given here.

I have omitted three Theoricus Adeptus Minor papers from this book. The first is the Ring and Disk which is published by Regardie in his *Complete Golden Dawn* book. The other is the 'Convoluted Forces', which was published in my *Magical Tarot of the Golden Dawn*.

A third paper not listed was on Sidereal Astrology and was an A.O. paper. Up until 1900 the Golden Dawn used the Placidus system of Astrology, and after 1910 they switched to the Sidereal system, which comes from 0 degrees Leo. Francis King discussed this briefly in his 'Ritual Magic in England' and this system will be found in many astrological programes written under the name of D.K. (Alice Bailey's Astral teacher). It can be quite easily worked from a computer, but is something I was never happy with nor found accurate in any shape or form as compared to Placidus. I am unaware at what period of time the D.K.Mathers method of Astrology came into being in the Bailey organisation and can find no early reference to it other than an obscure statement in her 'Esoteric Astrology' that the Zodiac began in Leo.

I have given many additional lectures on diagrams for the Practicus Adeptus Minor level. There are some lectures at this level I have not published though I have included examples to show which direction I am going with my own research. The Practicus Adeptus Minor (P.A.M.) papers presented here are just lectures on Diagrams and are not the entire basis for that grade (though are an important aspect of it) as much of this level revolves around ritual analysis and projection. Some minor examples of this are in my book *Golden Dawn Rituals and Commentaries*. You'll note that I have omitted some diagrams like the Serpent of Wisdom, and I feel Bill Gray's Ladder of Lights more than adequately covers this subject in enough detail. Mathers has explained the Lineal Figures to the Planets enough in the combined lecture of the subject, published in Regardie's Golden Dawn volumes. The two alchemical diagrams taken for the Aesch Mezareph (Purifying Fire) was something that I have stated was 'ad hoc' and felt had no business being placed in the ritual and was based on a series of tabulations. A.E. Waite published a little known lecture on this subject, and this more than covers it. You will find this in the *Hermetic Papers of A.E.Waite*, edited by Bob Gilbert. The 21 page tract goes into enough detail. My own study of Kabbalistic Alchemy is seen from the perpective of the paths, not the Sephiroth, which is included in this text on Alchemy and the Tarot Keys. The other missing diagram for this level is one on Geomancy. Stephen Skinner has exhaustively covered that subject in a couple of excellent books and I doubt much if anyone will go further into the subject than he has. I have taken these at random to show how I approached the study of the sub grades. This is of course to be studied in conjunction with the previous book on Ritual Commentaries. There are couple of other Mathers papers referred to in the ThAM grade that as far as I am aware have not surfaced yet There are mentioned by him in the form as a teaser of 'more will be revealed at the next level'. I have commented on them at the conclusion of the Mathers 1=10 grade analysis. Perhaps one day they will turn up. Another that I know of is the discussion of Sandalphon and Metatron which is lengthy and used at the Grades above 5=6 in the AO and SM temples.

If my work, and that of Mathers, stimulates any ideas for temple chiefs to go further then I have done my job. If those out there can expand on what I have written then I say good luck to them. I am a firm believer in each temple constructing its own teaching, especially for the Inner Order level, providing they are built on the existing Golden Dawn framework. On reflection I do not think that there is a right or wrong methodology to teach the sub grades of the 5=6. They are just ways.

From time to time I have the old 'Oath Breaker' title thrown at me for revealing too much (not that I have really) but would like to inform those (again) that the oaths I took under Jack Taylor were not the same as the Golden Dawn and reworded to suit my particular path. So I have broken nothing! The accusation has a good sounding judgemental Apocalyptic ring to it and why spoil it with the truth getting in the way.

I would further add that I put this book together at a difficult time of my life, but I felt that it needed to be done, and apart from the Ego talking, I hope that there is some sort of message there in its creation. I wish you all luck out there doing the Golden Dawn work.

Finally I would like to thank a number of people who helped me, in their own way, getting this manuscript published. First is Chic and Tabby Cicero for allowing me the privilege of advertising it on their wonderful Golden Dawn web site (www. hermeticgoldendawn.org). To my late friend Bert Beer, who gave me unwavering support from day one, and whom I shared many a pint with. To Richard Dudschus for his Golden Dawn drawings of the trumps we worked on together for years. To my good friends Connel T. and Tony H. who always gave me their best when I asked for it, and even when I did not, and the talented Mary Greer who helped provide me with missing documentation. To Adam McLean a big thank-you for the diagram of Homer's Golden Chain.

A special thanks to Tony Fuller with whom I swapped papers over the years and without whose help this book would not be published. Though he has so far never published a book, and not well known in the public arena, he is one of the most knowledgeable individuals on the Golden Dawn history and technique I have ever come across. I hope one day Tony will publish as he has a lot to offer.

Pat Zalewski
The Rainy Season
Cairns, Australia 2005

Chapter 1

The Universe

The following description from Key 21 is taken from a Mathers paper that written for the Theoricus Adeptus Minor grade of the Golden Dawn. It is Part II ('Of the Tarot Trumps attributed to the Seven Planets') of a larger paper 'Order of the Ritual of the Heptagram'. I extended this paper, and issued it out for the Theoricus Adeptus Minor Grade as part of the explanation of Key 21 for the Practicus Ritual. Mathers had intended to give out more information on each card as one progressed through each level of the 5=6 grade. Though an excellent one, the Mathers paper I thought was too brief. It did manage to cover a few more points not included in the Theoricus Ritual. I added to the original document and elaborated on some of Mathers' explanations. I took this from my own observations, plus works from numerous sources that I came across over the years. Key 21 is a composite of all the Tarot Keys, and, one could easily write a book on the card and just about incorporate all the Golden Dawn ritual diagrams within it.

Part Two

Saturn

To Him is attributed the Twenty-First Key or Trump of the Tarot, known as the 'Universe'. The true design and colouring thereof are as follows:

At the four corners, are the representations of the four Kerubim, which are the vivified powers of the letters of the Name (YHVH) –the four living creatures. Thus, at the top of the left hand corner, the head of the Angel. At the top right hand corner the head of the Eagle: at the bottom right hand corner the head of the Lion: and at the bottom of the left hand the head of the Bull. Opposite, and corresponding to to each of these, there are, in the oval shaped forms, three larger circles, twelve in all. Attributed to the Zodiac signs.

The arrangement of them is, not by triplicities, but in their natural order. Thus opposite the Kerubic signs of the Lion, correspond to the letter Yod, are three larger circles, attributed to the three Zodiac signs of Leo, Virgo and Libra, and so on around the oval, which in part, symbolises the aura of either, the Universe, the Earth or Man, the Microcosm: and within each of these larger circles, are six smaller ones, two of which are attributed to the planet of each of the three decantes of that particular sign, and related to the positive and negative forces of the planet. Thus, in the first of the larger circles corresponding to the Sign of Leo, there are six smaller circles, of which two are referred to Saturn, two to Jupiter and two to Mars, and so on around the oval.

The representations of the heads of the Kerubs shall be depicted in the elemental colours and the details of markings shall be in the complementary or Flashing colours. Thus the head of the Bull shall be in black, with white markings. The head of the Angel is yellow and purple. The head of the eagle in blue and orange. The head of the lion in flame scarlet and green. The other twelve signs shall be in the colours of the sign of the Zodiac in the colours of the (paths) King Scale. The seventy two smaller circles in the colours of the planets - one of each pair in the colours of the King Scale and the other in that of the Queen Scale respectively.

This Oval symboliseth, amongst other things, the ring of the binding limitation, which, even in fancy, they cannot pierce. For the material Universe, it typifieth the ring which is termed Ring Pass Not: and for each material man the limitations of his senses, and which, in our planetary system, is typified by the ring of the planet Saturn - and all this under the control of the four elemental letters of the Great Name YOD HEH VAU HEH. Within the oval, is the Qabalistic queen, Isis of nature, shown as a female form of great beauty, nude, save for a green scarf that floats around her. Her long hair is in flowing golden locks, symbolic of the gold of the Sun, and she is crowned with the Lunar crescent in silver.

In her left hand she holds a green wand with a red tip and bands, pointed upwards to receive form above the influence of Gedulah or Chesed, and in her right hand she has a red wand with a green tip and bands, representing the influence of Geburah. She bears, traced over her, the Signet Star of the Venus,which symbolises the seven Churches which be in Asia or Assiah.

Another title of this key of the Universe is the 'Great One of the Night of Time'.

End of Mathers transcription

Part Two
Planetary Association to the 72 Smaller Circles

Letter of Name	Sign	Decante	Number	Angel	Colour
Yod	Leo	Saturn	1	Vahuaiah	Indigo
			2	Yelavel	Blackish Red
		Jupiter	3	Saitael	Violet
			4	Nghelamiah	Blue
		Mars	5	Mahashiah	Scarlet
			6	Lelahel	Scarlet Red
	Virgo	Sun	7	Akaiah	Orange
			8	Kethethel	Yellow Gold
		Venus	9	Hazeyael	Emerald Green
			10	Eladiah	Emerald
		Mercury	11	Leviah	Yellow
			12	Hihaiah	Orange
	Libra	Moon	13	Lezalel	Blue
			14	Mebahael	Violet
		Saturn	15	Harayel	Indigo
			16	Hoqamaih	Blackish Red
		Jupiter	17	Laviah	Violet
			18	Keliel	Blue
Heh	Scorpio	Mars	19	Livoiah	Scarlet
			20	Pheleliah	Scarlet Red
		Sun	21	Nelakhel	Yellow
			22	Yeiael	Yellow Gold

		Venus	23	Malahel	Emerald Green
			24	Hahauiah	Emerald
	Sagittarius	Mercury	25	Nethhiah	Yellow
			26	Heeiah	Orange
		Moon	27	Irthel	Blue
			28	Sehaiah	Violet
		Saturn	29	Rayayel	Indigo
	Capricorn		30	Eviamel	Blackish Red
		Jupiter	31	Lekabel	Violet
			32	Vesheriah	Blue
		Mars	33	Yechuivah	Scarlet
			34	Lehahaiah	Scarlet Red
		Sun	35	Keveqaiah	Orange
Vav			36	Mendiel	Yellow Gold
	Aquarius	Venus	37	Anaiel	Emerald Green
			38	Chaamaih	Emerald
		Mercury	39	Reheael	Yellow
			40	Yeizael	Orange
		Moon	41	Kehihel	Blue
			42	Mikhael	Violet
	Pisces	Saturn	43	Vavaliah	Indigo
			44	Iihaiah	Blackish Red
		Jupiter	45	Saelaiah	Violet
			46	Ngharaiel	Blue

		Mars	47	Asiaah	Scarlet
			48	Mihel	Scarlet Red
	Aries		49	Uhauel	Scarlet
			50	Deneyael	Scarlet Red
		Sun	51	Kechasheiah	Orange
			52	Amamiah	Yellow Gold
		Venus	53	Nanael	Emerald Green
			54	Nithael	Emerald
Heh (F)	Taurus	Mercury	55	Mibahaiah	Yellow
			56	Pviael	Orange
		Moon	57	Nemamaiah	Blue
			58	Yeuileel	Violet
		Saturn	59	Herachael	Indigo
			60	Metzrael	Blackish Red
	Gemini	Jupiter	61	Vamibael	Violet
			62	Iahahel	Blue
		Mars	63	Nghaneavel	Scarlet
			64	Mochaiel	Scarlet Red
		Sun	65	Dambaiah	Orange
			66	Mengal	Yellow Gold
	Cancer	Venus	67	Aiael	Emerald Gold
			68	Chbeoiah	Emerald
		Mercury	69	Rohael	Yellow
			70	Yebamaiah	Orange
		Moon	71	Heyaiel	Blue
			72	Mevamiah	Violet

Part Three
The Oval
'Ring Pass Not'

When Mathers associated the 'Ring Pass Not' to the oval spheres of the Twenty-First Key, it opened a door to an entirely new dimension in meaning to this Key:

> *The Ring-Pass-Not is a term (used both Macrocosmic and Microcosmicly PZ) to denote the periphery of the sphere of influence of any central life force, and is applied equally to all atoms of the Solar System. The Ring-Pass-Not of the average human being is the spherotical form of his (or her) Mental Body, which extends considerably beyond the physical and enables him (or her) to function on the lower levels of the Mental Plane.*
> *(Treatise of Cosmic Fire –Alice Bailey)*

The Ring-Pass-not is a division or separation between the external and Internal systems. It is shown in this Key by the 12 larger circles. From the outside of the circles to boundaries of this Key we have the energy of the 'Ring Chaos'. It is classed as a source of devolution. It is a spinning force –sometimes considered negative. It is a reactionary force forming the Ring of the Cosmos (shown by the four beasts). The 'Ring Cosmos' is shown by the 72 smaller circles and its primary objective is to let in and filter rays that come into our solar system. Now you have the 'Ring Chaos' pushing outwards and the 'Ring Cosmos' pushing inwards. The point between each is the Ring-Pass-Not. This is the holding point of neutrality between the forces of Expansion and Contraction - shown in the larger 12 circles.

The influence of these three rings is not static and they are constantly counter-balancing each other. The Ring-Pass-Not, acting as a type of buffer for unwanted energy and returning it back to its source. For this is the founding principle on which esoteric evolution is based. Dion Fortune, in her book *Cosmic Doctrine* says:

> *You will perceive that each phase of evolution begets an organised system of forces. These forces react to all influences that play upon them, and they register the*

reaction in the movements of space that are under their influences. They are therefore sentient, because they react and register through experience. So that even the three primal rings are sentient and capable of development, but they are so vast, these rings, and so simple (because the influences that act upon them are so few) that the individuality, though it exceeds the span of all imagination, is exceedingly primitive. Yet it is upon this vast and simple type that your individuality is built up. Therefore, it is that you - small as you are – have your affinities with those cosmic beings and are influenced by their phases, form the 'absolute' down to the atom of your own earth. This it is which in essence is the Secret Wisdom. For uninitiated man is acted upon by these forces, but the Initiate, by his knowledge, transcends their influence, and uses them for his own ends. Should his ends be those of the cosmic evolution, he grows and delivers though all its phases till he attains that static condition which is completeness and, following the laws of the great organisms of which he is now one, he gives rise to a system.

It is important to note that there are 12 fundamental rays - colours of the spheres, and the motion of the Ring Cosmos gives rise to the seven circles shown by the Heptagram over the figure. From the circle of the Ring-Pass-Not are the twelve rays.

The angels of the months equate to the Theosophical 'Lords of Flame'. They work on motion - mainly on magnetism, reaction and vibration. Underneath them, are the 'Lords of Form' and below them the 'Lords of Mind'. The angels, as Lords of Form, are prime movers for if the Ring-Pass-Not is associated to this card - all its implications must be considered as well. Each of these three main Lords work on the seven planes, as shown by the Heptagram. They all in turn influence the 'Swarms', or souls incarnating on this planet. Within each ray or globe, the 'Lords of Flame' rule the 'Lords of Form' and 'Mind'. The Heptagram here has yet another layer of meaning, the points are all related to Cosmic Laws:

Number	Sign	Colour	Angel of the Month
1	Aries	Scarlet	Machidiel
2	Taurus	Red-Orange	Asmodel
3	Gemini	Orange	Ambriel
4	Cancer	Amber	Muriel
5	Leo	Greenish Yellow	Verchiel
6	Virgo	Yellow Green	Hamaliel
7	Libra	Emerald Green	Zuriel
8	Scorpio	Green Blue	Barbiel
9	Sagittarius	Blue	Advachiel
10	Capricorn	Indigo	Hannael
11	Aquarius	Violet	Cambriel
12	Pisces	Ultra Violet Crimson	Barchiel

Law of Action and reaction-equal and opposite.
Law of Polarity
Law of Impaction (transmissions of the action of one plane into another.)
Law of Attraction of the Centre.
Law of Attraction to Outer Space.
Law of Limitation.
Law of the Seven Deaths.

The action of each of the twelve spheres is the key and can be either positive or negative, depending on the phase the ring is in juxtaposition with each other.

The Oval
'The Cosmic Egg'

The Spheretical symbol of the Oval or Egg shown on this Key shows a new birth state. From this state, we have the three-fold principle of the ancients. The first is the Gaea or Mother concept associate to the earth. The second is the emergence of Man on earth. The third is the Soul of Man - Adam Kadmon, the Perfected Man, and the emergence of Kronis (time). Using the Greek reality as a model, we have with time, an Alpha et Omega - a Beginning and an End. This relates to the quality of opposites. The Wands held in the hands of the Dancing Figure are symbolic of these concepts. We should look at the formation of the World Egg on the Pottery Wheel of the Egyptian deity Ptah. The emergence of both Seb and Nut, are one such example. In Greek myths we have the birth of Caster and Pollux. Basilius Valentinus says: 'I am the Egg of Nature, known to the Sages only…'

From the Hindu pantheon we have a parallel when we look at the Egg of Brahman. Plutarch stated that the image of the Oval-Egg is like a mini universe. The figure in the centre of the egg can represent the embryo or pre birth state of things to come and represents the concept of potentiality. The figure within the Oval can be linked with the Aspiring Adept and the reflective power within. The Oval is now transformed into yet another level and becomes the auric boundaries of the Self which can only be seen with the Third Eye or Brow Chakra. The figures trapped within the Egg shows a figure in a transparent alchemical vessel - showing the way of promise - the cloaked layer around the figure (scarf) reflecting the colours of the experiment. There is a link with the broken Egg and the figure then represents the attainment of unity with the macrocosm around us. Both meanings show different aspects of the Spiral - whether one is Ascending or Descending.

Manley Palmer Hall states:

The Auric Egg is so complex in its structure that all the descriptions which applies to the Universal System' is equally applicable to the Human Auric Envelope. Within man's aura are the zones and belts, the stars, the planets,

and the elements, the gods the angels and the demons.
Man is a universe, and at his present state of
development, his physical personality is a golden embryo
suspended within a brilliant shell of his auric sheaths.
As the Rosicrucians would say he is a proper womb
quickly preparing himself to come glorious forth with
all the radience and beauty of the orphic phanes

So within the Oval of the Twenty-First Key, its mysteries are multi-layered. Paul Foster Case makes the point that the measurement of the Sphere is five units by eight high, the number of the squares on the wall of the Vault of the Adepti. The Heptagram shows that the seven sides express these so seven expresses the Oval and zodiac circles.

Twenty first Key
and the Holy Oblation
The Foundation of the Geometric
Pattern of the Universe

Holy Obligation

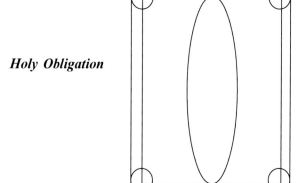

The basic structure of the Twenty-First Key comes from the ground plan of the Heavenly Temple of Jerusalem. The four beasts of that vision are equated with what is described in the Apocalypse, with the four Gospels (see Ms Add. 18633 British Library). For the mathematical equation of this, Ezekiel states that the sides of the celestial city are 25,000 reeds. Divided by the number of the 12 Tribes this comes to 375. This figure is combination of the Sun's orbit - together with that of Venus (according to the old Egyptian system). The orbit of Saturn, being 2,046, the diameter of the Sun. This is contained within the outer square of the diagram. The outer square being 2083 and one third. This shows the Holy Oblation is a square enclosed by 2 lines and is represented by the number 2083 and one third (mean dimension). The outer line will measure 2093. A circle within a square (whole sides are 1480) relates to the firmament of the heavens. The Christeos has the Greek numerical value of 1480 - the measurement of the God's body. The Greek numeration of the five planets comes to 3976 (one less than the radius of circle 25,000 units in circumference).

'That great city, the Holy Jerusalem descending out of the heaven' is called 'The bride of the lamb's wife, and her light was like unto a stone most precious, even like a jasper stone clear as crystal'. This is the Bride of the kabbalah (kalah) under the figure of the Heavenly city. The Vesica here corresponds with the four circles (Mercury's orbit). The circumference of the two circles being nearly 360 – the heavenly Equator and Elliptic. In the 2nd Chapter of Numbers, the four corners relate to the encampment around the Tabernacle (four companies of three tribes each. The planets have a built in maths in proportion to the figure.

The Dancing Figure and the Twenty-First Key

The figure in the Twenty-First Key, we are told in the 2=9 ritual that she is 'Kallah the Bride' – the Bride of the Microssopus. This is the 'restored Kingdom' after the Kings of Edom unbalanced the first 'perfected Kingdom'. Expressed in the geometric terms of the Tree of Life the two following diagrams show the figure in the before and after the Fall.

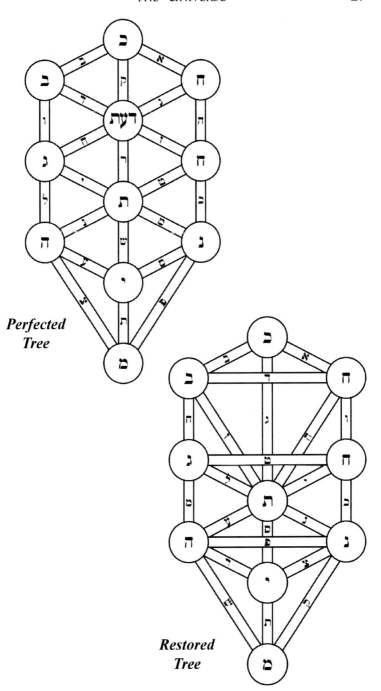

Perfected Tree

Restored Tree

In the Perfected Tree, Daath was a Sephirah and Malkuth was not attached. The emanations reached into the Supernal. In order for the Tree to survive, it had to accept 'Kallah the Bride' from the lower echelon of the Tree. By accepting Kallah, the Tree had to accept matter, for Kallah was both. Daath was then closed and the Abyss was then implemented. Kallah is the entranceway to the Tree, through the World of Assiah - our world and she shows us the way. The destruction of the perfected Tree was due to the premature openings of the Chakras. With Kallah now on the restored Tree, a safety check is now there to prevent these unbalanced energies erupting again. She shows us the way to the correct path for enlightenment.

The Heptagram traced over the figure is a reminder, and alludes to the fact that the aspirant will have to accept her way and conditions before she will grant access to the Higher Realms - initiated above her. She is constantly on guard against the Qlippothic shells of the Lower Tree, now under her control, shown by the rods of balance that she holds. She is balancing the entire energy of the Tree through the lower Sephiroth, represented by one aspect of the Heptagram. The Jews consider their Torah to be likened to an aspect of the Shekinah (upper Tree) for the Dancing Figure reflects these ideals as well. In the book *On the Kabbalah and its Symbolism*:

> *The Torah releases a word and emerges it from her sheath and then quickly hides herself again. This she does for those who know her...The Torah is alike a beautiful woman, hidden in a secret chamber, in her palace, with a secret lover...This lover constantly passes through the gate of her house, searching for her...She opens her chamber door and reveals her face to him but for an instant - he alone sees it.*

The figure in the Twenty-First Key is clothed in a scarf. The scarf is important here for this represents the allegorical (teaching) words in Kabbalistic doctrine. Once this is understood she will then reveal her full self to the initiate and the secrets that this implies, for only then will her true meaning be revealed. The figure, as Kallah, is in a form reminiscent of the Shekinah, which some consider her a lesser aspect of her divine energies. The colour of the scarf (according to Mathers) is green, an aspect of the earth element and Assiah. For green is the colour of nature-growth, and this is what she promises. Because the figure is dancing, she is dancing in a pre-arranged step. It is this step that the aspirant must seek to learn to emulate, for without knowledge of it, she will not reveal her secrets. As the Dancer, she is 'Isis of Nature', and the aspirant must travel in the 'footsteps of nature' before he can understand her, or to travel to the upper reaches of the Tree. But the study of her must be balanced, shown by the wands. Kallah is much the 'Princess of Assiah'. The Katha Upanishad states (3.12):

Though hidden in all things
The world soul shines not forth;
Yet is seen by subtle seers
Of superior, subtle intellect.

The Golden hair that Mathers attributed to the figure is a reflection of the light of Tiphareth, which in turn, reflects to the Heptagram. It shows luminosity, the enlightened state of awareness. This is the Philosophical Gold of the alchemists. It is the golden sun over the green nature that inspires warmth and growth. Her dancing implies (as a rehearsed step) ritual. She shows the way to rise up through the Tree which is like the initiatory steps of ritual and study. The feet in the figure represents Malkuth, but one foot has risen, which implies advancement up the Tree. The rising foot is there ready to tread on the Qlippothic elements lest they get too close.

The allegorical alchemical aspects should be understood as well. The Figure is Mercury, shown by its outline, the lunar current above and the crossed feet below.

Mercury

As Mercury, we have the figure as the Divine essence imprisoned in matter. He/She is now the androgenous character that is present in the beginning of the Work (Key 0) and the end (Key 21). When Key 21 is looked at in terms of ascent, this process is then reversed. The figure is the Primea Materia or first matter of the alchemists, and the state of the Nigrido - the Blackening step of alchemy where the first stage Purification/Transformation has begun. The figure shows, or rather represents the Separation process and the Conjunction, both at the same time. Mercury is representative of motion, hence another reason why the figure is dancing (continuous movement). The figure is the 'Anima Mundi' the 'World Soul' or Spirit within all things. The association of this Key to both Saturn and Earth is relevant here for this is the densist part of the work, The elusive Spirit is now either, seen, glimpsed or felt. The layers around her must be peeled off like that of an onion. The Heptagram before her shows that while she is glimpsed, there are seven alchemical stages to go through before she is met.

1. Calcination
2. Sublimation
3. Solution
4. Putrefaction
5. Distillation
6. Coagulation
7. Tincture/Lapidication

These are the planing stages of the work that the figure requires. Though they are not all undergone in Key 21, they are planned out here. Each stage is placed in the correct order. The figure has shown herself in part, but before unification, the practical steps must be undertaken first. She brings awareness and order to the aspirant that wishes to climb the tree. As mentioned earlier, the green of nature must be understood first before the gold is reached.

The gold though is reflected from Yesod and Tiphareth, and even if her Crown is taken, it is but one step of transformation

The Oval shape around the figure is no accident, for this is a symbol of the hermetic vessel that has sealed in its essence the Lunar symbol above the head of the figure which can be taken both as a part of and a force external to the figure. This is the 'Regimen of Lunar', the joining of both the winged and the wingless dragon (of the zodiac) with the Virgin Queen. (Kallah the Bride) with the King, shown by the points of the Heptagram which represents the 'Lords who wander'. Once they are joined they must be separated as well. This is the secret doctrine of the Emerald Tablet in which the 'above' must join the 'below'.

Origin of the Dancing Figure

One of the main origins of the Dancing Figure is from the Roman Ceres and the Greek Demeter, mother of Persephone. The old concept of this Key was a garland of flowers or wheat surrounding the figure. According to one legend, Persephone was raped near Mt. Nyssa, which in hermetic terms is equated with Mt. Abgigenus – the Mountain of the Adepts. The rape shows the extreme way and symbolises a sacrifice so that she could enter the next world – typified as the underworld. Numerous portraits show the myth of Demeter and Persephone; they are shown holding torches, usually two, sometimes more. The origin of the two rods held by the figure appear to be torches bringing in the Light, as Demeter searches for reunification with her daughter. The link with the myths is with Hecate the Moon goddess, for the Moon applies to Persephone and Diana. We must remember that during the Ceres/Demeter time in the Underworld no crops were grown. The old concept of using wheat as an oval around the figure mirrored their own journey for with wheat it lies fallow in the ground during winter and comes out in spring. This is yet another reminder of the dark period of nil growth, hence the wands/torches of light are to guide us.

In the Eleusian mysteries the instruction was clear, a single ear of grain-initiation, which is the entireity of Key 21. Demeter instructs us in following the footsteps of nature for our growth. The time of Persephone with Hades in the Underworld is a variant of the theme of death and rebirth. The Golden Dawn, by placing the 12 Signs (symbolising one year) relates to the cyclic format of nature that influences the figure:

> Aries: Spring-rising of temperatures and growth, buds bursting and the rising of sap.
> Taurus: Rapid growth where sap is strongest.
> Gemini : Sap giving off fragrance, growth.
> Cancer: Maximum growth, consolidation.
> Leo: Swelling of fruit to a ripening state
> Virgo: Gradual drying of vegetation and harvesting.
> Libra: Division of the harvest.
> Scorpio: Downward growth - plants decomposing
> Sagittarius: Start of plant growth under the soil.
> Capricorn: Fertilisation of soil
> Aquarius: New life in roots
> Pisces: New Growth

All of this seen from the perspective of nature shows the concept of growth as seen in the cyclic performance of nature. The steps of Demeter guided by the torch light to find her nature. Shelley's song of Proserpine (Persephone) typifies this :

> *Sacred Goddess, Mother earth,*
> *Thou form whose immortal bosom,*
> *Gods, and men, and beasts gave birth,*
> *Leaf and blade, and bud and blossom,*
> *Breathe they influence mist divine,*
> *Own thine own child Proserpine.*

The myth of Demeter is her journey to find her off spring with Light guiding her journey. For the aspiring Adept the journey is similar, the light being the guide to the end. It is an entrance to the Labyrinth of the Tree of Life, a journey where the Adept will face his darkest hours as he faces his fears as he searches for his reunification with the Self. By following Nature with its cyclic spiral it reflects the soul search and the many different levels of the Tree. The Golden Dawn, by extending the original wreath concept to encompass the Zodiac takes Nature in Microcosm and expands it to the Macrocosm of the Stars themselves. It widens the scope of the card from the 'World' to the 'Universe'.

The entire structure of Key 21 shows balance and to live in the realm of the mortals and gods of the Underworld one cannot remain both and balance must be maintained for proper study. In a single Tree Malkuth is the World of Assiah and is part Assiah and part Yetsirah, hence the dual association of the figure leaving one world to enter another. The Dancing figure walks out of Malkuth and the material world of Assiah. This is the journey of Demeter into the Underworld. Her daughter's name Persephone means 'Light' or 'search of Light'. Here she explores her own fears holding the wands to light the way. Light brought into darkness. The descent into darkness shows her descent into the material state of mortality, where birth and death are a regular occurrence. Trying to find the Light (her daughter) in Darkness and bring it out into the material world, shows the climb to a higher level of Yetsirah –the Astral/ Mental World. Since Demeter knows that Persephone's visits to the Underworld are regular ones, her daughter must find her way out again after each visit. This is the constant cycle of death and rebirth as the Soul (Demeter) searches for Light in each existence. The Upraised leg of the figure shows the withdrawal from the world of Assiah. The Moon above her is the Astral - that shows the light to the figure. Demeter as Ceres, was a sorceress that transformed men into swine, showing magical power reflected in the wands she holds. For the light instead of showing the way is now used as a power source.

If we look further back into the pre-Demeter myth associated with the dancing figure, we might find a possible origin in the Babylonian story of Ishtar's descent into the Kingdom of Hades. Here entrance to Hades is like an initiation ceremony. The Queen of Hades, Allatau, tells the gate keeper that Ishtar is to be treated like any other who comes.

At the 1st gate her crown is removed

At the 2nd gate her earrings are removed.

At the 3rd gate her necklace is removed.

At the 4th gate the ornaments around her breasts are removed.

At the 5th gate her waist girdle is removed.

At the 6th gate her bracelets are removed from her
                          hands and feet.

At the 7th gate her robe is removed.

These seven gates remind us of the Heptagram over the Dancing figure. Ishtar, Queen of Heaven reminds us of the descent of Metatron into Sandalphon. Like Masonry, the seven gates show the gradual loss of the material so that one can seek the spiritual. The Lunar cresent she wears in this instance stands for the Queen of the Underworld, Allatu, for through Heaven is in the realms of Allatu, Ishtar was rescued by Nadushu –Namir (a sphinx like creature-man/lion). In this instance we have the four Kerubs of the card guarding Ishtar. She then returns through the same seven gates she entered by – retrieving all her possessions on her journey upwards. Another pre-Hellinic myth is from Robert Graves's *Greek Myths*;

> *In the beginning, Eurynome, the goddess of all things, rose naked from Chaos but nothing substantial for her feet to rest upon, and therefore divided the sea from the sky, dancing lonely upon its waves. She danced towards the South and the Wind set in motion. Behind her some things seemed new and apart which to begin the work of creation. Wheeling about she got hold of the North Wind and rubbed it between her hands, and behold! The great Serpent Ophion, Eurynome danced to warm herself wildly and more wildly, until Ophion had grown lustful and coiled about her (she laid the universal egg). Out tumbled all things that exist, her children, Sun, Moon and planets and stars... Earth and living creatures... (later Ophion) vexed her by claiming to be the author of the Universe, forthwith she bruised his hand with her heel.*

Though part of the Universe card it is much like the Crowley description of his version of this Key though both are one and the same.

The Twin Wands of the Dancing Figure

It would be impossible to study the Dancing Figure in the Twenty-First Key without relating it to Shiva, the Indian God of Destruction, equated with Saturn. He is often depicted seated, with a Luna crescent on his forehead and holding a trident, His spiritual function is to wipe out incurred karmic debts. The destruction aspect associated to him is not only wiping out karma but the negative traits of the personality that holds him back. One can hardly talk about Shiva without bringing in his other half, Durga 'the impenetrable' - his consort. Both of these deities are part and parcel of the same concept. Durga is linked to Kali. She is shown riding a lion, representing power held in check and not as yet unleashed. As Kali, Druga is both the destructive and creative principle. Kali represents the vital force (Shatki) that awakens Shiva from his meditations. The heads he was shown with represented the false values the enlightened Soul must work through.

The two wands represents the two outer channels that help stabilise the Kundaline energy when it rises through the seven chakras, the points of the Heptagram. The left wand is analogous to the IDA and the right hand to the PINGALA, the two channels that the rising Kundaline ascends through. The complementary colours (red and green) of the wands shows that each wand reflects the power of its opposite. The IDA and PINGALA actually end or join at a spot between the eyebrows - the top point of the Heptagram.

The Dancing Figure is considered by many as the rising Kundaline itself and it's visions are from Indian mystics, such as Gopi Krishna. Of here when he underwent the kundaline experience that have perpetuated the connection of the dancing figure with the Kundaline archetype.

It is the experience of joy and ecstasy that makes the figure dance – due to the stimulation and rising, activated about by initiation. The four beasts are likened to the four petals of the base chakra. So the entire card could be sent to act as a blueprint for the kundaline energy - activated by stimulation.

The Wand being symbols of the initiatory process can be judged on four basic levels.

1. Stimulation of the latent power within.
2. Synthesizing these powers so that they are activated in balance to each other.
3. To increase your overall vibratory rate within matter so the force above you will empathise with the force above you that you wish to contact.

4. Expansion of the Subtle bodies - especially the
Causal, that represents the fourfold nature of the
initiation through the wands of power.

The Lunar Crescent

The image of the Lunar Crescent (a half circle) historically is
inseparable from the circular symbol of the Sun. The Lunar crescent
being the lower half of the Solar disk showing the symbol of
reflected light. Its position to Yesod, on the Tree of Life, where it
reflects the Light of Tiphareth seems to equate with the old symbol
given above. There is a strong link here right back to ancient
Babylon which links in with the Saturn myths. Ninurta, the old
Babylonian name for Saturn (which was often depicted as a
scimitar or sickle) and the weapon was called Sraursargar 'who
governs the cosmos' and babbanulla 'hurricane which spares
nothing'. It is this crescent shaped weapon used in mythology as
that of the destroyer. With every form of death comes renewal.
So the Lunar crescent is linked, firmly with Saturn (The Egyptians
called this sword a khepesh 'two hand to heaven').

It is interesting to note, that almost without exception, that all the
old goddesses of the Moon were Earth goddesses as well. The
dual association here is to link the earth and its satellite, for one
does not move without the other. A symbol of the circle of the
Moon, an enclosed crescent represents the island of the beginning
(in ancient texts) – earth. Within the Luna influence we have the
dual situation revolving between Light and darkness. This state is
reflected by the twin wands held by the figure, the crescent symbol
being above and central to each. The wands in turn are related to
Janus, the two faced god, sometimes depicted with a sky hat and
whose identity is linked to both Saturn.

The crescent symbol is representative of the barque of Saturn in
his primordial around the earth. The lunar symbol is now shown as
a barque. It is worth noting that this is shown in many old coins
which had Janus's face on the reverse side. The Lunar crescent
symbol represents the Egyptian symbol of the Egyptian 'Ka' , an
almost identical image of the Golden Dawn Theoricus Sign, which
is roughly translated as a double image. Florence Farr says of the
'Ka' in her book *Egyptian Magic*:

> *The Ka could progress in its celestial evolution,
> just as the body could progress in its terrestrial
> evolution...For the Ka or Ego can only grow and
> become potent through ardent patient
> perseverance and struggle.*

The 'Ka' of course, equates with an aspect of the spiritual nature of man. The upraised hands are a sign of protection. As a matter of coincidence the Egyptian word for 'Ka" and 'bull' are the same. The upraised hands can be compared with the wings. This in turn links to the winged goddess Nut, goddess of the heavens who shows the flight of the spiritual nature away from the material.

The wings and the sky ship (barque) are analogous to each other. In studying the 21st Key you will see that the point of the Heptagram rests in the pineal gland or brow chakra of the figure. This is in turn shows the awakened state of awareness within the figure, shown by the golden hair. The brow chakra rules the past lives and makes the individual aware of karmic debt. For this is the Slayer aspect of the Luna symbolism. The dark hidden side that is unrevealed, only reflected by our actions.

The Heptagram and its relationship to the Seven Churches of the Apocalypse

In the Theoricus ritual, we are told that in the Twenty-First Key, by way of analogy, is likened to the Seven Churches of the Apocalypse. If we examine the Heptagram traced over the Dancing Figure (a symbol in this instance of the Higher Self) we are then shown the Seven Churches interacting with the figure. Because the points are placed out of the figure that they are related to the seven points in man – the Chakras. However, to simply give a description of these chakras and leave it at that is too simplistic. The real key in this focus is the Seven Churches and it is my proposal to examine them and their effect. It must be considered that what we have here is an initiatory process of the soul, through Assiah, the material world, hence the references to the palaces of Assiah in the ritual description of this Key. Though the World of Assiah relates to the experinces of the soul, we must be reminded that the glands and chakras work through the triple process of Mind-Body-Spirit.

Church of Ephoses - Base Chakra

If we examine the Biblical geography of the Churches in Asia

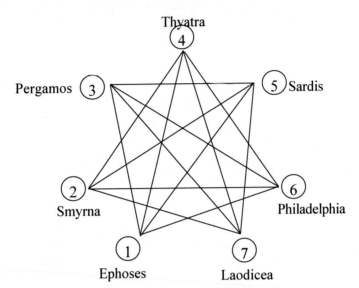

Number	City	Beast	Seal	Governs	Chakra
1	Ephoses	Bull	White Horse	Desire Lust	Base
2	Smyrna	Man	Black Horse	Temptation	Sacral
3	Pergamos	Eagle	Red Horse	Re-enforcement	Solar Plexus
4	Thyatra	Lion	Pale Horse	Learning Past Lessons	Heart
5	Sardis		Souls slain	Access to Higher Mind	Throat
6	Phildelphia		Upheavals	Awareness	Brow
7	Laodicea		Silence	Higher Communication	Crown

Minor, then we will find that each church corresponds to a point in the Heptagram. The lowest geographical church corresponds with the lowest point in the Heptagram. This point represents the City of Ephoses. This is related to the Base Chakra, and some have associated it with the gonads in man. In Chapter 2 of the Apocalypse, there is a reference to hating the deeds of the Nicolatiatans. This is relevant here, for if one looks at the function of this group it will be shown that is sexually orientated in its theology and its abhorrence of it, and dedication to purity of the Body and Spirit. This is the general area covering Desire and Lust, for this church teaches us to look higher than our own humanity and overcome desire. Control of this centre or chakra, is in a psycho spiritual state, which relates to healing and harmony, in both the material and spiritual. This is further reflected by the Winged Bull in the Twenty-First Key, for the Bull is the closest animal to that point in the Heptagram.

Church of Smyrna - Sacral Chakra

Going clockwise, the next point on the Heptagram relates to Smyrna and the Sacral chakra. Its spiritual teachings is that we must go through trial and tribulations to understand man's purpose on this earth. The virture is Suffering and the faults are Insincerity. What man must learn to handle here is Temptation. The reference in the Apocalypse is the second death and relates to a relapse into the old ways so that the first lesson has to be learnt again and again, with the cycle restarting until the lesson is learned. The ten day period referred to in the Biblical text relates to a complete cycle of the Tree of Life. A new period of Purification. The reward for the Purification process undergone, is the Crown of Life. The State of Perfection –shown by the corner beast on the Key as Man.

Church of Pergamos - Solar Plexus Chakra

The third point of the Heptagram is the Church of Pergamos and this is linked to the Solar Plexus chakra and the adrenal glands. By analogy, it is related to the Eagle, the next beast on the card (going clockwise) on the right corner of the Twenty-First Key. The Solar Plexus chakra relates to impulse activity (uplifting or rising movement). Some of its major functions are its effects on other glands. In short, it acts as a catalyst to other centres, through Meditation and any form of other such attunement. It acts a release mechanism for latent forces in the body to manifest to both positive and negative.

Church of Thyatria - Heart Chakra

The fourth point of the Heptagram is the Church of Thyatria, which in turn relates to the Heart chakra and the Thymus gland. Here one has to deal with past demons before transcendence can occur. The reference to Jezebel in the Biblical texts means the overcoming of sexual excesses, and of misdirecting the sexual creative forces. In many respects this is the make or break centre. If the Self refuses to learn the lesson that it endures, then decay sets in, and the soul has to restart the journey. In the 2=9 ritual, we are shown this when the candidate circumambulates around the Hall, and is stopped by the gods Nu, Mau, Heka and Satem. These show the journey of the soul as it embarks on its quest of knowledge and experience. It experiences the eastern sun at the beginning of its journey, the Sun in Strength, then the Sun Setting as the Sun at Night - going into the unknown. The beast in the Twenty-First Key: this refers to is the winged Lion.

Church of Sardis - Throat Chakra

The fifth point in the Heptagram represents the Church of Sardis and this is linked to the Throat chakra and the Thyroid gland. When this centre is operating correctly, it is in the area of the Perfection of the Self. This shows the overcoming of earthly designs and accesses to the creative forces – through meditation. The seven stars mentioned in the Apocalypse relate to the higher state of mind, the impulses which come through the seven stars of Ursa Minor, are the ones that influence all of humanity.

Church of Philadelphia - Brow Chakra

The sixth point of the Heptagram represents the Church of Philadelphia and the Brow Chakra. This is the centre of Virtue and Opportunity and the pineal gland. This is the area where past lives can be accessed. The Biblical reference to Satan relates to the unregenerative cells, while the term 'New Jerusalem' refers to the new state of awareness that one has access through this centre.

Church of Laodicea - Crown Chakra

The seventh point of the Heptagram represents the Church of Laodicea and the pituitary gland. This is the state of awareness where one communicates and becomes part of the greater logos. This is further shown by the Luna symbol above the head of the dancing Figure. For not only does it represent the state of Yesod above Malkuth, but represents Selene, the Luna goddess who controlled the four seasons – the four beasts the card's corners.

The Heptagram and the Qlippoth

In the 2=9 ritual description of the Key, we are told that the Heptagram can relate to the Qlippoth. This is shown primarily through the diagram of the 'Seven Infernal Mansions and the Four Seas' which is the darker nature of the Heptagram in Key 21. For these negative forces are the mirror image of the Seven Churches and are broken into two parts, the Seven Earths and the Seven Infernal Habitations. All these diagrams shown in this ritual being directly or indirectly interconnected with the Key 21. The earths show the states of awareness or consciousness. They are reflections of the Chakras' negative energies and representative of the dross left to man on his expulsion from Eden. In many respects these are the shells of the Kingdoms of Edom, which were destroyed by their imperfect ability to accept God's light; and are only shadows of their former glory. The entire concept here is to show the falsity of matter over spirit. The earths represent the material side of man, his passions and desires, which eventually will crumble with time, as shown by Aretz, the Earth furthermost away from our present. When applies to the Heptagram, the number sequence is then reversed to that of Churches. The Infernal Habitations are the experiences of one who has passed through the Seven Earths.

All of this is a warning of premature openings of the Chakras. The Twenty-First Key is the entrance to the Path of Tau and the first level one must rise to. In the *Book of Concealed Mystery* we are shown how yet other aspects of the heptagram and its relationship to the letters of the name YHVH, - the four beasts of the Twenty-First Key.

> *Seven are the paths (if Tetragrammaton be written in this way –partially complete). ID,HH,V,H (where the father and mother are written in full; Microprosopous and his bride are written uncovered, if here the last and first letters are to be combined, and the penultimate and second, and therefore the paths at either extremity, so that they may form the letters HI and VV (mother and son), then are produced (3 middle letters) HH, D (which are the symbols of the queen, heavy with judgements. But if mother and daughter combined) HVI and HH (then) is produced forth VV (or Microprosopous) aswell as DV(or the androgyn who is a condition of judgements), for occultry Adam is demoted, or the male and female, who are that DV(concerning who it is written)...*

Kabbalah Unveiled by Mathers.

What this passage tells us is that the Heptagram is formed in secret meaning from the supernal of the Tree. The Heptagram is linked

Church	Seven Earths	Seven Infernal Habitations
1. Ephoses	7. Thebal	7. Gehinnon
2. Smyrna	6. Areqa	6. Shaari Moth
3. Pergamos	5. Tziah	5. Tzelmoth
4. Thyatria	4. Neshiah	4. Bar Shasketh
5. Sardis	3. Gia	3. Tithion
6. Philadelphia	2. Adamah	2. Abaddon
7. Laodicea	1. Aretz	1. Shoel

to the seven headed beast of the Apocalypse, as shown on the floor of the vault of the Adepti. This shows the serpent (made from the Rod of Moses) Nogah (splendour), the seat of Venus. We are told that in the 'Book of Concealed Mystery' the serpent of Nogath has 370 leaps, formed by the 32 letters of the Name, plus the five letters ALHIM (totalling 37) which comes to 370 when multiplied by the decad. In Cant ii we are told that the serpent leaps high above the 'other shells' though it is linked to them. What we have here is the serpent formula of the 'Convoluted Forces' placed on the staff of Hermes, to form the caduceus of Hermes, for the shape of the figure with Luna crescent and crossed legs, the hidden meanings of the shape of Mercury in its alchemical essence, is revealed to the initiate, Thoth of the Egyptians - originator of the Tarot.

Tau and the Twenty-first Key

Tau (Th) has a numerical value of 400, In the T'shape it was a builders square, used to level the angles of building and as a form measurement. The actual numerical value of 407 which equates with the word ThBH-meaning 'ark'(of Noah). This concept relates to a vessel built from specific measurements to house the chosen to house those chosen to live. In many respects Key 21 is like this for the measurement is form and structure-dogma, while the Kerubs show containment. The ark itself was built to carry the word of God so that it would survive. Tau is representative of the hidden knowledge that the Tarot will unlock . It is significant of Kabbalistic teachings as well - through the power of esoteric Orders and their work.

   Using Theosophic reduction with Tau, we find that it reduces to 4, the number of the Kerubs that oversee this Key. This in turn relates back directly to visions of Ezekiel. Another reduction is to forty which brings this key in empathy to Mem (40) for this is a symbolism of baptism and self sacrifice to gain knowledge. The Tau symbolism is shown in the old versions of the 'Hanged Man' where the figure hangs from it. The reduction of 400 to its square root of 20 relates to the fraternities and prophetic vision (ThVH). The word instruction (MShKIL) has a value of 400 (which equates with the title of Yesod). Key 21 bridges the space between Malkuth and Yesod and leads directly in the latter. The modern symbolic form of Tau is a cross. This is the fourfold nature of the universe subdivided into the Father, Mother, Son and Daughter principles which is the abstract essence of YHVH. Four divisions are necessary for the application of both form and structure. The cross is further shown by the crossed legs of the Dancing figure. The oval represents the whole or the unconscious state. The cross at its centre shows the mapping of the unconscious area by a study of form, the same principles which govern the Cube of Space.

Astrology and the Twenty-First Key

Considering that the mythology of Saturn is usually related to the male deity, some have considered the feminine form in this key to be distinctly out of place. In the 2=9 ritual we are told of the link to Netzach and Isis. This is because Saturn is exalted in Libra, a sign ruled by Venus. The Kabbalistic relationship places a strong emphasis on 'Kallah' as well. We must consider that Kronos was an androgenous figure as well. Kronos had the man-Woman title attributed to him (Great Magical Papyrus –4thC.AD) which was considered the primal beginning of manifestation. The relationship of Saturn and the title 'the Universe' for this Key is well worth noting. The works of G.S.Faber shows that "the great Father (Kronos) was sometimes seen as an 'animating soul' and sometimes the husband of the Universe while the Universe was sometimes reckoned the body and sometimes the wife of the intelligent being: and, as the one theory supposed a union as perfect as that of the Soul and Body in one man, so that the other produced a similar union by blending together husband and wife into one hermaphrodite".

For many years Saturn was considered a negative (malefic) planet in astrological terms. In modern terms, Saturn has been considered as a main form or structure of learning as one goes through. In many respects Saturn is much a planet that typifies that one goes through, In many respects Saturn has inherited that dogma of traditional values. It is much a planet that shows the learning experience. From a karmic perspective, Saturn is a planet of transformation and change. This is brought about by the relearning various lessons through the reincarnation cycle until the change occurs. It shows the conscious striving for perfection and achievement. It is a planet of intense focus. Saturn is the great rectifier, it brings an individual back on the correct path of awareness and hence the concept of the 'hard task master'. We must consider that when the Astrological concept of Saturn is merged with the Twenty-First Key, the Key modifies to a certain extent Saturn's nature to fit its meaning.

Key 21 shows the Saturn influence through dogmatic belief structures, such as ritual, religious and carefully pre-structured forms of learning such as Hermetic Orders. Saturn is a slow moving planet and change or transformation does not come quickly, and is a patience tester. For Saturn is like the true nature of the Higher self calling us back on the golden path of the Tao (way). When we stray off that path Saturn will push us back on it again. That is one of reasons that Saturn is called the 'Great Instigator' or 'Initiator' for it gets us moving in the right direction. It brings the spiritual perspective through in the material world of Assiah and produces a path of learning for us.

Michaud and Hillerson in their book *The Saturn/Pluto Phenomenon* say:

> *The Saturn energy is a gateway to the choice between restricted and unrestricted consciousness. Frequently the Saturn experience is two sides of the same coin: uncompromising demand to produce unlimited blessings. The wisdom of the ancients perceived Saturn as a reproach rather than a curse. The Saturn influence must, of necessity, challenge human consciousness to question superficial social existence. The Saturn Phenomenon is an indication of potential and as positive force in self awareness. This is why Saturn rules the final card in the Tarot's arcanum 'the World'.*

The 'World' represents the ultimate in individual achievement. It is symbolised by a naked dancing figure - a hermaphrodite. It is the dance of Shiva and all the initiated throughout time, and indicates that only through a spiritually directed movement can the world and truth of existence truly be realised. The world dancer is a celebration of the Great Work accomplished. This is the potential offered to all seekers by the Saturn Phenomenon.

The American psychic Arthur Ford stated:

> *Saturn is where one goes for spiritual uplift, and it is reserved by most until other planetary influences have been met* (through various reincarnation cycles PZ), *to achieve perfection Saturn is important. That (most are) not yet ready for that ultimate testing of the Soul and would first run the course of the others.*

YHVH and the Twenty-First Key

YHVH or Tetragrammaton, is associated to the Schemahamphoresch which is reflected in the 72 oval circles on Key 21. YHVH can be a name of 12 letters and the four Kerubs. You would be hard pressed to find a better explanation of the YHVH than that Leo Schayo gives in his *Universal meaning of the Kabbalah* :

YOD

> *The letter Yod in YHVH and Yah, is revealed on the discursive level as the sacred ideogram of the undifferentiated unity of the 10 Sephiroth - For the Yod has the numerical value of 10 - and is in particular of the unity of the 2 Supreme Sephiroth:- Kether, 'the Crown' and Chokmah, 'Wisdom'. The fine upper point of 'Crown' of the Yod designates Kether; it is the supreme root, the root being (AHIH) in the midst of super being (Ain), itself 'symbolised' by empty space, the absence of any symbol. From this infinitesmial point, lost in the superintelligible, springs the first cognitive and active emanation Chokmah - The 'Father'- shown by the thick, horizontal stroke of the Yod and ending in the fine descending line which symbolises Being, as it turns towards manifestation.*

The Yod force is reflective of the Lion which relates to the protective and procreative power of the Order of the Golden Dawn through Initiation. It is a symbol of power and force and must be under control at all times.

HEH

This is second letter of YHVH and Yah, the Heh, is called the supreme 'Mother', symbolism of Binah, the ontocosmological, 'Intelligence of God', or his receptivity, which is the passive cause. This is the second emanation of Kether, the 3rd Sephiroth, together with the last two, constitutes the name Yah, the 'transcendental half' of YHVH. According to the Zohar, the union of the Yod ('Father' or active, Chokmah with the Heh (the Mother or passive cause Binah) produces Vau, called the 'Son'.

The Eagle related to the letter Heh, is a source of power and vibration and in some cultures represents the ascent into heaven. It show, in the Death Trump, as the spirit forever rising through the initiatory rite of death. It is the volatile nature leaving behind the material, the liberation of the spirit. To a lesser extent is represents the aspiration on the part of the initiate. In the death card, the eagle soars while in this trump the eagle is stationary and relates to a specific place in the heavens that already exists, a place of refuge of the spirit. The eagle and its solar associations relate to the Tiphareth 'point depart'.

VAU

The letter Vau has the numerical value of the six creative Sephiroth of the cosmic construction: Chesed, Din, Tifereth, Netsah, Hod and Yesod. The Vau or Son, is allocalled Daath (I dispute this point PZ) *universal 'knowledge' omniscience or conscious man of all God's ontological emanations and cosmic manifestations, which transmit the Sephiroth heritage to the Daughter.*

The Kerubic symbol of man shows consciousness realised, a state of being.

HEH(F)

> *The 'Daughter' is the last heh(f) name of YHVH. The symbol of the Sephiroth Malkuth, 'Kingdom'; This is the last of the 7 Sephiroth of cosmic 'construction', namely their passive aspect, in other words, the receptive cosmological principle, the uncreated and created substance, fed by the 'Son', or active mediator, form which it receives all the Sephoritic emanations and projects them onto the Cosmic Fire...*

The Bull is the Kerubic animal associated here. In the context of this card it represents the symbol of sacrifice for the long journey into the heavens. The Eagle will guide the spirit while the Bull carries it in Hebrew literature. It is the Bull of YHVH, its power and might. For the initiate, the Bull gives and shows the strength of character needed on the occult path.

Chapter 2

The Diagram Of The Table Of Consecrated Bread; and the Exemplification of the 12 Signs or Gates Of The Zodiac

This was issued to the TH.A.M in the old Golden Dawn by Mathers. This was one of the first papers that Mathers did explaining the ritual diagrams in more detail. This paper also could be applied as a partial description of Key 21 and I believe there were a number of parts added to this paper as I uncovered one in New Zealand given in my book 'Golden Dawn Enochian Magic'. A special thanks to Mary Greer for supplying me with this paper and to Tony Fuller who uncovered the A.O. colouring scheme of the diagram, which came through an ex Whare Ra member's papers.

Table of Shewbread

In the Second Point of the 1=10 grade of Zelator, this diagram is placed in the Northern quarter, the Temple being arranged to symbolize the "Holy Place" and the Hegemon explains to the Candidate, or rather Aspirant Zelator, the signification of the Symbol of the Table of Shewbread. Why in the Temple should this diagram be placed in the North; and why is it that the Hegemon is the Officer to whom is allotted its theme and meaning? ShLChN, is the word employed to denote "Table", means a flat surface for placing offerings. ZR denotes "Rim" rather than "Crown" in its description in Exodus. In the Tabernacle the "Table of Shewbread" was placed to the Northward; and upon it, it is said, that Twelve Consecrated called of Bread were daily displayed to symbolise the Twelve Tribes or, as Josephus says, the Twelve Months of the Year, with which we associate the Twelve Signs of the Zodiac.

The custom of offering Consecrated Cakes before a Deity was already usual in Egypt and would appear to derive from the remotest antiquity; for Plutarch states that in the Festival of "Coming of Isis out of Phoenicia", the Egyptians used to stamp upon the Consecrated Cakes, the symbol of the Hippopotamus bound, to symbolise the restriction of the Evil Power of Typhon; while in the months of Paoni and Phaophi, the device employed was that of an Ass bound, as referred to the quality of obstinacy accompanied by ignorance. A remnant of the custom of stamping Consecrated cakes with a symbol is still evident in the Crosses marked on Good-Friday buns. In the Book of Jeremiah (cxliv,v19) the offering of Consecrated Cakes to the Queen of Heaven is alluded to. The Consecrated Hostia, or Bread, of the sacrament is still one of the most sacred Symbols of the Christian faith; and especially refers to the Ritual Linking of Man unto God. And as the Hegemon is the representative to the Aspirant, both of reconciler and of Guide, so it is fitting that he should expound to him the Diagram of the "Table of Shewbread".

Among the religious Symbols of an immemorial antiquity, handed down to us from Ages forgotten, prominent have been those connected with growth and cultivation of the Corn. Callimachus, in his Hymn to Demeter sings:

To Kalatho Kationos epiphthenxasthe, Gunaikes;
Dah-mahther, megga, chaireth, Polutropheh,
Poolumedimneh;
Ton kalathon kationta, Chamai thaseistheh
Behbahloi. Etc.

I have endeavoured in this translation to give an idea of the peculiar Mantric ring of the above lines, which, with some others, in the same Hymn to Demeter, are evidently far anterior to the time of Callimachus, and have a certain Dorico-Ionic swell. Here follows the rendering:

As the Kalathos cometh forth, raise in choir the
Hymn, ye Women:
Hail! Demeter, Hail! O great One, Thou, the
Nourisher of All: Thou of all the Filling Measures!
As the Kalathos cometh by, lower your eyes to the
ground, ye Profane.
Raise the Mystic Chant, ye Maidens; raise in Choir
the Hymn, ye Mothers;
Hail! Demeter, Hail! O great One, Thou the
Nourisher of All,
Thou of all the Filled Measures!

Prominent of the Sacred Symbols of the Mysteries was the Kalathos, or Consecrated basket, and like the Accessories of the Hebrew Tabernacle, it was frequently covered with a Veil of Blue. A principal reference of it was the Soul of the Initiate, the Human Soul. In the ceremonies of the Goddess Demeter (Ceres), in many ways similar to the Amazon Goddess, the Kalathios, as a symbol of the presence of the Goddess herself was drawn in a Chariot by four Consecrated White Horses, referring among other things to the Four Seasons. In the Hebrew Tabernacle, the Kalathos was employed to hold the Consecrated Bread, and the word employed for such a Cake was ChLth+Chalath, Like the first two syllables of Kalathos. See Exodus (c.29.v.23)

The Winnowing fan is another symbol derived from the cultivation of Corn, as also the hoe – for labour in the Elysian Fields: while the Corn itself is used as an illustration of the Resurrection. In the sense also it is referred in Corinthians (cxv, v.36), to the exemplification of that idea.

Technically the North would be the darkest part of the tabernacle, as the Station of the Sun below the Horizon; that is to say, corresponding to the Night and darkness. Wherefore the table with the Shewbread would be placed in that Quarter as alluding to the Sowing, Death and Resurrection of the Corn and its transmutation in the form of the Shew-Bread into a Sacred Symbol. And from this transmutation into the likeness of a 'Hostia' and its connection with the Tribes and with the Signs, so was there interwoven in its symbolism, the idea of a certain Resolving Power, to aid the human race, as those Tribes had been, as it were, rescued and aided to escape from a condition of bondage.

Having thus considered the symbolism of the "Table" and of the "Hostia" offered thereon, let us examine the particular references, formulae and symbols of the actual Diagram itself. To a further extent than these are given in the Grade of Zelator in the Outer Order.

Clustered together after the fashion of the Petals of a Rose, that Mystic Rose symbolic of an Eternal Creation, that Rose whose heart shaped Emanations, distinct each one, yet form an integral part of a varying yet perfect harmony. Thus are the lines and circles of this Diagram arranged to ally it with the symbol of a created and Creating Universe whose Creation is unceasing. Hear thou, therefore, and understand, O Theoricus Adeptus Minor! Surely the Rose is a symbol of the Infinite and harmonious Separation of nature; assuredly this is its Interpretation. And its petals of double-bosomed outline, repeat the Symbol of the many breasts of the Aegis of the Amazon-Goddess of Ephesus, the Eternal Diana. The cleaving of the Axes of her Amazon Guards, under the Presidence of the Separation – Goddesses in the Bosom of the 'Mysterium Magnum". For the 'Mysterium Magnum' is the Infinite and Veiled Mother whence be the Great Separations, from the 'Prima Materia' unto the 'Ultima materia' in which latter is Death or the Re-Solution into the 'Principium'. Even as the Exordium of the 'Book M' commenceth:

"Mysterium Magnum"   -   The Vast Mystery
"Magna Mater:"   -   The Mighty Mother
"Studium Universale"   -   The Wisdom Universal

And this discern thou in the Central Pentagram of the Drawing enclosing the Place of the Lamp, the Symbol of the Central Spiritual Sun!

And this Pentagram hath allusion to Heh on its Planes; whether of IHVH, whether of AHIH; whether of Tetragrammaton, whether Eh-yeh. Even as Her Speech is, (Song of Solomon, cii:v.1), "I the Opening Rose of Sharon developing the Lily (or the six-fold Lily) of the deep and profound Valley."

Also by Three and by Four is the Designing of the Diagram, for about the Central Pentagram be Four triangles interlaced; and upon them their interweavings, guarding the Centre, be the Four Circles charged with Archangelic names and with the Kerubim symbols. Also each circle of the Twelve Circles hath its triangle, allied with a banner of Separation of the Great Name YHVH, a Tribe and with a Letter. Twelve be the Banners of this Great Name, thus returned or varied within Itself. Again it is said, (Song of Solomon, cvi.v4,10) "AIMAH KNDGLVTh with (or as) Banners."

About the Central Pentagram are Four Circles, charged with the Symbols of the Kerubim and the Names of the Four Archangels, and placed between the Centre and the Zodiacal-Tribal Circles, and even as Moses with Aaron and Miriam and the Three Sections of the Levites encamped about the tabernacle towards the Four Cardinal Points; and between it and the outer Borders formed by the encampments of the Twelve Tribes each under its own Banner.

These Four Circles be the Symbols, not alone of the Four Archangels, not alone of the Four Kerubim, not alone of the Four Elements; but also especially of the FOUR SEPARATIONS, What then, is the Separation regarded as, distinct from these? This matter of the Separations is not of the Natural Sphere of the Treatise on this diagram, but is rather a question linked hereunto, even as the formulae of the Separations is bound with the Inner of all Manifestations of the Visible Universe. For this Separation is not mere division and Cleavage, neither is it the Rendering Asunder of Matter. Of Separation, it is written, in the 'Book M' thus: "BEGINNING, MOTHER and GENETRIX of all Generation was Separation; for Separation is the Greatest Miracle of all Things!" and again; "Withersoever the Hidden Aether diffuseth itself, thither so far extendeth the Orb of the Mysterium Magnum".

From the Bosom of the Mysterium Magnum be the Separations; there is a triple separation and a triple form; there is also a last and latest Separation; and after this latter none other or further is made. Even as in the names AHI-H and YHV-H there be three letters and a Fourth 'H' repeated, as it were a closing of the Separations (or Successive Generations) thereof. And when Sh is added to YHVH so that it becometh IHShVH , this is placed within the midst thereof and not added to the end. Wherefore also it is written "Unto the third and Fourth Generation" *(This may appear a vague statement by Mathers, but it becomes a reality when the Table of Shewbread Diagram is coloured for the first time. The four and fivefold nature of the colours integrating with each other on the intersected triangles of the mandalla of the Shewbread diagram. That is the larger triangles facing the smaller one in the circle with the astrological sign on them.P.Z)* This is placed within the midst and not added to the end. Wherefore also it is written "Unto the Third and Fourth Generation" and after this latter is there not further mention of generation made. For by generations here, that is separations, is not to be understood a continued production of the same kind to itself, as from a Plant is produced the Flower, from the flower of the Seed, form the Seed the plant again; but a production of a different nature which doth not reproduce itself again. Even as (to use the near frequent illustration), Milk can produce Cream; and Cream again Butter etc., but the latter doth not in its turn again become Milk: so that in this example Milk is as it were the especial Mysterium from which the Cream and the Butter are two successive Separations. Also, be it noted, that in the Commandments, where it is said; "Unto the Third and Fourth (generations)", that this word "Generations" is supplied by the Translators, the actual expression being; "unto the Third and Fourth", i.e. preferably "Unto the Third and Fourth Separation" rather than "Generation". For as it is before said, Separation is not the same Formula as Generation. It is an important Phenomenon of the Elements of Being. For the War-Axe of the Amazon-Queen-Goddess, the Sacred Axe or Labrys of the "Labrandian Zeus" to Whom she has passed it as her Ensign of Authorisation, is the Great symbol of the harmonious Separations of the Infinite, of the Power of the Divine Spirit in the Manifestation of Creation. As it is written: "More penetrating than a two edge Sword..." etc. And the Circling Belt of the Zodiac is the War-Belt symbol of the Amazon Queen. And the above reasons is the Axe, the Egyptian Hieroglyph of a God, as also a Banner unrolling!

In thine own Soul, O Theoricus Adept, strive to comprehend this Great Mystery of the "Separations" as distinct from the "Generations", for herein is the inexplicable Wonder of the Mysteries of Eternal Nature, of the Formulated Thought of the Divine Mind in Creation. Seek why in AHI-AH there is a symbol of a Triple Separation, and of a Fourth which its Second Letter repeated. Seek why in YHV-H there is the same formula repeated! The Triple Separation, and a Fourth completing its development, this is it which is implied in the misunderstood Formula which has been handed down to us in the Aenigma of the Sphinx:- "Esti dipon epi ges, kai tetrapoun, 'ourmia phone'" etc.

> (Translation) *There is upon our Earth, (or Fundamental Plane), that which is of a dual divided Foundation of nature; that is also that of a Fourth adherent to the which alone is the faculty of Death: also there is a Third (between the Two and the Four). Also there is a Faculty of Change in its Oneness of Nature, even as it may be set in movement upon the Earth after the manner of the Serpent, throughout the Air and along the Deep of the Sea. But whensoever on its onward Course it is cast forward with most Foot Formation, then doth most its speed relax; then doth most its movement become lamed and halting.*

Here then is the enigma of the Sphinx and its presentation of the enigma of the Separations. For the Speech of AEMAIN, or HARMAIN, the voice of the Secret Wisdom is "WISDOM HIDDEN IN AENIGMA IN MY NAME". And there is the response of the Sphinx-Kerub unto the ill-formulated curiosity of Man. For the reply of Oedipus is but a Simulated Formula, and an Illusion-response; whence the De-materialisation of the Sphinx, whence the profound Expiration of Oedipus. From henceforth he remaineth the symbol of the Ignorant Aspirant of the Eternal Mysteries, who contented with a hasty interpretation thinketh that thus he hath comprehended the vast Portent Key of the Universe! (Note of S.R.M.D: I here append a more ordinary rendering, together with the reply of Oedipus).

> *There is upon Earth a two-footed thing, also a four footed, of which there is one slaughter, Also three-footed; and it changeth its one form, similar upon the earth; Unto reptiles it is set in movement, also through the air, also across the sea. But whensoever it may move forward being urged onward with most feet, Straightway its speed becometh most feeble from being lame.*

The Solution of Oedipus

Hearken, even though unwilling, O ill-omened Muse of the Dead, Unto thine ending of offence through my voice. Thou hast described Man, who when he creepeth upon the earth, Four footed it is at first when an infant he hath been born from the womb; but when old age approacheth upon a staff as a third foot, bending his neck, bowed down with the weight of years.

Knowledge without wisdom is in the reply of Oedipus, that haste of analysis which overlooks differentiation. For Oedipus is ignorant of the Separations; still more is he ignorant of those Human races who be not of Adamite Man; of the Four Classifications of Interpretation he hath known but that which is revealed unto the Profane; of the Four sacred castes he hath but comprehended the Wisdom of the Sudra; that is, of the fourth and lowest, no matter what Caste he himself may have been considered to have belonged. And herein is the Sin of Oedipus, who had dared to think that be so shallow and petty an interpretation he has solved the Aenigma of the Eternal Mysterium.

For there are the Four Worlds and the Separations, the Letters of name, and the Elements, the Human races who descended not from Adamite Man, the Castes, and the Classes of the Interpretation, as well as other and many Formulations which he included in these Symbols of the Infinite. The Kerubim and the Presence, the Fountain of the Abiding River, the Source and the Flowings of Nature, their Flux and their re-flux, all these of the Wisdom of the Four Fold name Re-Turned. For like as there be three Letters in the Name and a Fourth which is repeated, the second 'Heh', so also do we constate a Great Reversive in the Separations, which halting in the Progressive, becomes the more agile in the Regressive, as thought were endowed with the power to turn backward the last Separating Force into the bosom of the Mysterium Magnum and even beyond. For in the Earth, that is solid, is nearest the Return. Throw unto the beyond of the Mysterium Magnum, wherefore in the Solid is more immediately manifest the Commencement of Corruption. Derived from the

Ancient Egyptian Wisdom, Four be the variations of the Plane of the Interpretations according to the Tradition of the Qabalah. For these represent the returning Flux of the Logos. Form the Fourth and last separation on unto the beyond of the Mysterium. Each interpretation is under a Degree; each Degree is under a Letter of the the name of paradise, that is PRDS, Pardes, hidden therein like the Egyptian Kylestis or Scared Bread within the Kalathos. And the word "Kylestis" somewhat recalls the Hebrew "Chalath"

> *Regarding the Separation, Death is as it were the Positive Zero, like the throw-back to zeros after the formulation of the Triad: that which is the Four as regarding the First Triad, but the Substitute Four only; for it is the Transition unto the True Four which is in Chesed!*
>
> Moina Mathers

It is written; "In Daath the Depths are broken up." Even as Daath is referred to NHR Nahar, whence be the Separations of the Four Rivers. What then is the meaning of PRDS? Pardes, Paradise? It is derived from PRD and DS, implying "The Hidden Place of the Separations"; for PRD is to separate and DS is to conceal: that is their root meaning.

These be the names of the Four Classes of Mystic Interpretation, in order from the Outermost to the Inner; They are PShTh, RMZ, DRSh, and SVD, whose Initial letters form the Name of Paradise, PRDS, whose Middle Letters are ShMRV, implying the Guarding thereof; and whose Terminal Letters are ThZShD, or the Separating Bosom of the Mother of Things.

PShTh, Pashuth, is the lowest, outermost and most exterior form of explanation or interpretation of a mystic script; that which is known unto the Profane; the material and too literal shell which too many Theologians and Superficial Occultists imagine to be the sole intended meaning.

The second form of Interpretation is RMZ, Remmez, or Simple Allegory: this again, though somewhat higher than the foregoing, is only that which is communicated to initiates of the lowest degree, and is frequently taken for the more profound sense by the Interpreters of little knowledge.

The Third Sense is DrSh, Derash, meaning Enquiry or Searching out. It is that Superior Symbolism which is only communicated to Advanced Initiates; and then only under the Seal of a profound Obligation

But SVD, is the Supreme Secret Meaning, wherein is implied the Indeseribable. It is said to be only conceivable through a species of Divine Extasia: that those who attain unto it could not reveal it, but that any Rabbin who attempted to do this, notwithstanding the absolute prohibition, either perished on the spot or underwent a fearful chastisement. From this extreme concealment it is called SVD, that is to say, a closed or barred Secret.

There were also said to be many variations of Qabalistic meaning from the letters of these Four Words by means of Notariqon and Gematria.

The titles of the First Three Sephiroth with Daath have some analogy with the above definitions of Interpretations:-

Daath	Knowledge of Matter, as distinct from Understanding;
Binah	Understanding thereof, as distinct from Wisdom;
Chokmah	Wisdom , as distinct from the Crown or Summit of the Interpretation.

The Kether – Crown, which links back to the Divine light, even as it touched the AIN SOPH AUR. Some have applied Chokmah with the idea of the "Faculty of Abstraction"; Binah with that of "Generalisation"; Daath with that of "Reasoning"; while endeavouring to conceive the Holy Spirit, on the plane of Christian Theology, as the Reciprocal Divine Love breathed between the Father and the Son, (as Sainte Jeanne Chezard de Matel expresses it). But that great Initiate, Diotime, the beautiful and mysterious stranger, when Socrates asked her to define the origin of Love, replied: "Love was born from the Conjunction of Poros and Penia!" That is to say, the conjunction of the re-establishment of the Equilibrium between the redundant and the Deficient, between the plentitude and the Vacuity, between the Me and the Non-Me. For the Desire is for that is requisite unto Satisfaction. The Pros and Penia of the beautiful Mantinean are extremely difficult of translation; (Plentitude and vacuity scarcely expressed them); for she has employed them as Hieroglyphs of the Poles of Desire. (See the *Convivium* of Plato).

Now in the production of Things, each is at the same time Passive with regard to that which Produceth it and Active in reference unto that which it Produceth! These various reasonings being understood, it will be rendered for the Theoricus Adept to comprehend the Mutations of the Name YHVH.

The Axe of the Amazon Queen represents harmonious Cleavage, harmonious Separation; hence the Egyptian Axe or Unrolling Banner Hieroglyph for a God Force; hence its Consecration to the Idea of the Labrandian Jove, or rather Zeus; to Jupiter, the Thunderer, to Jupiter Tonans. But we do not find the Club of Hercules in this connection. For that represents, not the harmonious Separation, not Severance in nature in the Bosom of the Prima Materia of things, but instead a crushing and mistaken confounding of entities, beyond the Ultima Materia. Or to speak occultly, that which ultimates in that Poison-Development which brings him Death through the garment of Nessus the Slain Centaur.

Again a correlative of the Great Separations is to be found in the Four Hindoo Castes, whose character, however comprehended by Europeans as a fundamental Social Institution, is much rather a distinction from a point of view of Religion and Cultural Ceremony. The Castes also existed in Egypt, but in the time of Herodotus were divided into more classes than the Indian. It would also appear from the Pentateuch, that the Hebrews maintained the Caste Division: highest - the Priests and Levites, Like the Brahmins; next the Warriors, like the Indian Kshatriya, like the Egyptian Klashir. It is the Hymn of the Rik –Veda known as the "Pouroucha-Sourta" which formulates the origin of the Hindoo castes. Here is the best translation I have found hither of the Hymn:

> *Thousands be the heads of Pouroucha, thousands the eyes, thousands the feet! On every side enveloping the World, this Being exceedeth it by the ten fingers. This entire Universe is Pouroucha, all that which hath been, all that which Shall be! Lord of Immortality also is He; when well nourished he extendeth himself. Such is his*

*Greatness; and paroucha is superior even to this.
All existences united constitute but a Fourth of his
person; and the Three other Fourths are All that is
Immortal in the Heaven. (remark here the Idea of
the Three Separations and the Fourth) With the
Three Fourths, Pouroucha has ascended unto
the Heights. One Fourth of his is reborn afresh,
here below. This is then expanded into that which
is eaten, and unto that which is not eaten. From
him was born Viradj and from Viradj was born
Pouroucha. Once born he extendeth beyond the
earth, both behind and in front. Both behind and
in front. When the Gods celebrated the sacrifice
of Pouroucha for the Oblation, Spring was the
Ghee-Butter, Summer the Combustible; Autumn the
offering. (Compare the linking of the seasons to
the Idea of Separations.) This victim, Pouroucha,
born at the Beginning, him they, the Gods,
immolated upon the Turf of Sacrifice. It was with
him that the Gods, the Sadhyas, and the Richis
performed the Sacrifice. Universal sacrifice, the
Curd and the Ghee-Butter produced in abundance.
He formed the Aerial Creatures and the Animals,
both wild and Domestic. From this Universal
Sacrifice came forth the verses of Rik and of
Samon, the Metrical Chant and the Yadjour (That
is to say the Four Vedas, by the expression of the
`Metrical Chant', meaning the magical Hymns of
the Athra Veda.) From him were born the Horses,
all animals which have two ranges of teeth, Cattle,
Goats, and Sheep. When the Gods sacrificed the
pouroucha, into how many parts did they divide
him? What of his Mouth? What of his Arms? What
of his Thighs and Feet? It was the BRAHMAN that
was his Mouth; the RADJANIA, (or rather
Kshatriya) his Arms: that caste which is called
VAISYA, his Thighs; The SOUDRA came from his
Feet. Again also, the Moon was from his Soul; the*

> *Sun from his Eye; Indra and Agni from his Mouth;*
> *Vayou from his Breath; from his navel the Air; from*
> *his Head the Heaven; from his Feet the earth;*
> *and from his ears the Four Fourths and Quarters*
> *of the Universe. Thus it is that the Gods have*
> *fashioned the Worlds!*

Compare with this the Scandinavian Mythology of the Slain Ymir; in the Celtic, the Transformation of the Children of the vast and Shadowing Lir, the Numen or genius of the Deep of Things.

And the Four Separations be compounded of a Three and of a Fourth, so in the Diagram of the Shewbread, be the Four Circles corresponding there unto placed at the intersection of the Four Great Triangles, in allusion to that saying of Ancient Time:-

> *The Four Elements have a Three-fold*
> *Consideration, so that Four (i.e.multiplied by*
> *Three) becometh Twelve; and thence passing by*
> *Seven (i.e.the addition of Four and Three) into*
> *Ten (the Sephiroth in the Tree of Life there may be*
> *a progress of the Supreme Unity constated. (and*
> *the difference between the Four and the Three is*
> *One...the Seven hath conformity withn the Twelve:*
> *for as Three and Four make Seven, so Thrice Four*
> *becometh Twelve; and the numbers of the Celestial*
> *Planets and Signs resulting form the same radical*
> *Idea.*

Cornelius Agrippa in his *Occulta Philosophia* has cited these passages, but in an altered and less clear manner of wording. Thus then, attributed unto the Twelve Differentiations, do the Twelve Signs of the Zodiac and the Twelve Banners of the Mutations of the Name. And thus also with the Theoricus Adept comprehend that the name YHVH, like as also AHIH (with others such as ADNI and AGLA) as it were in Itself a Mightly and Completed pantheon of God-Forces acting together in a harmonious though varying Unity of being, of Essence and of Essential Operation: a plurality whose action is unified; and Unity whose nature is Pluralised. For what is the Mathematical Idea of unity, that is of one, but as a Unity only in relation to the Numbers which follow it;

while it is a Plurality in its root reference to the Zero which preceedeth it? Thus, necessarily, Pantheism is nearer in approximation to the Truth of Things than Monotheism; Though the collective and unvarying harmonious Action of an Interweaving and Isolated Pantheon may be nearly the conception of the Different and Complemental Persons of an Unified Deity.

And as regards to the attribution of so Universal a name as YHVH to the Twelve Signs of the Zodiac by the banners of the Mutations, these latter may be attributed in a varying manner thereunto without error or Signification. But perhaps the most applicable is that given in the Diagram of the "Table of Shewbread" as under. At times also the Names ADNI and AHIH are also hereunto allotted, so that the Mutations of these Names may be attributed to the thirty six decanates, thus: those of YHVH to the first Decante of each Sign; those of ADNI to the medial; those of AHIH to the Final. YHVH to the initiative force; those of ADNI to the reigning power in the centre of the Zodiacal Sign; those of AHIH to the Linking Faculty, thus:

Aries	IHV H ADNI AHIH(f)
Libra	VHIH(f) NDAY HAH(f)
Taurus	IHH(f) NDAY AHH(f)I
Gemini	IV HH(f) ANDI AIHH(f)
Cancer	HVH(f)I DNIA HIH(f)A
Leo	HVIH(f) DNAI HIAH(f)
Virgo	HVH(f)I DINA HH(f)IA
Libra	VHIH(f) NDAY IHAH(f)
Scorpio	VHH(f)I NDIA IHH(f)A
Sagittarius	VIHH(f) NADI IAHH(f)
Capricorn	H(f)IHV IADN H(f)AHI
Aquarius	H(f)IV H IAND H(f)AIH
Pisces	H(f)HIV IDAN H(f)HAI

And as implied in the preceeding paragraph, there may be other modes of attribution, as with IHVH the three commencing with H to the watery Triplicity, the three commencing with V to the Airy; and three with the H final to the Earthy. And in the Diagram of the Grade of Zelator here subjoined a certain harmonious of the orthography of the name so noticeable between those between those Signs which are opposite in the Zodiac. And the Four Cherubic Symbols are not in usual relative sequence, to indicate their more Universal Character, as before implied.

The Tetragrammaton being thus applied to many and various attributions, it is interesting to constate the alleged speech of God to Noah in the Sibylline Verse: "Enna grammat" echo, Tetrasullabos eimi noeime!". This may be translated as : "I have nine characters (letters or Hieroglyphics), yet I am Four syllabled: perceive!" or "I have Nine methods of writing; yet perceive me as the Four syllabled I AM (i.e.AHIH)!"

"In some Magical Conjurations the knowledge of the Magical employment of certain Divine Names is attributed to Noah"...e.g.... the Name EL which Noah heard and saved himself with all his family from the Deluge...the name of IOD which Noah heard and knew God the Almighty One...the name Tetragrammaton Elohim, which expresseth and signifieth the grandeur of so lofty a Majesty, that Noah, having pronounced it, saved himself, and protected himself with his whole household from the waters of the Deluge".

In connection with the foregoing Sibylline verses, it is to be remarked that the Name of IHVH ALHIM of nine letters, as also IHVH TzBAVTh, IHVH TzDQNU etc. There is also a Sibylline verse which implied a connection between the name of HADES and that of ADAM, the latter spelt as in the Greek, with four letters; and these again in their turn are taken as the initials of these Names of the cardinal Points:-

"Autolien te Dusin te, Mesembrian te, Arkton" = Adma + ADAM.

"The Rising point, the Setting, the Noon-Meridian, and the region of the Bear (the North)."

Most Sibylline verses have a peculiar mantric modulation in them. For example:

"Estai kai Samos ammos, eseitai Delos adelos" meaning "Samos shall be sand, and Delos no longer known."

Concerning The Usual Hieroglyphic Form of the Symbols of the Signs Of The Zodiac

That "Venerable name of Sleepless Revolution", as Proclus expresses it, being above considered, the actual Symbols of the Zodiac next demand examination. As is the case of the Astrological Symbols of the Planets, those of the Twelve Signs of the Zodiac can also be applied to the "TREE OF LIFE", with the difference, however, namely that the latter confined to the Seven Lower Sephiroth with Daath; the Zodiac being by its nature the belt of Constellated Stars about the Universe.

> *Further still understand, O Tat, that these Decans are impassive to things which the other Stars suffer. For neither being detained do they stop their course, nor being impeded do they recede: nor are they like the other Stars concealed as with a veil by the light of the Sun. But being liberated above all things, they comprehended the Universe as the Guardians and accurate inspectors of it in the Nuktemeron (Night and Day). They possess with respect us, the greatest Power.*

This is from a Ms. of Stobaeus, cited by Gale in his notes to Iamblichos. The word 'Decans' evidently is understood from a preceding passage and it might be better supplied as including the generic idea of the Zodiac Constellations as well. 'Inspector' is Episkopos = 'Overseer' whence 'Episcopal'.

As before remarked, the Symbols of the Signs of the Zodiac on the 'Tree of Life' are confined to the Seven Lower Sephiroth with Daath: "For in Daath the depths are broken up, and the Clouds drop down the dew".

And here in the Cardinal Signs would appear to be as a Triad of Centres.

Sign of Virgo on the Tree of Life

Here VIRGO , while comprehending both the Pillars, clearly manifests excess on the side of Mercy, seeking to bring that Force into actions upon Malkuth. It touches but does not include Daath. A rather more powerful Symbol than Scorpio, for it includes the Seven Lower Sephiroth though not in a fully balanced form.

Sign of Libra on the Tree of Life

LIBRA is as it were, hung trembling in balanced form from Daath, ready to incline unto either side were it not for limiting Pillars. Strong as comprehending both of these in a balanced form, Nor enough basis beneath.

Egyptian Hieroglyphic 'Hor of the Solar Mountain'

Compare this diagram with that of Libra.

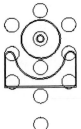

Sign of Scorpio on the Tree of Life

SCORPIO shows excess in the pronounced degree on the side of Severity, even almost menacing the side of Mercy, where the dart shaped tail terminates in Chesed. It touches but does not include Daath. Not enough basis below.

Sign of Sagittarius on the Tree of Life

In the ordinary symbol of SAGITTARIUS, the Arrow has been launched, not in a straight , but an inclined line. Were it vertical, thus, on the Tree, it would be very strong, as representing keen and well balanced aspiration. But inclined, it approaches Chokmah and does not formulate either Pillar, Daath, Chesed, Tiphareth, Netzach and Yesod, directing towards Chokmah.

Inclined form of Sagittarius on the Tree of Life

The inclined form of Sagittarius diagram 12 as above analysed

Sign of Capricorn on the Tree of Life

This symbol of CAPRICORNICUS would appear at first sight to be very powerful, as including all the Lower Sephiroth together with Daath. But it is an unbalanced form, and only clearly showing the Pillar of Severity: Uncertain.

Second Sign of Capricornicus on the Tree of Life

A second and less usual form of Capricornicus. Rests upon Malkuth and with this exception includes the same Sephiroth as the former.

Sign of Aquarius on the Tree of Life

Though fluctuating in form, the Symbol of AQUARIUS is balanced and unties the Forces of the two Pillars without, however, marking their form. Furthermore, it depasses them on either side. Unstable.

The Sign of Pisces On the Tree of Life

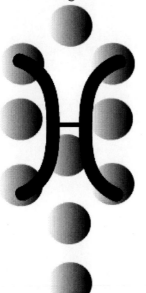

The Sign of PISCES shews forth the forces of the Two Pillars bound across through Tiphareth, which the curves touch, but do not include, while the bar stretches across to the Pillar on either side. Although strong and well balanced, its operation is fluctuating. There is not enough basis below.

The Sign of Aries on the Tree of Life

The Symbol of ARIES touches, but does not include Daath. It comprehends the whole equally united force of the Seven Lower Sephiroth in a balanced form, and ready to act together, It concentrates the force of the Pillars towards the centre and clearly affirms the Central Pillar, but without Daath.

The Sign of Taurus on the Tree of Life

The Sign of TAURUS includes all the lower Sephiroth with the exception of Daath and Malkuth, which latter it touches upon. It includes the force of both Pillars, and in a balanced form, although neither is distinctly formulated. Stronger in appearance than in reality.

The Sign of Gemini on the Tree of Life

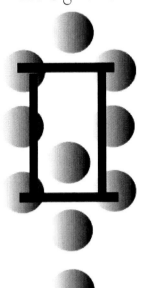

GEMINI shews the two Pillars clearly formulated, but nothing more. It touches but does not include Daath and Yesod. It is too separated though parallel and twin. Therefore rather strong and in detail than in comprehension of the whole.

The Sign of Cancer on the Tree of Life

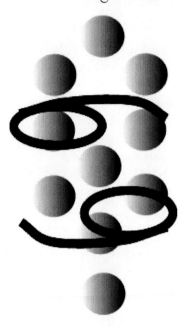

Cancer includes Daath and all but Malkuth and Tiphareth, which latter but touches. Yet it does not formulate the shape of the Pillars and thereon is more fluctuating.

The Sign of Leo on the Tree of Life

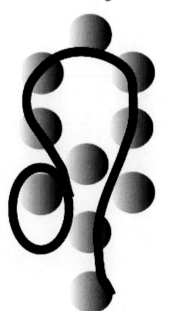

Leo includes all but Malkuth, which it touches. But it is not in balanced form, neither does it formulate either Pillar.

One Outer head and well known classification of the Zodiacal Signs is as Hieroglyphs of the forms they are supposed to represent (see table).

♈	Head and horns of a ram
♉	Bull's horns
♊	Two exactly similar columns
♋	Claws of a crab or a lobster
♌	Outline of the head of a Lion
♍	A corruption of the word Virgo
♎	Hieroglyph of Balance
♏	Knotted tail and sting of a scorpion
♐	Dart of an arrow
♑	Hieroglyph of the profile, head, neck, chest, and forelegs of a goat
♒	Two lines pouring water from the jar of a water bearer
♓	Two Dolphins linked together

Signs of the Hieroglyphs

Such attemped derivations as Aries form the period lambing, Taurus from that of calving, Cancer form the apparent sideways or crab-like movement of the Sun at Summer Solstice, Leo form the raging heat etc. insufficient in Occult value.

The attributions of the Signs of the Zodiac to the various parts of the body is sufficiently well-known; but their Hieroglyphic similarity to those parts is worthy of consideration here. Thus, though not absolute, the following resemblances are clearly traceable:-

> ARIES: The lines of the eyebrows and nose.
> TAURUS: The outline of the lower part of the face and neck.
> GEMINI: The twin lengths of the arms.
> PISCES: The splayed shape of the extremities, especially of the feet.
> CAPRICORN: The lines of the knees seen in profile; and the rise of the muscles of the calf.
> SAGITTARIUS: The single bone of the thigh.
> AQUARIUS: The double bones from knees to ankle.
> LIBRA: The lines of the back and above and below the haunches.
> VIRGO: Perhaps the lines of the bowels and the exterior folds of the outer skin of the stomach and abdomen.
> SCORPIO: Perhaps those of the genitalia.
> CANCER: The chest, and the breast of a woman.
> LEO: The female breast seen in profile, the ascending curve of the shoulder, the descending line of the spine.

But a further and interesting correlation is traceable between those Zodiacal Hieroglyphics and the forms assumed by their cognate Elements in nature, as shewn below:-

Triplicity Of Fire

> ARIES   — Ascending flames.
> LEO   — Rushing Flames.
> SAGITTARIUS — Darting Flames

The Triplicity Of Earth

TAURUS   — Fertile land in a valley
VIRGO   — Undulating land and low hills.
CAPRICORNICUS — Precipitous, rocky and barren land

The Triplicity Of Air

GEMINI   — Cirrhous and flecked cloud
AQUARIUS   — Rain descending from clouds.

Triplicity Of Water

CANCER   — Eddies of swirling water
SCORPIO   — Undulating surface of water.
PISCES   — Breaking waves over the sea.

The attribution of the permutations of the Four Lettered Name IHVH attributed to the Twelve Signs of the Zodiac:

ARIES   A Great ruling Force.
TAURUS   A Force exalted.
GEMINI   A Powerful Force.
CANCER   A Force that renders Powerful.
LEO   A Force Wise.
VIRGO   A Force Wise
LIBRA   A Force Illustrious.
SCORPIO   A Wisely Dispensing Force
SAGITTARIUS   A Force Great and Potent.
CAPRICORNICUS   A Force Strong and Mighty
AQUARIUS   A Force manifesting and
                   Manifested
PISCES   A Force Avenging

And thus is the operation of the Pantheon in the Four Fold Name.

Correspondence Of Vibrations

Varying attributions and correspondences of the gamut of the Musical Octave have been given by writers on Occult Symbolism, but the True Rosicrucian attribution is based on the Rainbow correspondence of the Vault, thus; though the consideration of the Octave itself fall necessarily under the Symbolism of the Seven Branched Candle Stick; while it is the Twelve Semi-tones which find their correlation in the Zodiac.

Yet for the succession of the Octaves themselves, we must attribute the lowest to Saturn, the next above to Jupiter, the next again to Mars, then to Sol, Venus, Mercury; and Luna the highest.

Red	Mars	F in the first space	Fa
Orange	Sun	G on the second line	Sol
Yellow	Mercury	A in the second place	La
Green	Venus	B on the middle line	Si
Blue	Moon	C in the third space	Do or Ut
Indigo	Saturn	D on the fourth line	Re
Violet	Jupiter	E on the fourth line	Me

The twelve Semi-tones be attributed to the Twelve Signs of the Zodiac

Although it is usually stated by musicians, that the whole tone is only divisible into nine Comae, Komai, Chomai, or distinctions of vibratory tone, we find in the Rosicrucian secret knowledge the ten Sephiroth : so that in the Ideal Tone we have an exact Semi-tone corresponding to the exact half of its Comae, and avoid the anomaly of a dieze, or #, which varies in position from four to five Comac above the natural notes, and of a hemol, which varies to the same extent below. For of what truth is a system which admits the Ideal of a Semi-tone and yet at the same time expresses it by a varying barring? Unless indeed the # be fixed at only four Comae above the note and the at only four below: but then neither is a true Semi-tone; and where is fixed the locations of the Modes?

Red	Aries	F	Fa
Red-Orange	Taurus	F or G	Fa dieze or Sol bemol
Orange	Gemini	G	Sol
Amber	Cancer	G or A	Sol dieze or Si bemol
Yellow	Leo	A	La
Grass Green	Virgo	A or B	La dieze or si bemol
Green	Libra	B	Se
Greenish-blue	Scorpio	C	Do ut
Blue	Sagittarius	C or D	Do or Ut dieze or Re bemol

Indigo	Capricorn	D	Re
Violet	Aquarius	D or E	re dieze or Mi bemol
Ultra Violet Crimson	Pisces	E	Far

Table Of Shewbread
Part 2.
By Pat Zalewski
For The Theoricus Adeptus Minor Grade

This paper is an extension of the previous one of Mathers, and incorporates three separate parts.

1. The Twelve Tribes and the Neophyte Ceremony.
2. Early associations of the Constellations and the Fixed Stars.
3. The Twelve Stones on the High Priest's Breast Plate.

The 12 tribes and the Neophyte Ceremony

The following Signs are in their Astrological Order, and show some of the 12 hidden Key Points within the Ceremony of the Neophyte. This is but a further subdivision of the Z2 formula.

1. The Tribe of Gad relates to the 'Opening' of the Neophyte ceremony, for Gad is the son who won against all adversity and increased his numbers with the Blessing of YHVH. For this is the Opening of the Temple which also hopes to swell the number of members of the Order, by obeying the ways of YHVH by using the ancient Wisdom through the teachings of the Order. From Chron.12.14 tells us that those from the Tribe of Gad were the

first ones to cross the Jordan, the first month when it was overflowing its banks.

2. The Tribe of Ephraim is the preparation of the Candidate by the Hegemon and ensuring that the rope, robe and hoodwink are correctly on the Candidate. For this relates to Ephraim's strength and devotion and who will be rewarded for his struggling until Israel is reached. It provides the candidate with the necessary tools to perfom the task of preparation in the long years ahead.

3. Manesseh relates to the petition of the Candidate (by the Hegemon or the Kerux on his or her behalf) to seek entrance into the temple. For it was this Tribe that assimulated with the old inhabitants of Israel and were punished for their attitude. Here their attitude shows redemption for their sins, as they try to reinstate themselves within the Holy of Holies.

4. Issachar relates to the Entrance of the Candidate to the temple, and taken to the edge of the Portal within. He is guided because Issachar was Tribe of indolent leader less people in need of Guidance.

5. Judah relates to the Speech of Hierophant granting the admittance of the Candidate to the Temple, for Judah was the first Tribe to cross the Jordan.

6. Naphthali relates to the purification and consecration of the candidate. For Naphthali was one favoured with Blessings.

7. Asshur relates to the Cirumambulation of the Candidate, for that Tribe was the one that inherited the wealth of the land through application of their knowledge.

8. Dan relates to the advancement of the Candidate to the foot of the Altar, for it was Dan that lapsed into idolatry in want of God's truth.

9. Benjamin is the Tribe that relates to the taking of the Obligation. For Benjamin is 'beloved Of the Lord who shall dwell in safety by Him: The Lord shall cover him all day long and he shall dwell between his shoulder.' This last sentence shows the touch of the sword at the nape of the neck during the Obligation.

10. Zebulon was the Tribe that was preferred over Issachar. Now the oath is taken and the Motto is now used and it is like a new person, for the old ways have been left behind as a new Blessings and cicumambulation is given and the Candidate is passed

on. For Zebulon lived by the seashore and related to ships and travel.

11. Reuben is the beginning of Jacob's strength, and this is explained by the Exhoration of the Hierophant and the mixing of the blood and water symbolism which links this station and Sign with Aquarius, the water bearer and the entering of a more enlightened Age.

12.The Tribe of Simeon relates here to the closing of the Neophyte ceremony for Simeon (along with Levi - the second part of the two fishes of the Sign of Pisces) shows the Rule of Law, for this is what Simeon must uphold. The Law was made to banish the wicked or evil, and that is exactly the function of the Closing Ceremony. For this gets rid of unwanted negativity in the Temple.

The fixed stars in the 12 constellations, their ancient meaning and tarot associations
by Pat Zalewski
Aries

The constellation of Aries the Ram falls in the Jewish month of Nissan (March-April), In Egyptian times, Aries was called 'Tametouris Ammon - 'reign or government of Amon', and we are reminded here of the 4th Key of the Tarot, 'The Emperor", and the strong symbolism of the Ram being depicted in it, directed by the seated figure on the throne, who represents a form of government.

The Tarot Queen of Wands also relates to a large portion of Aries. The three stone crystals which are shaped like a tripod (on the throne and scepter) of the card, comes from the Arabic 'Athaflyy' – trivet or tripod). The lioness in the card relates to the symbol of Aries (according to Teucros) and in the hourly cycles relates to Bast, the lion headed goddess.

If we examine the three cards in the Minor Arcana that are related to Aries, then we have:

2 of Wands – Lord of Dominion.
3 of Wands – Lord of Established Strength.
4 of Wands – Lord of Perfected Work.

If you view the titles of each card successively then you have: 'The Jews were dominated (controlled) and they gain strength and left Egypt'. All three of these cards relate to the meaning of some of the main individual fixed Stars of Aries.

There are 66 stars in this constellation, with the main star being called 'El Nath' meaning 'wounded' or 'slain'. The next star of importance is 'Al Sheraton', the' bruised' or 'wounded', while another important star is 'Mersatim' – 'bound'. All three of these main stars are in harmony with their associated meanings.

The Akkadian name for Aries was 'Braziggar' meaning 'correct or right sacrifice'. This is the time of Passover (Spring Equinox) when the Angel of Death visited the Jews in captivity and killed the first born of every household that did not have the Blood of the Lamb on the door:

'In the tenth day of this month they shall take to them every man a lamb, according to the house of their fathers, a lamb for a house'

It is also noted in this month that the Exodus began (according to Josephus) from Egypt. The Angel of Aries is Melchidael (also Machidiel) meaning 'fullness of God'. He is an angel of procreation.

Taurus

The Chaldee name for Taura is 'Tor', while its Arabic name is 'Al Thaur', while the Greek is 'Tauros'. The Hebrew name for this constellation is 'Shur' meaning 'coming or rising', while the Hebrew name for Bull is Reem. This relates to a lofty approach or ideal, pre-eminent or high father. From this we get the idea behind the fifth Tarot Key, the Hierophant. The symbol of the Bull is self evident in this Trump. The Prince of Disks rules from 20 degrees Aries to 20 degrees Taurus, and he also has the Taurean symbols depeicted in his card, with the symbol of the hexagram or Star of David, as the Jewish people are united for the first time under this symbol as a single nation.

The three cards under this Sign:

    5 of Disks   –   Lord of Material Trouble.
    6 of Disks   –   Lord of Material Success.
    7 of Disks   –   Lord of Success Unfulfilled.

'Through trouble comes success which is only momentary'.

There are 141 stars in this constellation and two important star groups. The main star is 'Al Debaran' meaning 'Leader or Governor'. The Pleiades has a meaning of 'congregation, judge or ruler' and comes through the Hebrew 'Camih' – 'accumulation'. The Hyades is another star group of note in the Taurus constellation and its meaning is identical to that of Pleiades. Some of the main stars are 'Patlilicium- 'belonging to a judge'; 'Wasat' - 'foundation'; 'Al Thuraiyia' - 'abundance' and 'Vergilae - centre' .

The two tribes of Ephraim and Manasseh are associated to Taurus, as the following quote shows:

The firstling of his bullock majesty is his, And his horns are the horns of the wild ox. With them he shall push the peoples, all of them, even to the ends of the earth. And they are the ten thousands of Ephraim, and they are the thousands of Manasseh. (Deut. 37:17)

Asmodel is the angel of Taurus, and was formerly one of the chiefs of the Cherubim, and is now considered an angel of punishment for any evil doing. The punishment aspect of this angel relates to the strength and power of the Bull of Taurus.

Gemini

The Egyptian for this constellation was 'Cluss' (or Claustrum Hor), meaning 'he who cometh', which shows two human figures together. Both the Coptic (Pi-mahi) and the Hebrew 'Thaumin' have a common meaning of 'united'. There are 85 Stars in this system and it was originally called Apollo and Hercules, the Romans changed this to Castor and Pollux. In keeping with the original tradition of 'he who cometh', the Golden Dawn association of the sixth Key of the tarot, is to Perseus who comes to rescue Andromeda from Cetus the sea monster. Because of their love for each other, both were placed in a constellation in the heavens and were united forever, or so the story goes. The Court card association here is the Prince of Swords, who rules from 30 degrees Taurus to 20 degrees Gemini.

The three Minor Arcana cards under this Sign are:

    8 of Swords   –   Lord of Shortened Force.
    9 of Swords   –   Lord of Despair and Cruelty.
    10 of Swords –   Lord of Ruin.

All of these cards are not good and show punishment, cruelty and despair, much is outlined by the 6th Key, as Andromeda awaits her rescuer, fearful that Cetus will get to her first.

The first major star worthy of consideration is in the head of the right figure. This star is called Apollo and means 'ruler'. The star in the head of the other twin is called is Hercules 'who comes to labour or suffer'. Another star of importance is 'Al Henah' meaning 'hurt' or 'wounded.' The point to consider is that this constellation shows victory after the rescue or battle, and to this is a point not lost on the meaning of the Sixth Key (note how the club and bow are held in the relaxed position). This is also shown by the star name, in the figure of Apollo, who is called 'Mebusta', meaning 'treading under feet', yet another inference to victory won. Others stars in this constellation are the Hebrew 'Popus' meaning 'the branch or spreading';'Al Gaiuza' - 'palm branch' and 'Al Dira' - 'seed or branch'. The use of the branch is also given in some pictorial representations of the twins.

The angel of this Sign is Ambriel, one of the chief officers for the 12 hours of the night. One of his main functions is the protection against evil.

Cancer

In the Egyptian Zodiac, Cancer is associated to a Scarabaeus or beetle. The Egyptian name in the Denderah Zodiac is Klari or 'cattle pens' or 'folds'. Its Arabic name is 'Al Sartan' meaning 'he who holds' or 'binds' and is very close to the Hebrew ASR, meaning 'to bind together'. It has a similar meaning in Syriac and the Greek name is 'Karkionos', which also means 'holding' or 'encircling'. A breakdown of the modern names is from 'Kahn' and 'Inn' or 'resting place'. The Akkadian name is 'Sukulna' - 'seizer' or 'possessor of seed'. The Seventh Tarot Key of the Tarot, the Chariot, is associated here as well. The binding concept is shown in this Key by the Chariot of a ruler who holds and protects his realm, through force. The concern of the Golden Dawn is the methodology used to keep all the lands of the Kingdom bound together is through patrol of his realm. The Court card association is the Queen of Cups and the crayfish symbol for Cancer is prominently displayed from the cup she holds. The Ibis also shown on this card is part of the description from the early Egyptian designs. She governs from 20 degrees Gemini to 20 degrees Cancer. The three Minor Arcana cards under this Sign are:

    2 of Cups – Lord of Love.
    3 of Cups – Lord of Abundance.
    4 of Cups – Lord of Blended Pleasure.

All of these cards are of a positive nature, and work on an emotional level of perception.

This constellation contains 83 stars. The brightest star is called 'Tegmine', meaning 'holding', other stars of importance are 'Acuben' - 'sheltering' or 'hiding place'; 'Maalaph' -'assembled thousands'; 'Al Himeran' - 'kids' or 'lambs'. There are some star clusters worth noting in Cancer, 'Asellus Boreas' - 'Northern Ass' and 'Asellus Australias' -'Southern Ass' (both of these represent the astrological symbol of Cancer).

The angel governing Cancer is called Nuriel. He is invoked from the South and is said to be able to aid in Astral projection. His direct superior is Veguaniel, ruler of the third hour of the day.

Leo

In the Egyptian zodiac. Leo is shown as a lion treading upon a serpent, it is called 'Pi Mentekeon', meaning 'pouring out' (originally the shape was in that of a Babylonian 'dog'). The whole concept shows that the serpent had issued forth from the cup and is held in check by superior strength. In the map of the heavens, this shows the lion above the constellation of Hydra, the serpent. The early Egyptian figure of Leo included the added constellations of the Crater and the Bird (Corvu). The Eighth Key of the Tarot is called 'Strength', and shows a woman controlling the superior force of the Lion, the Lion is at point of docility. In Egyptian symbolism the woman is called 'Her-ua'- 'great enemy' and she represents the constellation of Corvu, where she holds two cups that indicates part of her nature is poisonous, for from the spilled cup the serpent comes forth. The Golden Dawn theme, like the Egyptian actually incorporates more than one constellation's meaning.

Another name for Leo is the Egyptian 'Knem' -'who conquers' hence victory over the serpent. The Hebrew name Leo is 'Arieh' -'rendering lion' (there are 6 variations of this; 'Gor' - 'lion's whelp'; 'Ciphir' - 'young lion'; 'Sachil'- 'mature lion'; 'Laish - 'fierce lion'; 'Laiba' - 'lioness'). The Syriac name is 'Aryo' which is the same as the Hebrew, while the Arabic name is 'Al Asad' - 'Lion coming forth'.The King of Disks rules 20 degrees Leo to 20 degrees Virgo. The emblem of the stag on his crest is also Solar in nature, and is often depicted standing on a serpent, like the old Egyptian symbolism.

The three cards of the Minor Arcana representing Leo are as follows:

> 5 of Wands – Lord of Strife.
> 6 of Wands – Lord of Victory.
> 7 of Wands – Lord of Valour.

This constellation has 95 stars. The brightest star is called 'Cor Leonis' -'heart of a lion' (also called 'Regulus' - 'treading under foot'. Other stars of interest are 'Denebola' - 'Lord who cometh'; 'Al Geibha - 'exaltation'. 'Zosma' - 'Shining forth'; 'Sarcan - 'joining'; 'Minchir al Asad'- 'punishing Lion'; 'Al Dafera' - 'enemy put down'.

The angel governing Leo is Verchiel who also helps rule the Thrones that are associated to Binah. This angel is also a governor of the Sun, hence its Solar association to Leo.

Virgo

The constellation shows a woman with a branch in one hand, and an ear of corn in another. The earliest Sumerian title for her is 'Absin -'whose father was sin'. In Assyrian time she was called 'Baaltis' (Belat, Belit) or 'Bel's wife'. In Egyptian times she was related to Isis ('Aspolia' - 'ear of corn') . the Syriac and Hebrew name for this Sign is identical , 'Bethulah' – a 'branch'. Another Arabic title is 'Sunbul' -'ear of corn', while the Latin name simply means 'virgin'. Her Persian title was 'Khosa' - 'ear of wheat' , and 'Secdeidos de Darzama' -'virgin in maiden neatness'. The Ninth Key of the Tarot 'The Hermit' , at first glance bears no resemblance to Virgo. The only connection is a lobe figure holding a staff (branch). Since Mercury rules Virgo, the mercurial concept is linked to the figure of the Kerux, whose function is to show the way – by example. This is also one of the functions of Virgo. There are some very strong links with the hermit and some of the meanings of the fixed stars relate to the coming of a messenger or someone of importance. The Court card associated here is the Queen of Swords, who rules from 20 degrees Virgo to 20 degrees Libra. The child's kerubic emblem worn by the Queen is another form of Eros (Cupid) and as such is linked directly to Mercury.

The cards of the Minor Arcana in Virgo all follow the general meaning of the Sign and the fixed stars:

8 of Disks   – Lord of Prudence.
9 of Disks   – Lord of Material Gain.
10 of Disks – Lord of Wealth.

There are 110 stars in Virgo. The brightest star is called 'Al Zimach' -'the branch', while its Hebrew title is 'Tzemech' (now called 'Spic') -'ear of corn'. The next star of major importance is 'Zavijaveh', meaning 'gloriously beautiful'; another is 'Al Mureddin' - 'who shall come down' or 'who shall have dominion'. Some other stars worth mentioning are 'Subilah -'who carries'; 'Al Azal'-'branch' and 'Sublion -'spike of corn'.

The angel of Virgo is Hamalie, who is also one of the rulers of the choir of Virtues, whose orientation is linked to Tiphareth.

Libra

The early Sumerian title for this constellation was 'Zibaana' meaning 'heavenly fate'. With this title alone , we are reminded of the Judgement scene in the 'Book of the Dead'. The Akkadian name for this Sign was 'Bir' meaning 'light', and its earliest time was shown as a circular altar, or depicted as a lamp on a altar. There used to be an overlap with this sign with the Claws of Scorpio. The translation of the Hebrew name for Libra was 'the scales ' or 'weighing'. Another old Akkadian name was 'Tulku' was 'sacred mound' or 'altar'. The Syrians called it 'Masatha', while the Persians called it 'Terazu', all related to 'weighing'. The Coptic title was 'Lambadia' 'station of the propitiation'. An Arabic title was 'Al Zubena' – meaning "purchase' or 'redemption'.

The modern astrological figure associated to Libra shows a beam in balanced disposition. In the 11th Key we have the title 'Justice' and its association to the 'Hall of Maat' and the 'Egyptian Book of the Dead', which is identical to the ancient meanings of this Sign. In the Court Cards we have the Prince of Cups who goes from 20 degrees Libra to 20 degrees Scorpio you have the Crab issuing forth from the cup.

The three cards of the Minor Arcana associated here are:

2 of Swords – Lord of Peace Restored.
3 of Swords – Lord of Sorrow.
4 of Swords – Lord of Rest from Strife.

All these titles relate in one way or another to the scales of justice as applied to the 'Egyptian Book of the Dead'.

There are 51 stars in this constellation. One of the brightest is 'Zebulon al Genubi' - 'purchase - or 'price which is deficient'; 'Zuben al ahemali' - 'price which covers'; 'Zuben Akrabi' - 'price of conflict'.

The angel associated to this Sign is Zuriel ('my rock is God'). According to Numbers (3.35), he is 'chief of the House of the father of the families of Merari'. He is also said to offer assistance in curing the stupidity of man.

Scorpio

The earliest name for this Sign was from the Sumerian 'Girtab' meaning 'which claws and cuts'. The Coptic title for Scorpio was 'Isidis' - 'attack of the enemy' or 'oppression'. The Hebrew name for this Sign is Akrab, which can literally mean 'Scorpion' or 'conflict' or 'war'. One Arabic title is 'Al Akrab'- 'wounding him that cometh', while the Syriac name was 'Akreva', and for the Persians it was 'Ghezhdum'. The 13th Key of the Tarot is the 'Death Card' which relates to both death and renewal after conflict. The Court card associated here is the King of Cups and governs 20 degrees Libra to 20 degrees Scorpio. A look at this card will show the serpent coming out of the cup. This relates to the constellation of 'Ophiuchus'(which is still classed under the heading of Scorpio) who controls the Scorpion - who tries to bite him with its venom. The symbol of the Eagle in this card is an old one and its attributed to Scorpio by the patriarch Abraham (according to Sir William Drummond) which is also the on the armorial of the Tribe of Dan. The Minor Arcana associated to this Sign are;

5 of Cups   –   Lord of Loss in Pleasure.
6 of Cups   –   Lord of Pleasure.
7 of Cups   –   Lord of Illusionary Success.

There are 44 stars in this Sign. The brightest is 'Antares' , sometimes called 'Kalb al Akrab', meaning ' the wounding' (also called 'Cor Scorpio' in Roman Times). The next star of importance is in the stinger of the Scorpion's tail and is the Hebrew 'Lesath' meaning 'perverse'.

The angel of this Sign is Barchiel (Barakile) 'Lightning of God' and is said to bring success in games of chance when invoked along with Uriel and Rubiel.

Sagittarius

The Sumerian name for this Sign was 'Pabil', meaning 'defender'. The Persian name is 'Kaman' while the Syric was "Keshta', and the Hebrew 'Kestheth'; in Akkadian 'ban', all of these names relate to 'a bow', in their translations. A Coptic title of this Sign is 'Pi-Maere' -'graciousness, beauty, coming forth'. Early Cuneiform scripts designate this constellation with 'war' and 'strength', but as a defender. The 14th Key of the Tarot associated here in 'Temperance'. The Golden Dawn figure here, which is also a traditional Tarot design, shows one of stabilisation through adverse conditions., this is shown by the fine line the angel is treading, standing with one foot in water and the other on land (with volcanic activity). It shows that even in adverse conditions, the necessary adjustments are being made so that the balnce of power is maintained.

The Knight of Wands rules from 20 degrees Scorpio to 20 degrees Sagittarius. The symbol of the horse's head as his crest relates to the horse like attributes (centaur) of the archer.

The three cards of the Minor Arcana under this signs are:

8 of Wands – Lord of Swiftness.
9 of Wands – Lord of Great Strength.
10 of Wands– Lord of Oppression.

There are 69 stars in this constellation. The star group near the drawing hand is called 'Al Naam al Sadirahd' or 'returning Ostriches', while those on the head of the arrow are called 'Al naam al Warid' or 'going Ostriches'. These three concepts relate to the figure's prominence in the Milky Way, which is sometimes related to a vast celestial river.

The angel associated to this Sign is 'Advachiel', and he alternates with 'Phaleg' with his duties.

Capricorn

The ancient Sumerian name for this Sign was 'Suhur Mash' meaning 'goat fish'. The Persian name is 'Busggali', the Syriac 'Gadjo', all of which mean 'goat'. The Hebrew name is 'Gedi' meaning 'kid'. The Egyptians called it 'Chnum' or 'Knum' meaning 'God of waters'. The Golden Dawn have associated the 15th Key , the 'Devil' to this Sign. We must consider that the Biblical reference (Lev. 16-17) when we are told of two goats, one is called the goat of 'sin offering' and this is what many consider the 15th Key relates to. For this goat is doomed to pay the price for all the transgressions of the congregation, there is to be no escape.

The Court Card association here is the Queen of Disks, who governs 20 degrees of Sagittarius to 20 degrees Virgo. She sits on the throne with a goat emblem, while holding a cube, watery part of earth.

The cards of the Minor Arcana associated to Capricorn are :

2 of Disks   –   Lord of Harmonious Change.
3 of Disks   –   Lord of Material Works.
4 of Disks   –   Lord of Earthly Power.

There are 51 stars in this constellation. The two brightest are 'Prima' and 'Secunda Gieda', or collectively 'Al Gedi' which means 'kid'. The star in the forehead is called 'Uz'- 'the goat', by the Akkadians. The other star names are 'Al Dehabeth' meaning 'sacrifice slain' and 'Maasad' meaning 'slaying', 'Deneb al Gedi' or 'tail of the goat'.

The angel of this Sign is Hanael - 'Glory of the grace of God'. It was Hanael who took Enoch on his journey to heaven. The name Hanael was often used in talismen for protection against Evil.

Aquarius

The Sumerian name for this constellation was 'Gu', meaning 'lord of waters'. The Akkadian name was 'kukura' or 'seat of the flowing waters'. In the Egyptian Zodiac, it was called 'Hupei Tiron' - 'place of him coming down' or 'pour forth'. In Hebrew it is called 'Deli' or 'water urn', while the Arabians called it 'Al Dalw' meaning 'well bucket'. The 17th Key of the Tarot, is related to this principle, though the water pourer is feminine by nature, for she is on the Mercy Side of the Tree of Life.

The Court Card associated here is the King of Swords, who rules 20 degrees Capricorn to 20 degrees Aquarius.

The Minor Arcana associated to this Sign are:

5 of Swords – Lord of Defeat.
6 of Swords – Lord of Earned Success.
7 of Swords – Lord of Unstable Effort.

There are 108 stars in this Sign and four of the first magnitude. The star in the right shoulder (alpha) is called 'Sa'd al Melik' meaning 'pouring forth', other translators have called this star 'lucky one of the kingdom'; the star (beta) in the left shoulder is called 'Saad al Sund' meaning 'who goeth and returneth' or 'pourer out'. Another version names this star 'Sa'd al Suud' and is translated as 'luckiest'. One of the stars on the innermost edge of the urn is called 'Sadachbia' or 'Lucky star of hidden thing'. The star nearest the shin is called 'Scheat', which has the Hebrew meaning 'who goeth and returneth'. Another star was called 'Al bali' or 'good fortune of the swallower'.

The angel of this Sign is called Cambriel (Cambiel). This is the angel of 'Kavanah' or 'intention' and will help those obtain visionary experiences and help them try and interpret them, especially through ceremonial works of magick.

Pisces

The Sumerian name for this Sign is 'Simmah', meaning 'fishes'. The Egyptian name was 'Picot Orion' or 'the fishes of Him that cometh'. A Coptic variant is 'Piscis Hori'-'protection'. The Syriac name is 'Nuno' - 'fishes', which is very similar to the Hebrew, which is sometimes referred to as 'Dagaim'. The Babylonian name was 'Nunnu' and the Persian name is 'Mahik', all of course meaning 'fish'. We must also consider while there were but two fishes in this Sign, the 'band' that holds them together is also very important. The Egyptians called this the 'Uor' or he cometh' while an Arabic name is 'Al Rish' meaning 'the band 'or bridle'.

The 18th Key of the Tarot, 'the Moon', is associated here, and at first glance bears no resemblance to the Sign of Pisces. Yet the Water Sign of the fishes when related to its Egyptian meaning 'he cometh' - as the crayfish comes.

The Court card association is the Knight of Cups, who rules 20 degrees Aquarius to 20 degrees Pisces. He holds in his hand, the crab emerging from the Cup, just like the crayfish emerging from the pool.

The Minor Arcana associated to Pisces are:

8 of Cups   – Lord of Abandoned Success.
9 of Cups   – Lord of Material Happiness.
10 of Cups   – Lord of Perpetual Success.

There are approximately 113 stars (according to Heis there are 128) in this Sign. One of the brightest is 'Al Rischa, 'meaning 'cord' shown in the knot of the band of the cord binding the fishes. Another is 'Fum Al Samakh' or 'the fish's mouth'.

Amnitzel (Amitiel) is the angel of this sign, though sometimes it is Pasiel. This angel is called 'the angel of Truth and Peace.'

A study of the stones of the Breast Plate of the High Priest
By Pat Zalewski

Due to the number of differing opinions by scholars, the actual designation of what stone represented what Tribe of Israel, and what order they were placed in the Breast Plate is apt to give us some confusing testimonies. It should be pointed out that the early biblical description of the 12 stones varied with the experience of the writers to clarify and identify what stone was what, as the modern concept of a stone based on its crystalline structure was unknown in Biblical times. The first reliable scholar to identify them is Josephus ('Antiquities'). The first appearance of the stones in Exodus 28 and 39. There is a great deal of confusion also in what order the Tribes (stones) were given on the Breast Plate (whether they were right to left or left to right or top to bottom) though most historians work in the direction of Hebrew calligraphy (left to right). The following order is the astrological one, as the order given in Exodus is not necessarily consecutive.

Gad

The first stone on the High Priest's Breast Plate is called ADM in Hebrew (Odem or Adam) and signifies a 'blood red' coloured stone associated to the martial tribe of Gad. The stone here is thought to be a carnelian (also called Agate), which Josephus called sadius (sardonyx), both of these are in fact part of the modern description of Chalcedony. This stone stimulates feelings of spirituality through stimulation of the heart chakra, hence its spiritual and directional drive. On the vibrational level, it increases ethereal fluidium around the Etheric Body, giving it a protective layer of energy. It gives awareness and a fraternal bonding that brings about the ability to control the Mental Body. It also reinforces the Emotional Body and stimulates the nervous system and thus helps with the intuitive states of awareness in general. One of its prime forces is the help in connection with and speaking to group situations and also giving additional impetus to the flow of a speaker in trying to capture the imagination of those present around him. It is a gem stone that gives hope to those who need it most.

Ephraim

The second stone of importance is the Hebrew PTDH (Pitdah) and is associated to the Tribe of Ephraim. The stone associated here is called Peridot, and is a lemon-green in colour. This word comes from the Greek 'peri' meaning 'around', and 'doto' meaning 'donor'. Josephus calls this Topaz, though his description of the stone does not resemble what we now call Topaz, for the gem that had that ancient title has been lost. Peridot gives deep spiritual insight and aligns subtle bodies. It works mainly on tissue regeneration, through stimulation of the individual cells of the energy of the Etheric body. It enforces contact with Higher Self, so that the directions coming from it are more clear and concise. It works through the heart chakra, and repairs any weakening in the subtle bodies and also helps alleviate Miasms. It helps to understand karmic patterns. Especially if used with meditation through a reinforcement of the potency of the Astral Body. It is a slow acting gem that gives protection and helps give protection and purifies the entire system.

Manasseh

The third gemstone on the breast plate is from the Hebrew word 'BRQTh' (Bareketh) loosely translates as 'gleaming', 'flashing' or 'brilliant'. This gem is also associated to the Tribe of Levi. The description of Josephus simply called it 'smaragdus' (green) and some authorities have related it to the emerald. This stone helps meditation with its tranquil vibrations and fraternal love. This is governed by the actions of the Heart Chakra, for to obtain these vibrational levels by this, all the lower subtle bodies align (Astral/Emotional, Etheric and Lower Mental) though it will mainly work through the Astral/Emotional body increasing psychic awareness. It is a meditational stimulant and helps get rid of hidden fears.

Issachar

The fourth gemstone of the Breast Plate is called NPhK (Nophek) which I have placed as Turquoise, for the Tribe of Judah. Josephus calls this a 'carbuncle', which is red, while the Midrash clearly shows a stone of blue colouring and not red. Some writers have associated red stones here because of the link to the Lion of Judah. The ancient Chaldean name for this stone is Torkeja. Its function is to aid and strengthen the physical body through some tissue regeneration. It also helps the meditational states of awareness by aligning both the subtle bodies and the chakras. It's function is that of a healer, and works very well on cataract problems as well as stimulating circulation. Its colour shows a strong tendency to help with Astral Work.

Judah

The fifth gemstone on the Breast Plate is SPhIR (Sapphire), according to Josephus, though it is considered by most authorities that it does not refer to the gem we know of today, as sapphire, but is a black onyx. This is a variation of Chalcedony and has its name derived from the Greek 'onychos' meaning 'gingernail' or 'claw'. This is a stone that gravitates the wearer towards Spiritual awareness and insight to whatever forces are guiding you. It balances the positive and negative energies within the Self and opens the Solar Plexus, Base and Throat Chakras and helps control the Kundaline process that it stimulates. On the physical level it is a stone of tissue regeneration of the heart, kidney, nerve and skin.

Naphthali

The sixth stone of the Breast Plate is associated to a stone called 'YHLOM' (Yahalom). Some authorities have considered that this word Yahalom comes from 'halam' meaning 'to strike', and have given the English translation of this gemstone as a diamond, as it is described in the Midrash as a white stone (rock crystal). This is White Quartz and is a stone of communication. It removes the negative tendencies, thoughts and emotions, it also increases one's psychic awareness and helps in meditation. It is a stone of vision as well as helping to realign the Emotional and Etheric Bodies, and amplifying thought forms by strengthening the Brow, Crown and Solar plexus chakras.

Asshur

The seventh stone on the Breast Plate is 'LShM' (Leshem) has this has been attributed to Opal, from the Greek 'Opalus' meaning 'precious stone'. Opal is a variation of Quartz and was used in ancient days as the stone of prophecy. The Midrash gives the colour as blue. This stone works on the Crown chakra and opens the door to true mystical experiences by working through the Emotional Body. It helps with depression and aids and also transforms one's basic nature from sexual to the divine process of higher realisation of one's spiritual awareness. It helps modify thought forms, especially through meditation, and opens up to one's full creative potential. It helps align the Emotional and Mental Bodies.

Dan

The eight stone on the High Priest's Breast Plate is called ShBu (Shebo) which some have considered coming from the root 'to take prisoners' or 'capture'. The Midrash describes this stone as being grey in colour. The Moonstone (Adularia) is possibly the stone referred to here. It is a stone of peace and harmony and pulls one towards spiritual matters. The stone works through the emotional levels by aligning the Astral and Emotional bodies and activates the Brow and Crown Chakras. It also opens the abdominal chakra and helps it alleviate stress as well as helping with the birth process.

Benjamin

The ninth stone on the Breast Plate is from the Hebrew root 'AHLMH (Ahlamah) which is associated to the word 'Halom' - 'to dream', which relates well to this stone. Amethyst (a variety of quartz) was known in Egypt as 'Hemag' and related to the heart, and from this is it is no surprise that it directly effects the Heart Chakra. Amethyst is a stone of meditation, hence its title 'to dream', for it helps with certain visionary experiences. If correctly used, it can be used as a stone of protection against negative psychic influences. The Midrash described this stone has having a wine colour.

Zebulon

The tenth stone of the High Priest's Breast Plate is the 'TRShISh' (Tarshish), and the stone associated here is the Beryl. Beryl gets its name from the ancient Greek word 'Beryllos', whose origin is unknown, but is used to described green gems. It is a stone that aids spiritual development and stimulates the Base chakra and helps ease tension on the spinal column and the intestinal tract. It eases general tension in the physical body and can have a similar effect as a sedative. The Midrash colour to this stone describes it as being aquamarine in colour.

Reuben

This stone is called ShHM (Shoham) and relates to Obsidian. It derives its name from Obsidius, who discovered this mineral in Ethiopia. Its function works on the physical body by balancing up the intestinal tract and helping to ease any viral infections there. Its higher value is in aligning the Emotional and Mental Bodies and it is used frequently for divination and mediumship.

Simeon

This stone associate here is called YSPII (Yashphch) and the literal translation is Jasper (which is also a variety of quartz). The Midrash desribes this stone as multicoloured. It works on the cellular level of tissue regeneration and also aligns briefly the chakras so that messages from the Higher Self can be clearly understood. It depresses disorientation from overuse.

Flashing Talismatic Zodiac Colour Formation
By Pat Zalewski

When applying the flashing Colours of the Zodiac, the Adept will find that the exact opposite colour of the one being worked also relates back to the circular diagram of the colours, for the Flashing Colours will appear directly opposite the primary one being used. A good example of this is given in the following list, taken from an early description of the Golden Dawn Colour Scales.

So when colouring an object in the red of Aries (Cardinal Fire) the balanced colour of the Emerald Green of Libra(Cardinal Air) would be required as a complementary. Also the colours of Capricorn (Cardinal Earth) and Cancer (Cardinal Water) are also complementaries.

Now if we examine the Four Triplicities that are indicated in the Table of Shewbread Diagram (from the paths of the King Scale) we find that the Fire Signs of Aries, Leo and Sagittarius are related to the Three Primary colours of Red, Yellow and Blue (Fire Air and Water). The Airy triplicites are linked to the the Secondaries of Orange (Gemini), Green (Libra) and Aquarius (Violet). The Water Triplicities of Amber (Cancer), Green-Blue (Scorpio) and Crimson (Pisces) are closely related to the Quaternaries, and the Earth Triplicity of Red -Orange (Taurus), Capricorn (Indigo) and Virgo (Yellow Green).

In Talismatic work involving the Zodiac colours, the complementary colour comes from its polar opposite, so the energy colours of the circle can be balanced harmoniously. Its opposite colour, when applied to the Zodiac Signs is not a Sign antagonistic to it, but in harmony with it. For Fire and Air can be paired with each other and Earth and Water cannot. This also relates to the colours that they represent. So every complementary colour will be in a Sign favourable to the main one utilised (hence the term complementary) and this allows the two colours to work with each other in a support role, without interfering with the force and magnetic attraction one will provide for another. By breaking the Signs down into their elemental divisions, as in the Table of

Shewbread, one can show the generation of colour into four major divisions - these divisions are called 'Grand Trine' in Astrology and they are worth studying. (Dane Rudhyar's *Astrological Aspects* shows a deep intuitive understanding of the Trines and Elemental associations along with Bill Tierney's *Dynamics of Aspects Analysis*)

The 12 Zodiac colours are placed in Two Tarot Keys. The first is Tau, the 21st Key when the 12 Zodiac colours are given in Circles. The Four Elemental Colours given to the Kerubics of this Key manifest in the Table of Shewbread. The 10th Key of relating to Kaph, the 'Wheel of Fortune' is the second where the Zodiac colours are used and these in turn relate back to the symbol of the Lotus Wand.

Since the Three Mother letters of Aleph, Mem and Shin equate with the three primary colours, the secondary colours mixed together produce the Indigo colour, which is representative of the 32 path, shown by the letter Tau. Placed together you have the word AMETH, meaning 'Truth', for Aleph is the first letter and Tau the last letter of the Alphabet.

Colouring of the Shewbread Diagram

Aries	Red	Libra	Emerald Green
Taurus	Red-Orange	Scorpio	Blue
Gemini	Orange	Sagittarius	Blue
Cancer	Amber	Capricorn	Indigo
Leo	Lemon-Yellow	Aquarius	Violet
Virgo	Yellow-Green	Pisces	Crimson

A. The Outside Circles that encompass the Triangles with the Zodiac Sign within are in the Paths of the King Scale relating to that of the Sign.

B. The Triangles within these circles are in the colour of the Element of the Sign.

C. Colour of the Zodiac Sign in the Complementary colour of Path.

D. The Hebrew lettering in these circles are Complementary to that of the Path.

E. The Kerubic Circles are in the colour of the element with the drawing them in the Complementary.

F. The triangle below is an example of one portion of the colouring of this diagram:

1. Colour of the Path of Sign.
2. Colour of Sign mixed with its neighbouring Sign
3. Colour of Sign mixed with its neighbouring Sign
4. Mixture of two and three
5. Path and Element colours.

G. The Pentagram is red and the lamp orange.

The colouring of this diagram, revealed to the TH.A.M by Mathers (I am not sure which one designated the colouring but one copy did turn up at Whare Ra temple and passed on to me by Tony Fuller) and is complex in the extreme, and it becomes comparable to a meditation Mandala of Indian literature.

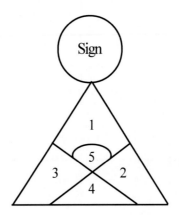

Chapter 3

The Order Of The Ritual Of The Heptagram
By Macgregor Mathers

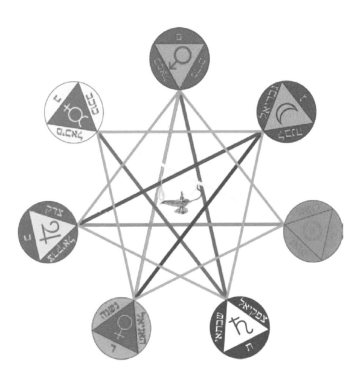

*This was originally in four parts, and I have only included
two, as the others are less than impressive.*

1. *General Symbolism of the Planets.*
2. *Of the Tarot Trumps attributed to the Planets.*
3. *Of the method of making symbol of the Heptagram.*
4. *Ritual of the Heptagram and planetary powers in every day life.*

I will include only part 2 and part 4. I was not impressed with this paper overall and even Mathers work on the Trumps relating to the planets was only good in parts and frankly is not good enough for the level of TH.A.M. That is one of the reasons I have opted to expand on each Trump, as I have done with the 'Universe' Key. I have omitted the description of the 'Universe' Key, taken from part two, which is given at the beginning of this book. Part 1 and 2 were very poorly done. The God form attribution in part 1, was barely a paragraph on each of the Roman and Greek gods of the Planets. The whole thing was put together to explain further deeper attributions of the diagram of the Heptagram shown in the 1=10 ritual. As far as I am aware, this paper is as far as Mathers got with the Trump explanations, the exception being in his A.O. 6=5 and 7=4 grade rituals. I have viewed the Tarot explanations of the 6=5 ritual and they are quite poorly done. Eventually even the A.O. opted for the Felkin/Westcott Trumps design. I have had some of the cards redrawn from the Mathers description to give an indication as to what he had in mind with the rest of the Trumps. PZ.

The Tarot Trumps Attributed To The Seven Planets And The True Designs And Interpretations Thereof.

Wheel of Fortune - Jupiter

To him is attributed the 10th Key or trump of the Tarot, known as 'The Wheel of Fortune' or 'Rota Fortunae'; and here notice that this word 'Rota'is, by Metathesis, the same as 'Taro' and this Key,

THE ORDER OF THE HEPTAGRAM 103

in a sense, epitomises and sets forth the symbol of the entire Tarot pack, even as Jupiter, the Father of the Gods, in himself unites symbolism of all Olympus. This card is also titled 'The Lord of Force of Life'.

The 'Wheel' is the shaft or handle of the Lotus - wand of the Zelator Adeptus Minor, bent round into a circle, and it is so bent because it typifieth an External Power momentarily exerted on the Works of a particular coloured band, which is grasped by the power of Jupiter. Therefore is the rims of the wheel divided into twelve segments having the Colours of the bands of the shaft of the Lotus Wand, and having Twelve spokes therefrom, bearing the same colours, and banded with the complementaries thereof: and, at the centre or hub of the Wheel, is the Lotus flower itself, which thus becomes the point of rest. And if thou wilt colour this card for thyself, take heed that the carmine tint of Pisces shall lead the eye with no break round to Aries again with its blood red colour. And the uppermost band or segment of the Wheel shall be the yellow band of Leo; the reason thereof shall at once appear. For the bands shall be grouped into threes, and to each three there is assigned a Kerubic or Talismatic Figure of a Sphinx, uniting in itself and shewing forth the symbology of those Three Signs, thus forming the figures which, in the ordinary and corrupt packs, appear as if bound to the wheel. Thus, the uppermost figure is formed from Leo, Virgo and Libra, and the form above it is a woman's head and shoulders and bust, save for a light scarf of Yellowish Green that floats around her. Her hair is Light Golden, and she wears a Golden crown, and bears the sword and Scales of Justice and Equilibrium: and her hinder parts are those of a Tawny Lion, with on his side, a Red Star. and this star is Regulus, the Prince, or Cor Leonis, the Heart of the Lion, which being the starting Point of the Zodiac, comes appropriately at the top. And the Sphinx faces to the left hand of the observer when looking at the card.

And the next Sphinx, descending on the left hand, half way down, is formed from the Triad of Scorpio, Sagittarius and Capricornicus; and it is somewhat like a centaur - that is, a grey bearded man's head and trunk, bearing a bow and arrows, over the forelegs and feet of a goat, and the hair of the goat of a dark purplish blue; and the hinder parts are the tail of a Scorpion, of a dark purplish green. But the man has a cloak hung over his shoulders of a vivid blue, and thereon, in orange, the symbol of an Arrow. This figure is often depicted in Assyrian sculptures, and by Assyriologists is called the 'Scorpion Man' or 'Scorpion Horse'.

And the lowest Talismatic figure is formed from Aquarius, Pisces, and Aries. And of these, because Aries or the Ram is itself the symbol of Jupiter, according to Greek and Roman Mythology, and so dominateth the entire symbol, so the Symbol of the Ram itself entereth only slightly into the design of this sphinx, least, in the Works of Jupiter, it should be over strong, and should destroy the equilibrium of the card. The form of the Sphinx, therefore, is that of a Mermaid, a beautiful woman, wholly nude to the waist, save for a leopard skin wrapped round her: and the tail of a Fish - and these are in their natural colours, save that the fish hath somewhat the hue of the red mullet, which by some is considered to be the fish specially related to this Sign. And, on the Head of the Woman, is the red Phrygian cap, in front thereof, a pair of a curled Ram's horns - and no further symbolism of Aries hath she.

And the Sphinx on the right hand side, which is rising, is formed from the remaining Signs of Taurus, Gemini and Cancer; and the Form thereof is the Human headed Assyrian Bull, but having the tail of a Bird and the reason of this Bird's tail pertianeth to a certain knowledge concerning the Sign Cancer which cannot be fully explained at this stage, for it belongs not to the knowledge of This Grade *(I presume Mathers is referring to the Magical powers of the Ibis, the bird associated to the Sign by the Egyptians. I have covered this is part with the meaning of the fixed stars earlier in this book. PZ)* - and the head of the Assyrian man, Black headed: and the Bull lies dark in colour: but the tail is that of a Hawk or Eagle.

And these Four Figures, which are known as the 'Sphinx of Egypt', 'Scorpion man', 'The mermaid' and the 'Assyrian Bull', are round about the Wheel; and the Wheel itself is, as hath been said, the Shaft of the Lotus wand being in a circle, even as the Wand itself is the Circle straightened out. And upon the Wheel, on the base thereof, is inscribed the Word 'Asharoth' (Note: This appears to be the plural of the word AaShTRUTh, Ash'taroth or Ash'toroth, signifying the 'Statues of Ash'toreth, Astarte, the Goddess of the Planet Venus - probably the feminine of AshRH, and perhaps allied with, or from, the root Ashath, meaning 'made smooth' and 'shining'

CF Greek 'Aster', Latin 'Astrum', a star, luminous body or meteor) and refers to the title of this Key, which is 'Lord of the Forces of Life'.

And behind the whole, there is, faintly outlined, the Image of a Great Angel, affirming the Higher Forces of Spirit, which dominate even the Mightily and terrible Zodiac Forces.

The Tower Struck by Lightning - Mars

To Him is attributed the 16th Key or Trump of the Tarot, known as 'The Tower struck by Lightning". The true design and colouring thereof is as follows. The Tower representeth the World of Gross and Tangible Matter - such matter as was in the beginning created by the Word of God; but, by reason of the Fall of Man, God did divide his Word so that it became fourfold, and hence could men no longer comprehend each other, and the Tower, which before was the House of God, 'la Maison de Dieu', or Bab-El (BAB - a gate : EL - God) , The gate of God, became, by reason of that Confusion, the prison-house of Man, or the Tower of Babel. Hence are the stones of that Tower fitly coloured with the colours of Malkuth, counterchanged in their various layers. And the Tower standeth on a land, which is, on the right hand, a smiling landscape: but, on the left, an arid wilderness of rocks and dead leafless trees, under thick and lurid clouds. And, on the right hand side of the Tower, is the Tree of Life, as figured in the Minutus Mundus Diagram, with the Sephiroth and Paths thereof in their proper colours; and, on the left hand, are the Eleven Evil and Averse Sephiroth, arranged as on the Tree, but with Daath - and their colours are those of the Qlippoth. For, by the Fall of Man, was the Sephirotic System shattered, and Man no longer manifested in himself the Tree of Life. Yet fell he not entirely to the Qlippoth, but as it were, remained imprisoned in his House of Flesh between the two; and, over this prison-house, do the Lords of Unbalanced Force, typified by the Kings and Dukes of Edom, bear away. Hence must this prison-house be broken up, that Man may be set free; and this way be accomplished either by gradual disintegration, or by sudden and violent disruption. And this latter is the Force which is symbolised by this Key, being the Force of Will energised by Action, and bringing the Powers of the Triad to establish the them the tetrad, and hence the dominant symbol if this Key is (symbol to corrupted to reproduce - PZ) And, in the Clouds above the Tower and to the right hand thereof, is a circle, and from the Circle issueth a Lightning Flash terminating in a Triangle, thus forming the Astronomical symbol of Mars, and the colour therefore is red. And in the main Wall of the Tower are three holes rent in the form of a Triangle, the apex whereof are downward, symbolising the establishment of the Triad in the prison-house of man, whereby man may escape. And the Triad that is established is that of the Negative; but the Flash which establisheth it is of the Positive, or the triangle of Fire - and those twain mark on the Tower the Signet - Star of the Hexagram.

And the Crown or Summit of the Tower, which is falling, hath the Colours of Malkuth disposed in four bands, which signify Earth on the King's Scale, surmounted by Yellow or Golden battlements, which signify Earth in the Queen Scale; and thus are the Forces of the tetrad, which is materially and the Constraining Force thereof, overthrown by the sudden rush of energy which establisheth the Triad. And the men falling headlong are a King and Duke of Edom, representing the unbalanced Force. And upon the Crown of the Tower is inscribed the word, Hebrew, BBL. Note on Mathers's original drawings of this trump the BBL is not present so was added after the Th.A.M. was formed. PZ

And thus, this Key is, in a measure, the converese of the Thirteenth Key, which is 'Death'. For, whereas the latter is representeth the breaking up of the material prison house by slow and gradual disintegration, so doth this Key indicate the same violent disruption; and both show the dawn of a New Life from broken ruins of the old - the Light of a Golden Dawn after the shadows of Night. And the other title of this Key of the 'Blasted Tower' is 'Lord of the Hosts of the Mighty', and it denotes Ambition, Courage, Fighting and War - and its adverse aspect, Ruin, Danger, Fall and Destruction.

The Sun

To Him is attributed the 19th Key or Trump of the Tarot, known as the 'The Sun'. the design and colouring thereof are as follows. The upper half of the Card is occupied by the Golden Disk of the Sun, with traditional or conventional Face drawn thereon in red. From the circumference of this issue forth alternately six straight and six waved and salient rays, corresponding in their number to the six Masculine or Positive, and six Feminine or Negative Signs of the Zodiac; and they are coloured according to the Signs, beginning with Aries - but, seeing that although the Signs of the Zodiac there be six masculine and six feminine, yet, in their natural order, they are not alternated, neither, if they be arranged by Triplicities, are they alternated, therefore, in this arrangement, is each ray coloured as both masculine and feminine, and the alternation is preserved in their form. Thou shalt therefore colour each Ray both in the King's scale and the Queen's scale of that Sign; and, between each of the Rays, there shall be three finer rays representing the Decanates, and these shall be thus coloured to the colour of the ray, which they follow in order; and, in the case of Aries, Cancer, Leo, Virgo, Libra and Aquarius, two shall be in the Queen's scale, and the remaining one in the King's Scale. And, in the case of the other Signs, two shall be in the King's Scale, and the remaining one in the Queen's Scale. Thus of the three rays between Aries and Taurus, the two outer shall be in the colour of Aries of the King's Scale, and the middle one the colour of Aries in the Queen's Scale - and, for the remaining half of their length, they shall have the Colours of the Planets of the Decans - and between two of these Decan-rays, there shall be two Golden rays, very fine, making seventy Two in all; and these refer to the seventy two fold name of SHEMHAMPHORESCH. And, on each side of the Solar Disk, there are Seven Golden Yods, descending and bearing the Solar Influence or Solar Prana to the Earth. And the Earth below is, on the right side, fertile land: and on the left, a Crab is seen crawling out of the water (Note: Not in Drawings of this Key in G.D. ritual copies I have seen, unless this was added for the AO. PZ) typifying the Signs of Taurus and Cancer; and between the Two, are Two Children, standing respectively on the Earth and in the Water. And they are clothed in the colours of the Sign of Gemini, which they represent, in the colours of the King's and of the Queen's Scales respectively. And the Two Children are exchanging the Neophyte grip of the 0=0 Grade; and they represent the Influence of the Sun pouring down upon the moist Earth and bringing about fertility. And behind them is the Wall of the Zodiac. Circular and of the four courses; and there are Twelve Stones visible in each Course, and they are coloured as the Signs of the Zodiac, the Upper Course being in the scale of the King, and the second in the Scale of the Queen: the third in the Scale of the Prince and the fourth in the Scale of the Princess.

And the whole Key signifieth 'Apollo' or the 'Sun': on the Human Plane, the Will magnetically energised as embracing the Whole of Creation with his rays - or Solar prana, and bringing into action the generating influence of Earth and Water.

Another Title of this Key of the 'Sun' is 'The Lord of the Fire of the World' and it signifieth Glory and Riches: but, on its adverse side, Arrogance, Display and Vanity.

The Empress - Venus

To Her is attributed the 3rd Key or Trump of the Tarot, known as 'The Empress'. The true design and colouring thereof is as follows. The Telesmatic Figure of ANIAL (Aniel) and is this constructed: (*Note; this is from the Hebrew Letters associated to Angelic body parts to make a composite Angelic-Talismatic figure. Putting it here is very much an ad hoc concept that the early Golden Dawn tried. It was very much a hit and miss association. PZ*)

Aleph: A Winged, white, brilliant radiant Crown.

Nun: Arms bare and strong: on right, a shield, Golden and charged with a dove (the eagle on the Card in the ordinary pack is a corruption); in the left hand, three lilies, held like a Scepter, and the Crux Ansata or 'Nile Key' hanging form the left wrist - the colouring Bluish green.

Yod: A Yellowish Green Robe, covering a strong breast, on which is a square Golden lamen, in the angles of which are respectively the Crux Ansata: the Caestus: the conch shell: and the sigil of Venus traced in scarlet.

Aleph - Lamed EL: gives the usual angelic attribution of the termination AL or EL: and, in addition seeing that the letter Lamed is referred to the Sign Libra, it giveth a balanced andequilibrated figure of great beauty.

The whole figure, then is a more or less feminine counterpart of ADONI HA ARETZ - a beautiful female form with pale golden hair (for Aleph), wearing a radiant Crown of seven points (the number of Venus), and with large Golden Wings: Her Robe of brilliant light spring green, rayed with darker Olive: her Feet bare, with Golden Sandals: Her Shield and lamen have already been described: and about her waist a broad belt, bearing, in gold, the name Aniel.

This card dominateth the entire Heptagram, in as much as it is the Signet Star of Venus; and, in the brazen candlestick of Seven Lights, when set in a straight line, the metal was that of Venus, and to her was the central and Highest Light ascribed and 'The Daughter of the Mighty Ones' was her name.

The Magician - Mercury

To Him is attributed the first Key or Trump of the Tarot, known as the Magician, the true design and colouring of which is as follows. The Figure represents Mercury as a Minor Adept in the act of invoking with the Lotus Wand: the other implements (i.e. the Four lesser Implements) lie on the table before him. He wears the Rose Cross on his Breast, and the Magical sword at his left side, girded to the White sash of the 5=6 grade. His dress is yellow, over an Underdress or Tunic and hose of a pearly Grey. Round his waist is a belt of vivid purple, bearing, in Gold lettering, the Word MIKAL (Mikael). On his head is the winged cap of Mercury, and, on his feet, winged sandals. His hair is pale golden, raying out in all directions.

In addition to his title of 'The Magician' he is also called 'The Magus of Power'.

High Priestess - Luna

To her is attributed the second Key or Trump of the Tarot, known as the 'High Priestess'. The true design and colouring thereof is as follows. She is the Hegemon, seated between the Pillars. Her Robe is a dark blue, an over and under Robe of Silver, girt so as leave one breast bare. Her hair is dark and closely coiled. Her headdress is the Triple Crown, for she ruleth certain of the Elemental Kingdoms, and the waters of Earth, and the Land of Dreams: and, in front thereof is the Luna crescent. And around her waist is a belt of orange, bearing, in scarlet, the Hebrew word GBRIAL (Gabriel): and in her right hand is the Scepter of the Hegemon: and, in her left hand are the bow and arrows of Luna.

Note these last three cards have been little changed in modern designs, save only the colouring, which is here restored. And this much shall suffice of the true designs and colouring of these Tarot Trumps, and the Instructed Adept of our Order may, if he pleases, makes for himself cards, he shall mentally correct the Symbols and the Colouring.

And the manner of using them shall be shown hereafter.

Concerning The Formulae
Of Skrying
And Traveling In The Spirit Vision
Drawn From The Heptagram
Or
Seven Branched Light Bearer
Part IV

There may be such Formulae, as shall in due course be expounded unto the diligent Student of our mysteries: and, without doubt, the student who has acquired the general rules has practised simple and ordinary Formulae will discover methods peculiarly adapted to himself and his own temperament. But, first of all, he should endeavour to attain success in the simplest of all methods. Following the principles he has already been taught. Let him, then, realise that the HEPTAGRAM is the SIGNET STAR of VENUS, and that the peculiar Sephirah where unto this planet is attributed is Netzach. In Netzach, therefore, if in the Spirit Vision he can attain thereto, may he hope to obtain clear teaching regarding Venus and her Attributes, and to understand more completely the deep and hidden meanings of the Heptagram.

And first he will do well to make a careful Diagram of the Heptagram with its attributions as shown in the Ritual of the 1=10 Grade of Zelator. But let him make each angle thereof in its appropriate colour, with the letters and symbols marked there one in the Complementary colours; and this diagram he should keep by him for reference, as he hath already done with diagrams of the Pentagram and Hexagram (Note: the coloured diagram I was shown also had the paths in the King Scales colours of the Signs and elements in their order of progression. It was not over coloured like the detailed Shew Bread diagrams. PZ)

Now having prepared this diagram of the Heptagram and keeping it by him, let him understand that in the Rituals, and in the Signs, Grips, and Passwords of the Outer Grades, he has the Formulae of RISING IN THE PLANES, albeit no explanation is then given of their purport or meaning: and also that of body actions, sounds of words, and in the Notes of Music lieth a Power Ineffable to enable the Spirit to ascend withsoever he wills, and to receive teaching and instruction on any subject he desires. First then, seeing that before commencing any magical operation he should invoke the Highest names known to Him: and seeing that he is now in the Outer Material World, and about to enter the 'Immeasurable Region': let him humbly call upon the 'Lord of the Universe' by whatsoever name he designates the Supreme Being, saying over the 'Trisagion' or thrice repeated:

> *'Holy art Thou Lord of the Universe!*
> *Holy Art Thou whom nature hath not Formed!*
> *Holy art Thou, the vast and Mighty One!*
> *Lord of the Light and of the Darkness!'*

Facing to the east, let him raise his hands, bending the elbows at right angles, with the palms opened up and directed before him, and sink the right knee, as in the Egyptian Tomb pictures of the act of adoration. Then let him rise, and, standing upright, place himself is symbolic darkness by closing the eyes - symbolising thereby that he quits the Material Earth and seeks the Spiritual. Being then in darkness he must need to grope or seek a guiding hand. So let him slowly drop his hands till they are extended before him in the position of the 0=0 Saluting Sign: and in this position let him ask for the guidance of a hand. He must then imagine that a hand finds his in the darkness and he is led forward, seeking for the Entrance of the Temple of Truth - with slow hesitating step. But, being warned of the need for Absolute Silence as to the Secrets that may be revealed to him, he should here give the Sign of Silence by placing his left forefinger on his lip and repeating the Word HARPARKRAT, invoking Harpocrates, the Graeco Egyptian God of Silence. He may then open his eyes, and should build up before himself in fancy the Two Pillars of Hermes, of Seth, and of Solomon, between which he is about to be conducted. He should endeavor astrally to see himself passing between these. He is now in the Sephirah Malkuth; and before him hangs the Rainbow of Promise.

Immediately opposite him is the Path of Tau leading through the Astral World. Let him try to realise all he knows of the symbology of this Path, and of the Astral Plane. At this point, he is required to make a solemn asseveration that he seeks the Hidden Knowledge from pure and good motives only: not to do harm to any other; not gratify his vanity that he will preserve and preserve eternal silence as to Mysteries that will be shown, save only to the Initiates of this Order. To This effect let him raise his right hand in the position of taking an oath in many countries (Frater Sub Spe (Brodie Innes) here interpolates a Note 'As in the Scottish Courts'). And this position has also other symbologies cognates thereto. Thus it denotes the arm interposed to protect against the Qlippoth or Evil demons - also the hand raised to the point out and follow the flight of the arrow from Qesheth, the Bow as it cleaves upwards towards Tiphareth: and other meanings which shall be expounded in the GD Ceremony of the Adeptus Major.

But his present aim is set to reach Netzach, and this Sephirah lieth on his right hand. To this , then let him direct his attention and consider the Paths by which he must travel. But here let him know he must take up the burden of Knowledge. A New World is to open before him, and he must support it, even as upon the Shoulders of Atlas in the Greek fable rested the Material World. Let him, then, as he gives the two Signs of the outstretched arm and the Atlas position of the Supporting Globe, breathe the Names of ADONAI HA-ARTEZ. And SHADDAI EL CHAI.

Realising thereby that he calls upon the Lord of the Ruler of All the Created Universe, that is to say, not only of the Material Earth but of the Mental and Astral - by whose aid, therefore he can pass from the one to the other - from the Material and Physical, which is but a small part of the wider Astral Sphere itself - which is not a change but an enlargement of perception: even as though a blind man. Hither only able to perceive by touch, were made to see, and perceived, not only the things he could touch, also that are beyond his reach. All this can ADONAI HA ARETZ give unto the student who calls on him and, as he assumes the burden of the Astral and Spiritual World - so the burden of the Physical World falls from him, and he findeth the Astral and Spiritual far lighter to carry, by reason of his understanding the roots of things. As it said: 'The Children of the Kingdom fret not, neither are they dismayed, for they see the end and know good." Therefore, on taking this upon him, he should call on El Chai Shaddai, the vast and the Mighty One: who, indeed, is the same with ADONAI HA ARETZ , but with a different title referred to attributes the Student now desireth to invoke. And note: In this process he should in fancy build up these appearances before him of himself passing from the Outer World through darkness to Malkuth, and thence to the Astral Plane: rather than expect to see these by the mere giving of the Signs and breathing the Names. It is a conserving of power and saving of force, as it were, to build them up on the Astral Plane. Afterwards, when he is well accustomed to the exercise, these appearances will come readily to him; for he will be able to pass at will on to the wider plane, even as a man having closed his eyes may open them again.

Netzach, then, as he faces towards Kether (or physically towards the East) is on his right hand. Now, then, let him either look at, or imagine, the diagram he has made of the Heptagram. Let him regard it fixedly till it is strongly impressed on his sphere of Sensation (or Aura); and, in doing this, he will do well to sit in as comfortable a position as possible, facing East. Let him then deal with this diagram as though it were a Tattva card, enlarging it in thought till it becomes in dimension of at least double or treble his own height. Now let him imagine himself wearing a Mantle of Yellow Green of early Spring, with a Golden Girdle, and playing on any convenient musical instrument with which he is familiar, as for example, a small Irish harp, or a flute, fife, flageolet or any like instrument. Thereon let him imagine the seven notes of the scale, as directed and described in the Manuscript 'On the Seven Branch Candlestick', and by these notes demand to pass through the gateway of the Heptagram.

He will then pass through through the symbol, and will find himself in the Sphere of Venus, and will see the Signet Star of the Heptagram, shining with soft silvery radiance before him. The Sphere of Venus will appear very beautiful - a land of streams, misty woodlands and many flowers, chiefly of lily and lotus types, heavy scented. There should be no need for him to build up these appearances - he will see them.

Let him call for a guide. Probably one will appear in the form of a Nymph of Spring or Stream, who may bring him to one of the Great Forces belonging to the Planet. Let him ask to be shown the working of the plane, and of the Forces of Venus. He may ask for help in any mundane concerns, and for health, healing and contentment; and may ask to be taught the way to bring the astral conditions down to the physical plane. The accomplishment of this may take some practice, but will constantly acquire more power. When he has thus become familiar with this simple and elementary experience of working of the Heptagrams, more elaborate instruction will be given as to the working of more specialised Invocations. If he is not very familiar with the Ms known as the 'Microcosm', being 'Ritual V' of the ZAM series, he will do well to study it again, and try to realise how the teachings therein given are put into practice in this exercise.

Chapter 4

The Hermetic Cross:
Diagram Of The Table Of Sacred Bread:
The Twelve Signs Or Gates Of The Zodiac
By Mathers

This paper was in two parts. The first was a two or three page paper as an introduction to the Hermetic Cross and the second part is what is given here. There are parts of that are so badly faded I cannot make out some words or phrases and I have inserted question marks in brackets when this comes up. I cannot say I am overly impressed with this paper as it seems to be a Treatise on Mythology of the 19th century. P.Z.

11	24	7	20	3
4	12	25	8	16
17	5	13	21	9
10	18	1	14	22
23	6	19	2	15

Kamea of Mars

Clockwise Swastika on kamea

11	24	7	20	3
4	12	25	8	16
17	5	13	21	9
10	18	1	14	22
23	6	19	2	15

Anticlockwise Swastika on Tree

11	24	7	20	3
4	12	25	8	16
17	5	13	21	9
10	18	1	14	22
23	6	19	2	15

The Hermetic Cross, as here represented, forms the Admission badge of the Zelator in the first Order.

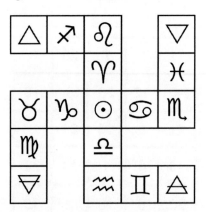

Hermetic Cross

It is here explained as being 'known equally under the Names of the Fylfot, the cross of Thor and the Swastika Cross and the elemental symbol of the Jains; as being composed of 17 squares taken out of a square of 25; the which 17 are referred to as the Sun, the four elements and 12 Signs of the Zodiac. It is a symbol of a whirling force, of a revolving Flail, the weapon of Zeus and Thor, the awakening of the Hidden Currents of nature. As it is written in the Qabalah:- (Idra Sutra, 429)

> *From a Light Bearer of insupportable brightness*
> *proceedeth a radiating Flame, dashing off like a*
> *vast and mighty hammer whose sparks which were*
> *the prior worlds.*

(The idea of a potent whirling Force is particularly noticeable in the Cuneiform inscription describing the armament of the Assyrian Merdoch. Besides whirlwind, hurricane or storm, he took with him, among others, 7 special weapons all more or less suggestive of revolving forces. They are thus enumerated:- The sword which turned four ways; the Whirling thunderbolt, the Bolt of Dual Flame; the Quadruple Bolt: the Bolt: and the Bolt of Crooked Fire.)

Turned as in the foregoing diagram, the Hermetic Cross will represent the direction and Order of the Zodiac signs; but when reversed, the course of the planets. Thus, each arm containing a Triplicity of the Signs under the Precedence of an Element, with the Sun as their general centre, the Elements and Triplicities can be applied to any arm, according to the effect desired: e.g.: employed as a 1=10 Admission badge, instead of he usual order from right to left, (of Fire, Water, Air and Earth), the Fire and Air counter change their position; but the passive Elements remain unaltered.

The Cross has been regarded as composed of Four Daleths, or of four axes, and has been called 'the Whirling Axe Cross'. Now Daleth + 4, and the sum of the arms is 16, + the centre + 17; i.e. the number of the squares of the Cross. 16 will represent the 4 Kerubim (each with four heads) of Ezekiel's Vision, under the precedence of Tetragrammaton, when the Hermetic Cross becomes a Symbol of the Rushing Chariot of IHVH. For Plane differentiates Symbol; a circumstance too frequently overlooked. There is some analogy between the Cross and the Dragon Formulas of the Revolutions of the Powers (symbolised by 4 tarot Aces round the Pole). Neither should be forgotten that in IHVH several Gods in harmonious unity of action implied, rather than a single or solitary Deity.

If we consider the Cross as composed of four Axes, we shall not find the foregoing Symbolism thereby impaired. For the Axe as a Hieroglyphic, is a symbol of Deity, and is referred to the idea of a God-Force penetrating the matter. Thus, composed of 4 single headed or Egyptian Axes, the significance of the Hermetic Cross will differ little from the foregoing, But the double headed Axe, or bipennis, was the symbol of the Labraidian Jove, and what is most especially worthy of note, of the Amazons; whose attributes, weapons and characteristics contain a most recondite symbolism: above all, the double headed Axe and the crescent shaped shield whose Formulas are the Light beyond Atziluth. Nor is it to be wondered at if we consider that according to ancient tradition, the Amazons were the allies of the Gods against the Evil Powers; for under the Goddess Athena, they aided the Great God Amoun against Kronos; and under their Queen Myrina, they allied themselves with Isis and Horus against Typhon, who had treacherously slain Osiris. After this, passing through Asia Minor, she and her comrades founded many cities and named them after the Amazon leaders. Notable among the Seven Cities of Asia so especially mentioned in the Apocalypse. It was against Myrina and her Amazons who in Samothrace instituted those august Mysteries in honour of the 'Magna Mater' or 'Great Mother of the Gods', which with the congeners of Eleusis, exercised so powerful an influence over the Mind of the Ancient World: At Ephesus the Amazons established the cult of the Great Goddess, later to be known as 'Diana of the Ephesians', the Protective Divine Force, the Goddess of many breasts, to whom they dedicated their own as symbolic of the Protective Energy of Nature; the which circumstances misled certain Greek writers into error of supposing instead that they amputated them, an idea refuted by a monument relating to the Amazons.

This Goddess is none other than the presentment of the Beneficent and Protective Power of AIMA or rather AMA Elohim, the Great Mother, the Goddess MAOUTH, shedding upon the wearied Earth the regenerating influence of the Divine Light. From her hands, the Eternal Current of Life streams down often symbolised, as in Egypt, by a chain of drops or of cruces anastae. The following are the mystic words said to have been graven upon the Zone of the Ephesian Goddess, (some say upon the feet as well), and their interpretation:-

'ASKI KATASKI HAIX TETRAX DAMAMENEUS
'AISION:

ASKI	'The same with Darkness'
KATASKI	'The same with Light'
HAIX	'The same with Self'
TETRAX	'The same with (Four-formed?)'
DAMNENEUS	'The same with Sun'
AISION	'The same with Truth'

These were called the 'Ephesiae Literae' or Ephesian Letters and were considered to be a powerful protective charm. Plutarch states that these were recited over persons possessed with devils; Kircher, that they were employed as incantations to procure success. They were considered as a curative. The translation of 'Tetrax' above what is given is somewhat uncertain. The words 'Damneneus' appears on a Gnostic in the 'De la Turba Collection'.

But while the Egyptian Goddess AUT or AOUTH may be taken to represent the Great Mother, it is rather the Goddess of the Starry Robe, stretching across the Heavens and above the Earth, Who corresponds to the Ephesian Diana, the Queen of the Path of the Souls to Earth, and before whose presence the varying Axes of Her Amazon Guards reflect the changing manifestations of the Light. For even the sacred Axe of the Carian Jupiter previously alluded to, was said to have been originally the battle axe of a Queen of the Amazons. It was borne as a sceptre in the hand of the Statue of Jove, who was thence called 'Labradeus' or 'Labrandius' from Labrys, signifying 'Axe'. It is said that he was the Giver of Rain = Jupiter Pluvius. The Sixth Avatar of the Indian Vishnou is that Paracou or Rama of the Axe. Off the Island of Tenedos in the Aegean, at a place called Asterion. According to Plutarch, the crabs caught, had on their shells, the figure of an axe, the sacred emblem of Tenedos, again derived from the Amazons and the worship of the 'Magna Mater'.

For this Goddess, (ill comprehended of modern Egyptologists; by them called Nupe, Nut or Nuit and attributed to the expanse of the heavens), is , the Goddess of the 'Via Lactea' or 'Milky Way' the Abundant Cause of Things. Hence the numerous stars in the Robe of (?); hence the numerous breasts of the Amazon Goddess at Ephesus the shape of the Stream of the stars of the (?) recalls the Hieroglyphic outline of the Egyptian Goddess stretched across the Sky. For this tremendous Constellation, sweeping athwart the heavens; this 'Milky Way in the sky, a meeting of gentle lights without a name', as Suckling, the poet, has elegantly described it, is as a Zone of Admittal, from the more material Star Sphere into a more vast and more subtle beyond. Hence its attribution as the 'Place of Souls'

The well known and eminent Astronomer of Edinburgh (our own G.H.Frater 'Veritas et Lux') *(Note: Sir William Peck PZ)*, in his admirable 'Handbook and Atlas of Astronomy', states that the Stars are not equally distributed in the heavens, but are much more condensed in some places than in others. They increase in number when the Milky Way is approached, while the Nebulae decrease, and are densely clustered in two places, situated perpendicular to it, or in parts of the heavens surrounding its poles. There are therefore in the heavens, two distinct regions – a region of stars lying principally in the plane of the Milky Way, and a region of Nebulae situated at right angles to it. The ordinary appearance of the 'Via Lactea' is that of a beautiful band of soft light stretching completely across the heavens. In the Northern Sphere it passes near the Constellations of Orion, Gemini and Taurus, entirely traversing Auriga, Perseus, Cassiopeia, Cepheus, Cyngus, Vulpecula, Sagitta and Serpens: in the Southern Heavens, Ophiuchus, Sagittarius, Scorpio, Ara, Centaurus, Crux and Argo, passing exactly between Canis Major and Canis Minor. Thence to Auriga it is fainter and more regular; hence it breaks up and before Aquila is divided in two, but reunited in Scorpio. Hence to Argo where there is an opening the form is exceedingly complex and the luminosity more conspicuous. This the Via Lactea completely encircles the Star Sphere, forming a luminous Great Circle, which proves that our Sun is interior to it and within bounds. 'Times without number' says our learned Frater, 'has the modern astronomer turned his most powerful instruments to the Milky Way, in the hope of sounding its mighty depths, for in it he knows is locked the secret of the structure of the Visible Universe…..The total number of stars distributed along the Via Lactea must be altogether beyond our conception….Herschel concluded that there were at least 20,000,000….Each small twinkling point of light is a sun. Each sun is the centre of a system of worlds.'

That the nature then of this vast constellation, tremendous, not alone in extent but in its depth, should represent a great Scission of the infinite, would seem even from a purely astronomical standpoint to be clearly tenable. The Minds of the Great Expanse, therefore, that is to say the Subtle Guiders of the Centres of Influence, whether radiating or wandering, would appear to derive themselves in varying ratio from the Fountain of Worlds and Systems.

The ancient Egyptian Wisdom regarded the Stars and the Constellations as being manifested Powers of the Gods rather than Gods Themselves, (as Imblichus, or perhaps we should say Ab-Ammon has clearly shown in the 'Answer to Prophyry', that is to say Their material Bases of Action, in other words, the masks of their power. Hence the extreme importance of the mask, whether Human or Animal, in the presentment of an Egyptian God, as marking at the same time alike the isolation and the Symbol of the Force manifesting, as well as the Nature of its Concentration.

Prophyry had remarked in his Epistle to Anebo and the Egyptian Prophetes: 'How, if the gods be utterly bodiless, will Helios and Selene and other heavenly bodies be manifested as God-forces?' In another place, Iambliches, or rather AB-Ammon, explains the frequently recurring Egyptian Hieroglyphic symbol of a God or Gods standing in a barque, as representing a Power intimately governing the world, and yet separate from it.

MSLUTh, Masloth, the Sphere of the Starry Heavens and of the Zodiac, (classed under Chokmah), is derived from the root SL meaning 'raised, elevated'. A variant of it is employed in the passage relating to Sisera, Judges, ch5 v.20. The Stars H-KUKS BHIH in their courses, or from their exalted heights etc. RAShITH H-GLGIM Rshith Ha –Galgalim, (classed under Kether) represents towards the Spheres of Assiah the Initiation of Initiative of movement, the Commencement of Whirling Force, the PRIMUM MOBILE . At least we can find its Administrative Energy, if not its source in the expanse of the most infinite Stellar System 'Via Lactea'.

The 'Milk which flows eternally from the breasts of the Great Goddess'; the 'Inexhaustable preservative Power which maintains the Universe in Being"; the 'Nourishing Light'; the 'Influx fromthe Limitless Ether'; such are the nature and Operation essentially implied in this particular appellation - VIA LACTEA: This idea then, of the Divine Breast, of the 'Supreme Mamelle'; of a Powerful and Protective Redundant Force ultimates on the Human Plane in the alternately vibrating Lunar and Solar Forces of the body, concentrating in the breasts (Compare the Formulas of the Swara, ultimating in the Ida and Pingala Breathings). These again differentiate in those Elemental Currents, which are symbolised in the Whirling Axe Cross. Herein lies one reason for the Amazon's customs of boldly exposing their breasts naked in battle, as thereby increasing their courage and strength by the correlation of the symbolism thus involved; besides such idea as those of clearly showing their sex in combat, of giving freer play to arm and shoulder in wielding their weapons.

Again, there is evidently a connection between the above symbolism and the varying manner of preparing the candidate in the Craft degrees of Freemasonry.

It is evident that the Ancients considered the heart and parts adjoining (or perhaps Solar Plexus), as the chief seat of emotion. And Homer employs Phrenes, (the plural of Phren, usually translated as the diaphragm or praecordia) in the sense of the seat of life, as opposed to Psuche when signifying the departed soul.

In Classical Mythology, the origin of the galaxy as well as that of the symbolic purity of the White Lily, are traced to the legend of (Hera) Juno and the infant Hercules. For Jupiter is represented as having placed Hercules to the breasts of Juno while the Goddess was asleep, wishing to thus bring about the relationship of fosterage between them. But the Milk of Juno gushed forth over the heavens, therein forming the thence entitled 'Via Lactea'; while a part, falling upon the earth, changed the colour of the lilies from purple to milk-white; for this was said to have been originally part of the crocus. A variant of the legend relates that Hera (Juno) voluntarily gave her breast to the infant Hercules by the advice of Athena; the child, however, having severely hurt her, she threw him out in disgust (Didor.Sicul).

For it is to be remembered that the Greek Heracles is a violent and brutal force, evil rather good. He is represented as a violator of the Mysteries, having forced entrance without the Golden Bough; and Charon was punished for thus aiding his passage of the Styx.

His Greek name was Herakles, derived from that of Hera (Juno) – as having gained fame against her opposition, but this derivation is shewn by Diodorus and others to be an error. Both Diodorus make especial distinction between the Greek and the Egyptian ideas of Hercules, further instancing the great difference of Epoch. Herodotus says: 'This Egyptian (Hercules), as I have been informed, one of the Twelve Great Gods; but of the Grecian Hercules, I could in no part of Egypt procure any knowledge. That this name was never borrowed by Egypt from Greece, but certainly certainly communicated by the Egyptians to the Greeks, and to those in particular who assign it to the son of Amphitryon, is among other arguments sufficiently evident from this, but both the reputed parents of Hercules, Alcmena and Amphitryon, were of Egyptian…. If they (the Egyptians) had ever borrowed the name of a God from Greece, the remembrance of these, so far from being less, must have been stronger… they would rather have been acquainted with the names of the other Deities than with that of Hercules. (The Egyptian) Hercules is certainly one of the most ancient Deities of Egypt; and as they themselves affirm, is one of the twelves who were produced from the eight Gods 17,000 years before the reign of Amasis (about 190 B.C.)'.

At Tyre, Herodotus found two temples of Hercules, one of which was 2,300 years old. The legends again differed from those of the Greeks, while at Thasus was another temple five generations before to Hercules, son of Amphitryon. The Greek story of Hercules and the Egyptian King Buriris is characterised by Herodotus as preposterous fable. While (observes J.de Rouge) the especial God of the Nome called by the Greeks Heracleopolis, was the ram headed form of Horus, (Har-shevi) or the warrior; the Greeks, embarrassed to find a name for this new variant of Horus, having chosen that Hercules because of the warlike nature indicated.

The derivation of the name Heracles signifies 'an appellation, (Klesis), of Har or Horus- Aroueris'.

But there is one Egyptian figure which does clearly resemble. Though in a squat and pigmy form, the appearance of the Grecian Hercules - I allude to BES with, the lion's skin and the mask. A glance at the representations of Hercules on the Greek and Etruscan Vases of the Archiac period where his type is more rude in treatment, will show this. Schweigger, in his work on mythology, remarks that at Samothrace Herculeus, as a pigmy but two feet high, was placed next to a fifteen feet high figure of DEMETER. But BES is evidently of a Typhonian classification: and Plutarch implies that Typhon was dwarfed and deformed at birth, though of immense strength. Now TYPHON is an evil Force and the antithesis of Horus. But there is a tradition that the name of the Egyptian Hercules was Chons, Chona, Ozo-chor, or Osor-chon; SHONS, KHONS or SHONS (compare the name John, Shaun) with reference to AMOUN and MAUT, is the correlative of HORUS as regards OSIRIS and ISIS. But neither SHONS nor HORUS do we find resemblance to the Grecian Hercules. In that Akkadian-Assyrian being, whose name has been variously read as Gilgames, Gizudar etc. and even Nimrod, some slight similarity both of type and legend may be discernable.

The ram headed form of HORUS-AROUERIS, (Har-shevi) before alluded to, has an evident connection with the story of Egyptian Hercules and (?) related by Herodotus.

Returning to the symbolism of the Great Goddess of 'Via Lactea'; the name of one of the chief's Telchini was Damanaenes which recalls one of the Mystic Words DAMNAMENEUS, inscribed upon the Zone of the Ephesian Diana. Damanaenes is said to mean 'The Power of Binding', as Epimendes, another Telchin, does that of 'Reflection and Counsel'. And there is certainly a connection in the Mysteries of Samothrace between Corybantes, the Idiac Dactyls and the Telchini, as Strabo and others have noticed, though this simply does not imply identity. This name Telchin, is usually derived from Thelgein, 'to stroke with magic power', 'to enchant'.

By the White Lily and the White Lotus is shewn a nature rising pure and unsullied above the mire of the earth or the turbid waters of the Nile, the which nevertheless afford it a physical basis, while it preserves the Descending Light it becomes fitted to receive against profanation or repellance; as is implied by the Symbol of Deity seated upon a Lotus, and of the Lily transformed to whiteness by the descending Milk of the Great Goddess. The witch, Nonnus describing as 'the dew of the breast of Hera (Juno), universal benefactor, preservative from evil'. The Qabalistic commentary on the passage, Song of Solomon 8.v.18 'And my breasts are like towers' expresses the same idea; 'Since they are full of nourishment of all things, because they are great rivers which flow forth from AIMA and the Supernal' (Idra Zuta, s. 733).

Conspicuous, therefore amongst the sacred Insignia of the Mysteries, are the Breast shaped vase and Libation of Milk, as is apparent from descriptions given in Clemens, Apuleius and others, of the symbols borne in the Sacred Procession. One form frequently employed for the Libation was suspended from the hand and the milk dripped slowly from its point. While another was much larger and rounded, ornamented with many breasts, through the extremities of which milk contained in the vessel could be made to flow with vary force. (this is somewhat analogous to the figure of the so called Canopus of the later Roman period in Egypt. the Brazen Sea of Solomon, with its adornment of the breast shaped knobs and lilies or Lotuses, may be cited in this connection). The vase of Milk was the Symbol of the Via Lactea, the place of the Reunion of Souls.

And that the vase was an especial attribute of the Great Egyptian Goddess of Might Constellation is clearly evident from her head-dress being surmounted by that symbol in the less frequent representations of Her as standing or seated: as well as by its constant recurrence in the Hieroglyphics of her name. The Constellation 'Crater' immediately following upon 'Leo' is in connection with this symbol.

The Amazon Goddess at Ephesus, the many breasted Diana, is at times represented with Symbol of the Vase above Her head dress, instead of the more frequent Tower shaped Crown, or with the Modius. This variation occurs on the reverse of some ancient coins, but in its rarer form.

And as, in the previously cited legend of Hercules, we find Hera (Juno) connected with the Via Lactea, so the celebration of the mysteries Hera, (the Heraia), at Argos the Amazon form again recurs. For girls and women dressed as Amazons took part therein, clad in short tunics reaching to the knee, the bosom bare, the hair flowing.

The Amazons with their Chieftainess Hippo, as the High Priestess, first erected the statue of Artemis at Ephesus, is evident from the Greek Hymn of Callimachus to the Deity: represents them as performing various dances in her honour, which were clearly in relation with those elements before Isis, and the predecessors both of the Corybantic and Pyrrhic in arms, according to the symbolism intended to be conveyed. And that there is again a connection between the Amazons and the Nymphs of Diana, (whose costume was closely similar C.F. Callimachus) appears from Diodorus Siculus (1.4 s.16), where he mentions three Nymphs of Artemis, Celaeno, Eurybia and Phoebe amongst the Amazons who fought against Hercules? This association is evident in Virgil, where the comrade feeling and sympathy of Opis the Nymph of Diana for the Volscian Amazon, Camilla, is clearly shewn.

That this Goddess of the Via Lactea was at times by the Egyptians represented in Double and even Triple Form is evident from the monuments (see Denon, plate 71). And as well Triads of 2 Goddess and God, or the reverse, Triads of 3 Goddesses or 3 Gods only occur. It was from such Triads that the Triple Diana and the Triple Hecate had their Origins.

'She strikes with terror, She illuminates, She acts;
She is Proserpine, Luna, Diana.
For Lowest and Highest in aspect, (O Goddess),
thou canst wield the Sceptre, the Lightning
Splendour, the Arrow.'

The distinction of each word by a comma (of the unreadable verse. P.Z.) suggest a Latin translation from an Egyptian Ideographic – Hieroglyphic original.

In many of the representations of the warrior angels, a certain similarity to the Amazon type is traceable; while the connecting link may be found in the Etruscan 'LASA', or Genius, a winged Amazon like figure frequently sculptured at the angles of relief on sarcophagi, as well as in the two Angelic forms at the extremities of the Amazon Sarcophagus in the Capitol at Rome, perhaps intended for figures of 'Victory'. Winckelman in his work on Ancient Art, has remarked on the purity and dignity of expression which characterises nearly all the representations of Amazons in Ancient Sculpture.

But whether we regard a Triune Goddess of the Via Lactea as the 'Tres Matres', the 'Three Mothers', of the Sepher Yetsirah, as a tremendous feminine Triad which precedes the 'Tres Patre', the 'Three Fathers', whether as those august and terrible Divinities refereed to by Plutarch as the 'Mothers'; equally this Goddess of the Via Lactea, this Goddess of the thousand Names, must be ever to us, of a clouded and erring World the great presidentia of the Translation of the Soul. Now in vain were the Rites of Isis' not in vain were those of the Amazon Goddess, handed down from an Epoch co-eternal with the Strife of the Great Force. What are time, and Death, the Son of Time, in the view of such Vastness, that time in KRONUS – SATURN , the Devourer of his Children. For he is but the Lucifer, the Light Bearer of a past galaxy, the Force that which is not, the Death Shrouded Formula that has been cast from the Path! The Empire of terror, the Initiation of Death, the false time formulae that has overshadowed the World of Brightness!

Such, then, is to us of a deeper knowledge of the false Serpent of the Myth of Genesis, the Stooping Dragon of the Stagnating Ether. Why, then, should he hailed by Mankind as the Symbol of the unutterable Wisdom! 'What is the chaff to the wheat! What are the just and the unjust!' Surely the vibrating Darkness under the Impact of Light; surely the Hollowed Shell of the Life Essence in the Ether!'

Here then is the mystery of the Dethroned Royalty of KRONUS-SATURN, whose dreams in his trance sleep duplicate the Acts of ZEUS – AMOUN! For the Shadow to Substance, as the Action to the Semblance; so is the Wisdom of Time to the Wisdom of the Gods! It is born but as the Shadow of an already existent Being; it is Fitting Subject of a finite Brain, instead of the Commensurate Object of an Infinite Power. Here, then, is the distinction between the Human and the Divine Mind, between the Expelled Shadow of thought Divine and the Thought itself! Here then is the difference between the Pseudo Wisdom of Human Reason and the Unborn Divine Wisdom Incomprehensible by its Shadow!

Who then is the fallen Kronis? He is LUCIFER; the Light Bearer: the Fallen Archangel of the Via Lactea; the Dragon chased from the 'Path of Souls'. He who is called at the same time 'The old God' and 'the strongest of the Gods'. That is to say 'he hath but Lesser Knowledge, or he would not be amenable to the quality of the Age'. For the True Wisdom is Young, and smiling and powerful; and it is but the false Wisdom that is Aging, and Treacherous and Weakening. Whence he is Destroying but not the renewing Wisdom; Shiva but not Vischnou. He is therefore in a sense the brutal (but not the spiritual) generative force, the Lust but not the Love. He is the false idea of a desire which is never satisfied, yet knows satiation; the Begetter of Shadows, of jealousy; of Death.

Szbo or Sbo, in the Egyptian meaning of time and Material Wisdom (Seb, Sibou, Shibbou, or Siva), why is he then given in the BOOK OF THE CONCOURSE OF FORCES the vibration of Szou Bal, or 'Star of Incense' Because he represents the transmutation as by burning of the Human Wisdom, to make its blasphemy a sacrifice of adoration unto true Wisdom of the Gods.

Thus then he is the transformer when not the Destroyer, the Transmuter of the shadows, the Excuser or rather Illusion of Death, the Hope of a Lost Image, the Desire of that Which is Not, The Reason - Veiling of Terror, the Mystery of a Feigned Extinction. This is then, and more than this in the disordered fall into a more material Chaos, this indeed is implied in the affirmed necessity of a Divine sacrifice, this is that which is shadowed in the Existence of a Past and Lost World. For as the Primal Law of Things to the Law of Human Reason, as the Law of Chaos to that of Substance, so is the Wisdom Supreme to the Pseudo Wisdom of Time. The One is born of the Infinite, the other is but a moment, for it is always subjected to the Illusionary Law of Time. Thus then our origin, this the True Wisdom, must be sought in that Great Path where Time is not.

And who be these forces, these Goddesses, these Gods, whose centre is cast for us in the Beyond; in the Revolutions of the Primum Mobile: in the Astral Veiling of the Planet Spheres, in the garments of the Soul Descending from the Abode of the vast Light? In the Rushings of the Planet Orbits; in the Vibration of the Hidden Ether; in those Tremendous Forces Whom we fear while we ignore. What be these, and what be They, Who be but shadowed forth to our

Substance; what Formulas of Creative nature do they not Initiate and contain?

Mortals say 'A God' or 'The Gods': these be but terms that veil our ignorance, Names allotted to those Vast Ones before Whose faces Time is Not. Thus time is indeed, but 'the Youngest of the Gods', for he is to our Human Reason but the Shadow that it can discern. The Great Dragon, the Stooping Dragon, cast from the path of the Limitless Ether. He who is but the shadow of that Whence he has fallen, but Which we may yet faintly discern by the Shadow that He Fallen casts across our Sphere: and where in is the Great and Unutterable Mystery of the Origin of what we call Evil. And yet it is that, false, bride of Human reason which may become to Mortals an instrument by the which, across the Fall of Saturn Lucifer, they may discern the Shadow of the Great Wisdom. For, be it well understood, the Fallen Lucifer is not the same as Satan, which latter is as menacing Resurrection of the Abyss, aided by the Shadow of the fallen Wisdom.

We will not here enter upon the Symbolism of the Wars between Ouranos and Kronos, those wars which preceded this Fall. Under many forms they mythed, under many names they figured, those Wars of the Forces that cease not. On the Human plane there is the War of Souls, there is the Scintilla of the Soul of Abel, there is the Scintilla of the Soul of Cain. Thus in Hebrew, there be the Sins of the Two Pillars: Unbalanced Mercy: Unbalanced Severity.

Compare thou now and consider the Fall of Sbo-Kronos, of Lucifer and of the Red Dragon, of Him Whose Time Wisdom is but the Veiling of Death. Who then is He, this Lucifer, fallen from the Infinite into Time; the Archangel cast out from the Via actea into the earth? He is father of the Children of Error and despair the restoration of the Infinite Wisdom into the Time Wisdom, the God of the Material Science of the World, and of the Falsity of its Presentment. He, who having been thus cast down, did yet in the Garden of Eden find means of action through the Tree of Knowledge of Good and Evil, so that in the Scene of Temptation in Genesis he was enabled to offer the veiled Death.

'How art Thou Fallen from Heaven, (M-ShMIM, Mi-shamayim), O Lucifer, son of the morning (HILL BN-ShChR, Haelael Ben Shachar); how art thou cut from the ground, thou did weaken the nations, (GUIM, Goyim). For thou hast said in my heart, I will ascend into heaven; I will exalt my throne, Star of God (LKhUKhBhIAL L'Khokn'vaei-MI) "What Stars of El"? Those who accompanied his casting out from the Via Lactea? Or Those whom with their aid he hoped yet to conquer and draw down?'

In the Phoenician Cosmogony of Sanhoniathon, KRONOS is called IL or ILOS (Like EL) ; and his followers thence Eloeim (probably rather 'Elim' or 'Elohim' than the Elohim'. There is a passage, (from Psalms) 'Give unto IHVH, O ye Sons of the Mighty (The Aelim), give unto IHVH Glory and Strength' Note the difference of vibration between EL and Ael. Compare Haeilael.

In the Apocalypse C.xii, is described the casting down of a Dragon. He is shewn as standing before the Woman clothed with the Sun (AIMA ELOHIM) waiting to devour her child Who is to rule the nations; exactly as in the classical Mythology Kronos-Saturn stands before Rhea, ready to devour her children as soon as they be born, and, in especial, Zeus-Jupiter, who is destined later to overthrow his power. And as Zeus is saved, so is the child in the Apocalyptic Vision saved and brought up to the Divine Throne. With his tail, the Dragon casts down the third part of the Stars of Heaven. Then follows the war between Michael and the Dragon who, with his angels, is cast out into the earth. (In Indian mythology, Meteors and falling or Shooting Stars are associated with KETU, or Cauda Draconis, the tail of the Dragon. While in the Mahometan Tradition, Meteors are flaming darts hurled by the Angels of Light when warring against the demons; like the Whirling Thunderbolt of Akkadian Legend, like the Whirling Axe Crosses, like the Lightning of Jove against the Titans).

And as the Dragon of Time is the chief attribute of Kronos-Saturn, and the Soaring Eagle that of Zeus – Jupiter, so does the Woman clothed with the Sun take the Wings of the Eagle to escape from persecution of the Dragon.

And let us note that 'Jove' and 'Jupiter' (which is a corruption of 'Jove Pater' = Jove our Father), is close to 'Jehovah' the pronunciation of IHVH (Jehovah, Joveh).

With these indications let us now examine that so called Hieroglyphic of the heaven and the Earth, so little understood by the Egyptologists, who see in it but a forcible separation of Seb and Nuit by Shu, as they are pleased to name them; though they have comprehended a kneeling Shu as the supporter of the Sky, and which latter we may assimilate on the ordinary celestial Globe to the Constellation of the Kneeler, miscalled 'Hercules'. Nuit or Nu is (?), as the Synthesized Goddess of the Via Lactea, the path of the Souls; Shu is Zeus; Seb is the cast down KRONOS; Ra is OURANOS, whence in the 'Concourse of Forces' his vibration is given as Pha-ouro; for OURANOS means 'the heavenly or celestial (?) , KING: Pha-Ours=The Pharaoh and therefore is Shu (as they will call him), represented as crowned with the plume feather of the Breathed Prayer and of Truth, or kneeling in adoration of the Divine Light; while he supports the Disc(whether of the veiled Sun or of the Heavens). He and the four groups of the 'Support Gods' who are in the Powers of the Four Fold Name.

In the Plate of Denon (lxxi) before alluded to, Sobo-Kronos is more plainly shewn in the position of one fallen from a height; the head low, the arms spread, the legs above; like a collapsed Hermetic Cross, whose central energy (the Central Square corresponding to the Sun) is paralysed. In the Hermetic Citations of Stobaeus such a conception is thus affirmed:-

> *And said Isis (in reply to Horus); the Earth lieth in the midst of All after the manner of Man fallen headlong backward, and looking toward the heaven.... And he Looketh towards Ouranos (the Heaven) as unto his Father, so that together with him he may undergo the same mutations.Toward the South Wind the Right Shoulder; toward that of the West the Left; under the Bear lieth the Feet, the Right beneath the Tail of the Bear, the Left beneath its Head...*

But Seb-Lucifer is not always an evil symbol. There is the Epoch previous to his Fall when Sebo-Lucifer-Kronos was Great in the Light, and the Star-God of the 'Place of Souls'. Recall the saying that Satan can be transformed into an angel of Light. And therefore in the Egyptian Assemblies of the Gods we see Seb often represented with Nu the Goddess of the Via Lactea, (Seb and Nu) And his Fall is the First fall, the Fall of the Male; which is why in the Scene of the Eden Temptation - the principal effort of the Serpent is to bring about if possible the Fall of Eve.

And against the Dragon Force we invoke 'the Lord of the Star, the Lord of the Star, the Lord of the terrible Star Come Again'. The Lord of the Star whose symbol is Sou Orion, SOU-N-HOON, the Avenging, the Risen, who with Isis-Southis in Sirius leads forth the new procession of a renewed Life-Power. With the Great Expanse is associated in Egypt the Qabalaistic Symbol of the 'Countenance', of which the Sun and the Moon be the Eyes. And the Symbol of the Abundant Nourishment of Things, the Great sacred cow of the Expanse, of Athor and of Isis, is shewn as concentrating force in Sirius, the Star blazoned between its horns. Plutarch has it that Saturn symbolises time, and that there is a certain religious Lament made over Him as 'he that dieth in the right region and born in the left". He says that the Priests have the sea in Abomination, while the Pythagoreans say that the sea is formed of the tears of Saturn, Implying at the same time the impurity and unsociable nature of the same Element.

In Rome we find the goose sacred the HERA (Juno), in Egypt as a symbol of SEB (Kronos) and both these associated with the Via Lactea. And what Harapollo gives as the significance of Swan may be here remarked, 'old age and musical Vibration', as well as the interpretation of the 'Drinker of the Infinite ether'.

No, let us consider the Name applied to the Goddess of the Via Lactea, remembering that in Greek a different character is employed to represent the long and the short E, whose pronunciation only varies in length of Stress; and that H aspirate is not a letter but expressed by an apostrophe turned backwards. Here are the variations of the three letters composing it and in which a certain cognate meaning is traceable;-

> hRea- With ease or pleasure: hRea the Goddess, the 'flowing One', 'The Flood of Life'
> hEra – Hera (Juno)
> Ear or Er – Spring:
> Era – to do a kindness, to be beneficent:
> Aer – The Air or Ether:
> HRa or Are – then, straightway, without hinderance:
> Ara or Are –Prayer, either as a blessings or imprecation, especially the latter.

It is evident from the Greek Deacan-List of Salmasius, that the Hieroglyphic representing the sky or the heaven and which is clearly derivable from the elongated form of the Goddess of the Via Lactea, has the power of Ar or Are, rather than the usually adopted Pe, and even will stand for Our or Ouare, Compare this with the variants of Rhea just given. Again the vase and the hemisphere will read MT as well as NT; and we have instead of '(?)' or 'Nut-Pe' the name of 'Nauth-Ouar' or 'Flowing Mother'; that is to say the 'Meth –Wer' of Plutarch, or the 'Cause of All Things'; and the identification by modern Egyptologists of Meth Wer, or METHUER with the Sacred Cow of the expanse does not invalidate the above reading: compare what has been said regarding the Cow of Sirius.

And as Orion is called Szou-n-Hoor, or the 'Star of Hoor', or of Milk; and the Star Capella Szou-th-Ehe-s, consecrated Szou-Thes, or the Star of the Cow; and Hor Thes is to Milk the Cow. Even in the Scandinavian Mythology we can find the 'Cow of the Sky' whose Milk is rain which makes the fertile the Earth.

But not alone in Egypt and in India was the Cow, sacred to the Great Goddess; for in Celtic Mythology of Scotland and Ireland it is equally associated with the Great Goddess, the Mother of the Gods, called from her TAUTHA TE ANAAN or the race of the Goddess Dana. Her Name and Symbols identify her with the Magna Mater, Rhea, Rhea, Cybele and the Ephesian Diana.

These are her Chief names or Titles; the Mohr-Reega, or Great Queen and Dana or De-Ana, that is, the Goddess Ana. The resemblance here to the name of Diana is impossible to be passed over, as the great writer on Celtic (Irish) Mythology, Standish O'Grady, has already remarked. She is called the 'Gloss of Cormac' - 'The Mother of the Iberian Gods' and that epithet of the Amazon Goddess meaning 'All variant Nature comprehending All Things' is the epithet to her.

Let us consider what Diodorus, the Scillian, relates as to the Great Goddess, the 'Megale Meter'. In his historical note on Atlantis, he states that 'She, whom he calls Basilia, Rhea, Pandora (or 'the Great Queen, the Flowing one, the All Gifted') was the Mother both of Helios and Selene, that is of the Sun and the Moon, the two Great Lights. Now this title of Basilea, or the 'Great Queen', is identical with the Celtic Mohr-Reega; and it recalls the expression of Jeremiah (?) translated as 'Queen of Heaven'; under whose worship the people said they were happy and prosperous.

But what then is the reason of the sacred character of the Horns, as so exemplified in Egyptian, Phoenician and other Cosmogonies? The Ruminant Beast with Horns, Hoofs Cloven and Four Fold Stomach; and antecedent to the Creation of Man! The Ancient Tradition is that this entity with such faculties of mammal, reproducer, of Mediator in Rumination, of pedal force dualised as in the Two Breathings and yet touching the Earth; as attracting the grosser Astral rays into its digestive system through the presence of the Four symbol, would thus through the Stellar influx, mounting to the Brain become not the Man Beast, but the Beast Man! Wherefore the redundant faculty mounting to the Brain was concentrated and diverted into the Excrescence of the Horns, onto which symbol sank in despairing effort Dragon Crowns of the Edomite Kings; and which are borne by the Divinities as a rescuing Sign; and even to this day used among some nations as a defence against the 'Evil Eye'.

We return for a moment to the symbolism of Sobo Kronos; and to that of the 'Lord of the Star Come Again' . The latter, as the Egyptian presentment of the Constellation of Orion is frequently represented in a Barque, with a striding –beckoning-adoring attitude which somewhat recalls the form of the Hermetic Cross, as though at the same time transmitting commands, invoking allied forces and acknowledging the Inspiration of the Infinite Beyond. But Sobo-Lucifer-Kronos, the fallen and collapsed Hermetic Cross, has at times the Star as his symbol in allusion to his former connection with the Via Lactea. While the former with Sothis, appears as leadings off the Stellar procession of the Constellations. Placed near the 'Gate of Man' , in Cancer, they stand, watching over the Descent of Souls; and they assimilated to Osiris and to Isis in many Egyptian Astronomical representations.

There is a connection between such names as Shabbathai, Sabbath (or Shobbas as many modern Jews inelegantly pronounce it), Sabbat, Sabazius, and the name of Seb, Sibou, or Sbo.

Our Soror 'Vesttiga Nulla restrorsum' is of the opinion that the whole style of Egyptian Portal Architecture has been based on the stretched out from of the Goddess of the Via Lactea, with the fallen Seb beneath representing the ground line. This would give the reason for the sweeping horozontal lines and for the sloping walls and would seem to be a perfectly tenable idea.

Let us now return to the symbolism of the Hermetic Cross itself. It is found in the Egyptian representation of Shu Zeus-like Atlas, supporting the Sky, kneeling, the arms raised in the Sign of the supported Disc above. It is found in the position of the kneeling man, with one arm raised in Invocation and the other touching the Earth. It is found in the position of the Candidate in the Grade of Zelator, with one hand touching the ground, with the other, he sprinkles salt presented to him or her, by the Kerux. Compare this attitude in the Zelator Grade with the Pythagorean dictum:- 'When it thundereth, touch ye the earth'. There is a distinct suggestion of a Hermetic Cross in the form of the letter Aleph, which has been compared to a man kneeling in the position just described.

We know the mathematical proportion of the construction of the Hermetic Cross is equal to that of 17 squares, taken out of a square of 25 squares. And this is the number of squares in the Kamea of Mars. Let us therefore now place the Hermetic Cross upon the Kamea of Mars, and examine the sums of the numbers that fall upon each arm:

The Hermetic Cross
On The Kamea Of Mars

Facing Left	*Facing Right*
Upper Left 11.24.7.25= 67 SZ	Upper Right 3.20.7.25 = 55 NH
Upper Right 3.16.9.21 = 49 MT	Upper Left 11.4.17.5 = 37 LZ
Centre = 13 IG	Centre 13
Lower Left 5.17.10.23 =55 NH	Lower Right 21.9.22.15 = 67 SZ
Lower Right 1.19.2.15 =37 LZ	Lower Left 1.19.6.23 = 49 MT

Whence we find that the position towards the right or left does not vary the totals of 67, 49, 55, 37, but simply throws them into an opposite situation not withstanding that these totals of the Arms are thus furnished by different numbers; the complete total of the arms remaining the same –208= RCh, meaning action or motion in the Air, or Ether, the Hebrew Root of RuCh, Ruach. If we add the number of the centre,13, the Grand Total is 221, = RKA, Raca, a variant of RQA Hraka, 'Mad with Vanity and Pride, Empty, Worthless'; this word is used as a term of opprobrium in 11 Samuel, vi.20, and Matthew, v.22.

The somewhat sinister number of 13 holds the Centre signifying Death, Change. IG means 'Afflicted, beaten down, in grief and punishment' 37, LZ, is a Hebrew Root-meaning 'To turn aside, to fall, to decline, to depart from the right way, to become perverse.' 55, NH, (NH signifying Beauty or Ornament) is derived from a different Root by prefixing N servile, while NH as a Root has N radical. As a Hebrew Root it means 'to bewail; to lament; to be in grevious, fallen, or terrible condition worthy of lament.' 49, MT, 'to slide, slip down, lapse fall'; 'to fall down swiftly as the Lightning fall from heaven' 67, SZ, as a Chaldaic derivate as a meaning of 'finished, some with'.

These sinister meanings have an evident applicability to the Fall of the Dragon, and the hurled thunderbolts in the war of the Great Forces. The application of the Tarot Keys to the above roots gives somewhat cognitive interpretations.

The sum of the four numbers not included in either position of the Cross - 12, 8, 18, 14 =52 BN.

Thus far is sufficient concerning the Via Lactea and the Hermetic Cross, the Admission Badge of a Zelator, the Key wherewith to unlock the Secrets and Mysteries of that Grade.

The Hermetic Cross And Its Mysteries
By Pat Zalewski

I wrote this paper as an introduction to the Hermetic Cross when I went through the ThAM grade, for my teacher, Jack Taylor, who asked me to give some explanation of it. I updated it in 1994. At that point I had not seen the previous paper of Mathers and planned to go back and do more in depth research. My idea was to link the Swastika with the Convoluted Forces paper in more depth later. I say this because there may be some of you out there that may wish to examine this aspect of its use for individual research.

The Hermetic Cross, Telraskelion, Gammadion, Fylfot or Swastika as it has been most recently referred to, has been with us since antiquity in almost every continent on the Globe. The actual shape of the Hermetic Cross is in the outline of the Hebrew Letter Aleph, both ascent and descent. Another association of the Hermetic Cross is to the First Tarot Key, The Fool, for it is the young child that stands in the shape of Aleph. The association of applying Beth to the Hermetic Cross comes to us through the Bahir or 'Book of Brilliance', when we are told that Beth resembles a man formed by God with Wisdom, closed on all sides but the front, so that it can be a recipient of the Divine White Brilliance. This triple dimension refers to the Supernal with Aleph as Kether, with Chokmah and Binah, as Wisdom and Understanding, which allows the Light to Shine through. The Bahir informs us that the tail of Beth is opened from the behind, and that man could not exist without this (speech and procreating). It states that Beth is not on the tail of Aleph then the world could not exist. For Aleph is the vehicle of power and manifestation that Beth augments. By analogy, the shape of the Hermetic Cross is Aleph and Beth is its individual arms that whirl into manifestation. For within the shape of the Hermetic Cross is that of the Words: LVX – LUX – LIGHT.

Mathers tells us:

> '...From the synthesis of the ten coruscations of
> the AOUR (Light) proceedeth the influence into
> EHEIEH, the Kether of Atziluth. And the influence
> of EHEIEH, the Kether of Atziluth. And the
> connecting thread of the AIN SOPH is extended
> through the worlds of the ten Sephiroth and is in
> every direction.'

Moses de Leon gives us this breakdown of the Light in varying
degrees, through the Sephiroth. The first three Sephiroth are beyond
the Abyss (Daath) and thus our present comprehension while the
lower ones are as follows:

Chesed	Good	TOV
Geburah	Glow	NOGAH
Tiphareth	Glory	KAVOD
Netzach	Brilliance	BAHIR
Hod	Radiance	ZOHAR
Yesod	Life	CHIAM

This process is further yet refined when it is applied to a lower
world, for each of the four arms of the Hermetic Cross reflects
Light in four levels. These four levels are the subdivison of Malkuth
acting on Kether, for we must never forget that in every Kether
there is a Malkuth above it, and each Malkuth is in but four
incorporeal divisions of the elements. Mathers states:

> '...There will be, not one, but four formulae of the
> application of the forces of Malkuth, unto the
> revolution of the Aces unto Kether, and these
> acting not singularly, but simultaneously and a
> different degree of force...Thence they are
> projected in a whirling convolution (yet according
> to their nature) through the lower cone of the hour
> glass symbol into Kether...'

1. Muhak Light   -   The power of the spectrum,
                        the Fire Arm.
2. Bahir Light   -   The power of reflection, the

			Water Arm.
3.	Zohar Light	-	The power of absorption, the Air Arm.
4.	Light from the Zohar	-	The power of visibility the written through absorption, the Earth Arm.

These four shapes of stages of Light equate with the four levels of flame shown to Moses on Mount Sinai.

When viewing the Hermetic Cross we find that it is associated with the Convoluted Forces. The Four outside Elements represent the Four Aces, for these are the Roots of Power, as they rotate around the central pole or column of the heavens. For those Aces are guided by the Invisible actions of the Four Kerubics and as such take some of their nature. As each arms of the Cross turns, then we find that an Ace or the Elemental squares of each wheel will move into the same position as the preceding Fixed Sign was in. This is the entire concept of the attraction and repulsion for forces, and is called the Lopped or Flying Formulae, which is more vertical than horizontal in action. For here we must start to see the Hermetic Cross in a three dimensional concept rather than as a flat wheel or disk.

The Revolving or Flowing formula is best described by Mathers, as its application is relevant:

> *This formula may be best symbolically represented by the Four Aces reveolving in a smaller wheel upon a great circle whose body is composed of the powers of the twelve Signs. So that this latter in its turn revolves upon the station above the zodiac. The effect of the revolution of the Wheel of Aces will be to excite, by the Ace of Wands, the Fiery Signs, by the Ace of Cups the Watery Signs, by the Ace of Swords the Airy Signs and by the Ace of Pentacles the earthy Signs. Yet the forces of the revolution of the Serpent as well, the forces of the Aces will be in their turn modified by the Zodiacal in the body of the Serpent.*

We must not forget that the Ace of Cups represents the Head of the Dragon, the Ace of Swords the Forepart, the Ace of Pentacles, the Hind part of the Ace of Wands, the Tail. The whole figure of the Hermetic Cross, with its four consecutive arms resembles the Great Dragon (Draco) of the heavens of the Northern Pole.

The 10th Key of the Tarot, the Wheel of Fortune, is strongly linked to this diagram. The Four Elements at the end of the Cross is identical to the form of the Sphinx resembling a mixture of the elements that the zodiac wheel below it must pass beneath. When compared with the Hermetic Cross the same principle is evident with each elemental arm being there only momentarily before the arm behind takes its place (this produces a mixture of both repellence and attraction of the forces of the elements for then harmony and balanced is maintained). It is the continuing turn of both wheels with the elements as the modifying force and the solar centre being equal to both. The Sphinx holds the Sword which is related to the Flaming Sword or Lightning Flash that ends the energy through the Higher Tree to make the wheel turn. For both wheels represent the evolutionary process of developments (through the elemental framework) which is amply shown by the Lotus Wand of the ZAM. Both wheels show the intermixture of the Four Kerubic Forces in Action.

Alchemically speaking, the Hermetic Cross represents the Primea Materia of first matter in the four worlds of the alchemist-Human, Animal, Vegetable and Mineral. The varying arms of the Cross-show the numerous hidden states (12 in number) that the matter has to be subjected to before it reaches its goal at the centre (shown as the Sun) where it is united with its spiritual essence. For each arm of the Hermetic Cross represents the four alchemical colours of the experiment:

Arm	Stage	Tarot
Fire	Blackening	Knights (on Horses)
Water	Whitening	Queens
Air	Yellowing	Princes
Earth	Reddening	Princesses

The Aces, being the root Power of the Element precedes the above associations. However, it must be remembered in the Convoluted

Forces that the Aces sit just above the Princesses and that the Princesses are Thrones for the Aces, hence the dual associations.

From this we can determine that while the Arms of the Cross appear to hold the thing in perfect balance, the effect of that balance differs considerably with the actions of each Sign and as such does effect the speed of the movement of the Cross. You could not expect the swift rapid movement of Fire to be equal with the slow penetration of Water and likewise Air with Earth.

With the Portal ritual, you were shown the diagrams of the Seraphim, and in particular the centre of the Wheel of Ezekiel's vision is the one that interests us in connection with the Hermetic Cross. It is in our best interests to restudy this diagram, for the ritual tells us:

> ...*The Kerubim of Ezekiel each have four faces;*
> *those of the Lion; the Eagle and the Man and the*
> *Bull – counterchanged with each other by*
> *revolution, whence the symbolic form of the wheels*
> *beside them wherein was Spirit...So the synthesis*
> *of the Kerubim is found in the revolving Cross.*

A careful examination of this diagram shows that each of the four wings is subdivided into various divisions of the Four Kerubs. These equate to the zodiacal divisions of the arms of the cross.

The Hermetic Cross is associated to the Hammer of Thor, for Thor was the Norse equivalent to Mars. The hammer was called the 'Mjollnir' and was like a boomerang, for it always returned to its place of origin. Its four arms represented the four main embodiments of the Thor mythology; consecration, fertility destruction and resurrection. All of these principles are the essence of the four elements and the Hermetic Cross.

Chapter 5

Golden Dawn Alchemical Papers
The Altar Of Incense
And Its Alchemical Considerations
By Pat Zalewski

This paper is an introduction to the Alchemical Mss 'Homer's Golden Chain' that was first circulated among the Zelator Adeptus Minor, but only to selective ones and was one of the restrictive Mss. I have appended it to the Altar of Incense because it fits better here than anywhere else. The Mss of the 'Chain' was first introduced into the Golden Dawn by a 5=6 watchmaker by the name of Henry Pattinson, which he published in a local magazine run by Wyn Westcott. The Mss is far from a complete version of Bacstrom, but it does cover the essentials and works in with the theory of the Divine Sparks. One practical alchemist , Joseph Lisiewski, in recent years, actually created a form of life in test tube by following this Mss. In the papers of the former A.O. Chief Langford Gastin, a coloured version of the ten steps was uncovered. In the 1=10 Grade there is no diagram for the described 'Altar of Incense', and the Postulant is simply taken to the central altar and an esoteric description of the Altar of Incense is given as a substitute. The Biblical Altar of Incense is called the 'Golden' or 'Brazen Altar'. Exodus 37;30 says:

> They made the Altar of Incense out of Acacia wood.
> It was square, a cubit long and a cubit wide, and
> two cubits high – its horns one piece with it. They

overlayed the top and all sides with pure gold. And made a gold moulding around it. They made two gold rings below the moulding – two on the opposite sides-to hold the poles and used to carry it. They made the poles of acacia wood and overlaid them with gold.

If you study the Central or Middle Pillar of the Tree of Life, you will find that the four elements are related to Earth and Malkuth. Once Malkuth has been left, as one advances up the Tree, the next stop above it is Yesod, the Foundation, which is described in the 2=9 ritual as the 'Holy of Holies' or DEBIR as it is sometimes called. Mathers says of this in an unpublished paper on the curtain colouring and shape around the vault:

...It has a value of 216 or the cube of 6, thereby shewing the Perfection of Tiphareth. Now, the Debir was separated from the temple by the veil PAROKETH. Shaped as a cube and lined with gold, it measured 20 cubits in all directions. The door of the DEBIR is believed to be the Pentagonal and herein lies a great secret...for the door is Daleth, symbolic of the Venus door of the Vault. The practical application of this identity is contained in a Mss of the 'Ritual of the Heptagram' wherein is fully set forth these great mysteries. Now, alluded here is the connection between the DEBIR and the Altar of the Incense. The incense that of which was burned on the altar that stood between the veil in the Holy Place...

The incense used exclusively for the altar, was onycha, galbanum and frankincense, which were representative of the Elemental nature. The times for the incense to be lit was at daylight and twilight. This was done after evening sacrifices and before drink offerings.

The shape of the outside curtaining around the Door of the Vault, is in the form of a cube. The DEBIR for both the altar of Incense and the Astrological symbol of Venus relate to the element of earth, for only through the Pentagram of the Four elements can one recapture the symbol of Venus, as the entrance to the Vault of the Adepti. For the colouring of the Veil of Pokaraeth that hides the cube of Venus is that of Capricorn. At Whare Ra temple, in New Zealand, there was a indigo curtain across the entrance way to the Vault. It covered the entire width of the dais. The left and right sides were used as changing rooms. In the middle area in front of the Vault door was a cube that separated them, though not revealed as such until the outside curtain was drawn back. A downward view would show the curtain in the form of a 'T' or Tau Cross. Once the indigo curtain was drawn back from this centre cube there was a double curtain of green, with a red Pentagram in front. I originally thought this was something Felkin instigated until I saw the paper on the DEBIR by Mathers for his A.O. temples.

In the Golden Dawn Altar of the 1=10, the three Mother letters are given, and these are represented as a symbol of transmuted gold that overlayed the Altar. These represent the alchemical states of:

Aleph - Separation - Ruach
Shin - Purification - Neshamah
Mem - Cohabation - Nephesch

Each must be strengthened separately and reunited as a Golden Quintessence. The whole process is a base for the Spiritual Transformation, of the Great Work. We are reminded of the words of Villanova, who says:

'That there abides in nature a certain pure matter, which, being discovered and brought about by art to perfection, converts to itself proportionately all imperfect bodies that it touches.'

This part of the spiritual purification process for the Altar of Incense, must transmute and get rid of the gross external nature through aromatics. The Sepher Yetzirah tells us:

Unite the end to the beginning, like a flame to a coal; for God saith he "is superlatively one and He hath no second"...Consider then what you seek: you seek an indissoluble, miraculous, transmuting uniting union; but such a tie cannot

be without the First Unity. "To create, saith one,
and transmute essentially and naturally, or without
any violence, is the only proper office of the First
Power, the First Wisdom and the First Love."
Without this the elements will never be married;
they will never inwardly and essentially unite,
which is in the end and perfection of magic...

For this is the preparation that is undertaken by studying the hidden symbology of the Altar of Incense. The 1=10 ritual tells us that the Altar is made of ten distinct parts. Though the number of these parts can be easily applied kabbalistically, there is yet another series of hidden steps that must be evaluated equally here when we talk of the transmutation process and that is of an alchemical nature. These ten parts or stages, can be alchemically associated to the manuscript 'Homer's Golden Chain' which has ten vital links:

1.   Chaos, the impregnated State.
2.   Birth of the State of Spirit descended into matter.
3.   Nitre, the male acidic state
4.   Salt, the Feminine state taken from the Male.
5.   Product of Union of the Male and Female.
6.   Animal World.
7.   Vegetable World.
8.   Mineral World.
9.   Extract.
10. Quintessence.

The Mss 'Homer's Golden Chain' is broken down into two main parts. Part one (consisting of the first ten chapters – one for each step) gives a theoretical discourse on the methodology of how to obtain the requirted results. Part Two is related to the practical considerations of mineral alchemy. Should the adept be at this advanced stage, that he or she wishes to go onto Part Two to perform mineral work, then the following instruction from Mathers on the practical working of the 'Aurei Catena Homeri' should be adhered to.

Introduction To Homer's Golden Chain
By Mathers

Let not the Adept, upon persual of this, wish to put into practise any experiements, forgetting the importance use of Invocations of the Flashing Tablets, seeing that without their employment in alchemy, no truly great result can be derived at; and that the constant practise of the material without the Higher, will gradually lead the Alchemist farther from the Divine Magic, until, at length he will become a mere blind practitioner of the Hermetic Mysteries, and little if any better than an ordinary so-called scientist. Therefore I earnestly recommend that this Mss be only circulated among those Adepts who have studied the portion of the 'Book of the Voice of Thoth' which is called 'The Enterer of the Threshold'.

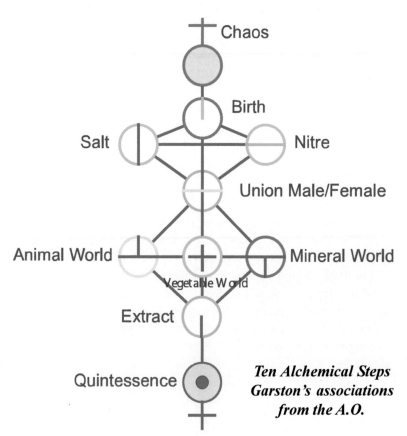

Chaos

Birth

Salt

Nitre

Union Male/Female

Animal World

Mineral World

Vegetable World

Extract

Quintessence

Ten Alchemical Steps Garston's associations from the A.O.

The Golden Chain Of Homer That Is A Description Of Nature And Natural Things.

How and from what they are generated and how they are destroyed again, and what that Subject is which generates, destroys and regenerates things. Franckfurt and Liepzic 1723. Translated from the German by Sigmund Bacstrom, M.D.1797.Revised from the unpublished Mss by V.H.Frater V.V.M.

Of The Generation Of Things

Chapter One
What Nature is

Nature comprehends the invisible and visible creatures of the whole universe. What we call nature especially is universal Fire or *Anima Mundi,* filling the whole system of the universe; and therefore it is a universal agent, omnipresent and endowed with an unerring instinct, which manifests itself in Fire and Light. It is the first creature of Divine omnipotence.

Anima Munda, as used here, does not mean animal life-principle, manifested or otherwise: but the *cause* of what we understand as the *Universal Life* principle.

Chapter Two
How all things proceed therefrom.

Thus God created first the Invisible Fire and endowed it with unerring instinct and a capacity to manifest itself in three principles.

1.   In its original most universal state it is perfectly invisible, immaterial, cold, and occupies no space; in this tranquil state it is of no use to us, yet in this unmoved state it is omnipresent.

2.   In its second state it is manifested by motion or agitation into *Light*. In this State it was separated out of Chaos, when God said, "Let there be Light, and there was Light." Yet it is Cold. When gently moved and agitated it manifests Warmth and Heat, as in the case in all friction, and in fermentations of moist things.

3.   When collected in a sufficient quantity and violently agitated it is manifested as Burning Fire. This continues to burn as long as it is agitated, and has a fit subject to act upon. When that fails, it returns to its first state of tranquil universality. In the character of Burning Fire, it manifests Heat and Light.

Thus we say in its primary universal state it is perfectly invisible and immaterial.

In its second state of manifestation it is visible as Light.

In its third state of heat and Burning Fire it is visible, hot or burning, and becomes somewhat material; as it occupies room or space whilst in this state.

You have now seen three distinct powers of the Universal Spirit. But it posesses more, and even some inconceivable powers.

We have told you the Universal Spirit is endowed with unerring instinct. Working by the simplest and nearest way, it has all besides its already mentioned conspicious qualities, two occult powers, *viz.,* attraction and repulsion, and these two powers are inconceivably great.

We see various instances of it in Thunder and Lightning, in Earthquakes, Hurricanes and in the surprising effects of gunpowder.

When God created this Universal Fire, he gave it a power to become material, that is to become Vapour, Humidity, Water and Earth, although that fire in its own universal nature is and remains centrally the same. Thus you see the beginning of the Four Elements. Burning Fire, Vapour and Humidity, mixed with cold Fire, constitutes atmospheric Air, which more condensed becomes Water and the Water becomes Earth. Originally it was but one element, Fire.

This Universal Fire becomes vapour of immense extent, which by further inspissation becomes Chaotic Water, and out of *this* Water, the Creator separated the Light, that is separated(*or subdivided*) the Universal Invisible Fire. Thus we see that the invisible Fire manifested in two principles - *Light* and *Humidity*. Therefore out of Light and (*chaotic*) Water, God has created all things.

Water was the first condensation of the Universal Fire, which nevertheless in its centre, was and remains *Fire,* full of life and activity, and the more so as it was assisted (*or equilibrated*) by its equal, the Light, separated out of it as much as was necessary for the creation of all immaterial and material Beings, and in succession of time, for their maintenance.

Of the Separated Light we have spoken of before.

We now have to consider its first Body, Humidity. Water differs in regard to Density (*or sub-division)*; if rarified to a certain degree, it constitutes Air, that is a predominance of Fire above Water. But if condensed to a certain degree it and becomes Humid Water, or Humidity predominating over Fire; nevertheless in both lies concealed the universal Fire or Spirit of the Universe.

As soon as the Air gets deprived of this Universal Fire, which animates it and renders it elastic, it becomes immediately putrid, and thereby declines (precipitates), becomes Humidity, Earth and Solid. It is the same case with Water, when deprived of Fire or animated Air, it becomes putrid and condenses further and becomes Earth.

God has ordained it, so that the Universal Spirit, by means of Humidity should work all things, because Humidity mixes easily with everything, by means of which the Spirit can soften, penetrate, generate, destroy and re-generate all things. This Humidity or Water, is the Body, the vehicle. But the Spirit or Fire is the operator, the Universal Agent, the *Anima et Spiritus Mundi* - the all working spirit and power of God; the Universal germ, the genuine agent, the only agent and fabricator of all natural things.

The Universal Fire fills that immense space of the Universe between the heavenly bodies, and as it has a power to become material, it generates a subtle vapour or invisible Humidity, its first passive principle. It causes therein a gentle reaction, and most subtle fermentation takes place universally, and by this reaction, the Universal Acid is everywhere generated, which can call nothing else than a most suitable incorporable *Nitre;* it is inwardly Fire and outwardly Cold.

This Spiritual *Nitre* or Universal *Acid* we call the invisible change of the Universal Fire generated out of chaotic invisible *Humidity* ; and as this approaches the atmosphere of the Heavenly Bodies it becomes gradually more and more material, until an alkaline passive principle whereine fixes itself and forms native *Nitre* so that from the universal spiritual Nitre it becomes material Nitre.

Thus we say not without good reason that the Solar Rays of light are nothing else than a most spiritual subtle Nitre which gradually becomes more and more nitrous as it approaches the Earth, but Sea Salt in the ocean, animating the atmosphere with Fire of Life, and thereby giving elasticity to the Air and Life and preservation to the Water.

We see between the Firmament and our Earth continual vapour, Clouds and Fogs, which ascend like a transpiration of the Earth; and are sublimed upwards by the central heat of the earth.

This Chaotic Water and Vapour, contain and are the First Matter of all things, and although this appears simple before our eyes, yet it is two fold, as it contains *Fire* and *Humidity*. The invisible in the visible - the Fire or spirit is the agent and the water is the mother or parent.

Whosoever wishes to arrive at the fountain of Secret Wisdom, let him study this well and let him go with the central point of truth to the circumference. And for ever imprint on his memory, that from Fire and water, or Spirit enclosed in Humidity, all things in the world are generated, preserved, destroyed and regenerated.

Whoever comprehends this will find no difficulty in analysing natural things. He may easily volatile the fixed - and fix the volatile: a putrid subject he may convert into a pleasent smelling one: out of poison he may make a salutary medicine, because he knows all things proceed from one root, and return to that root. The distinction is external, and regards only modification of the matter, which is more or less digested or fixed. Therefore the philosophers say that *their matter* is in all things. Yet they select subjects wherein the universal spirit is more abundantly contained, and more concentrated and thus easier to be obtained.

Chapter three
How all things are further generated

We have demonstrated that the Primordial vapour, or that Fire and Water are after God, the first matter of all things. This twofold vapour by inspissation becomes Water, this Water by the action of the Universal Spirit becomes defused, begins to ferment and thus generates Matter.

In the beginning, this Water was perfectly subtile and pure, but through the action of the inward Spirit, it became turbid and offensive, and thus generated Earth. It then subdivided into most spiritual and subtile Air, then into a less common Air, into a half corporeal *Water,* and into a body *Earth.* Thus it was the first one and two, but now it is two and three, likewise four and five.

At first, it was a simple Humidity; secondly, as a Water containing a Spirit; thirdly, when it was separated into volatile, fixed and half fixed, or chemically speaking into a volatile, acid and alkali *(Anima, Spiritus, Corpus);* fourthly, when it was divided into the so-called elements: Fire, Air, Water, Earth; fifthly, when it was by Art, assisted by nature, formed into an indestructable fiery quintessence.

When the Water by change becomes putrid, we may separate one subtle principle after another. The most volatile will ascend first, and so one principle after another, and the most dense the last of all. God has ordained that the different modifications of the Universal Spirit, in the four elements should continually generate and produce a *Universal Germ,* and for that reason He hath given to each individual thing its agent and sphere, to cause a reaction.

This is seen by the evaporation of various subjects which send forth this excess of humidity not required of them. This evaporation when from *above* is termed *enfluence.* But when from things here below, it is called *Effluvium.* God has given each individual thing its particular *Germ*, which depends upon the *Universal Germ* as their Ruler.

Chapter four
How the Universal Sperm is generated by the Four Elements

After God had divided or corporified the Anima or Spirit Mundi, the simple Chaos into four Elements, or predominating, leading principles; He called to them "increase and multiply". The Heavens and the Air, both animated by the Universal fire are the Father, the Male, the Agent or Operating principles. Water and earth are the Mother, the Female or Passive principle. These four are nevertheless only two, fire and water; They are forced to engender continually a regenerated Chaotic water or primordial Chaos out of their Centre, for the generation, preservation, destruction and regeneration of all Things, and this will continue until it pleases God to Calcine and regenerate the whole Earth!

These four so-called Elements, which must fabricate the Universal Sperm or regenerate the Chaos, when one Extreme is considered towards the other, seem quite contrary, and indeed as contraries they cannot effect any good; yet when they meet orderly, they are fully capable to execute that what God has ordained them for.

It is a natural and philosophical Axiom "Non transire posse abuno Extremo ad alterum absque medio," — that is: It is impossible to proceed from one Extreme to another Extreme without a Medium. This Axiom every Artist ought to mind, thousands err because they do not observe this Truth.

Fire cannot become water without air, and earth cannot become air without water. If you would unite fire, as being extremely volatile and subtle, with the earth, which is corporeal and fixed, you will never be able to do it; because the most Volatile will forsake the fixed and return to its Chaos. This is so in all Natural Things, that the most Volatile principle, cannot unite with the most fixed without its proper medium. An Artist ought to observe this constantly that he may not lose his time, his Matter, and Expenses.

Therefore if you want to unite Heaven or fire with the earth, or convert fire into earth, unite it first with its nearest volatile medium and they will unite immediately, when that is done, give them the water, as a medium between air and earth, and they will also unite; then add the earth, and thus you may unite fire with earth and fix it therein; and so vice versa turn the earth into water with water, then convert it into air, and the air into fire by means of air.

The Heaven or fire is extremely subtle, the air is also subtle, but one degree more corporeal than the fire; water is again a degree more corporeal than the air, and the earth is a degree more corporeal than the water. Thus we must proceed as Nature does, and we may then obtain a Quintessentificated Operation, if we do not mind this, we can do little or nothing.

Nature has its different degrees of subtilty, and mixes the most subtile fire with the less subtle, and that with the least subtle.

When they are united, they influence into the most subtil water, then into the less subtle, and into the grossest. Then it mixes gradually with the most subtle earth, with the less and least subtle, until it becomes Rocks and Stones.

In a chemical Anatomy we see how the most subtle comes over first, and how Nature regulates her Operations, and does not confound one principle with another, but lets go the most Volatile and most subtle first, and then the next less Volatile, and so on etc. for Example:

Take an earth out of a Field or Meadow or what Earth you please, pour Water upon it so as to dilate your Earth well, then let it stand a few days and you will find that the coarse heavy earth settles at the bottom of the Vessel, you must stir it 3 or 4 times a day. The water will in the meantime dissolve the most subtle earth which is its salt, this does unite with the water, as being a Virgin earth.

As soon as this salt, or Virgin earth is extracted out of the common earth, the water cannot dissolve it any further.

Now you must distil this water containing the salt, into a spiritual water, and you must cohobate so often until all the salt has come over with the water.

This water now has the power to dissolve again the next subtle earth, which can like the first salt be distilled over as a spiritual water.

With this Water you may proceed in dissolving more of the remaining earth, until by distillations and cohobations, you have dissolved the whole quantity and volatilised it into a spiritual water. This is a tedious Operation but of great moment: In the same manner Nature operates by dissolving and coagulating, until the Universal Sperm of all Things is generated, which is universal seed.

The Artist must observe that Nature proceeds gradually and regularly. and observes time weight, and measure, he must transpose the External into the Internal and Heavenly, and he will obtain more and more knowledge.

Chapter Five
In what manner the Divided Chaotic Water is Regenerated and becomes the Universal Gem of all things, called Anima or Spiritus Mundi

In what manner the divided Chaotic Water is regenerated and becomes the Universal Gem of all things, called Anima or Spiritus Mundi. The four so-called Elements have been separated out of the Chaos, but they proceed all from one. Form is Fire and the matter is Water. The form is one and the Matter is but one.

The difference consists in their external appearance. By Fermentation, Fire become Air, and Air becomes Water, and Water becomes Earth; but when Fire is fixed by Art or by Nature, it becomes Earth, and when the earth is volatised by water, it becomes Air and Fire. For one Element can be converted into another; if this were not true they would differ centrally, but they do not.

The Chaos which produced these elements was in the beginning Fire and Water only; these two have been divided into four by a further volatisation and concentration. By volatisation, extenuation, or rare-faction, Humidity becomes Air animated by Fire. But condensation of that primordial Humidity, the Earth has been formedwith Fire turned downwards towards the centre of the earth. The Hieroglyphic characters of the elements explain their nature exactly.

There is not a subject or substance under the Heavens, whether liquid or dry, which does not contain this universal Fire and Primordial Humidity. The first is called *Innate Heat,* the last is called *Radical Humidity.*

The Universal Fire became Humidity but remained Fire internally; being internally extreme spiritual and volatile it was of course extremely active and movable, and by that primitive mobility, excited warmth and fermentation, and by that fermentation the universal Spiritus Acidum was and is continually generated; and when this meets with a *proper body* or medium whether in Water or in earth, the Universal Germ becomes visible and corporeal, but whilst its is only a *Vapour* in the atmosphere, it is then the universal and incorporeal Germ. This is the influence we receive from Heaven by meaus of the Air. The Heavens give their influence, so do the Air, Water, and earth, and with united efforts they fabricate continually the Universal Germ of the World.

Chapter Six
Of the heavens and their influence.

After the separation of the Chaos, Fire is the First principle and becomes visible in Light. It is the most subtle as well as the most universal. When it generated Humidity, it became a most subtle vapour, pure and extremely volatile, and occupies the Highest station or the remotest form of the Atmosphere of the heavenly bodies.

To make this perfectly intelligible, understand it thus: Before God created the system of the Universe, He created by *emanation* the universal principle of Light and Fire, with a creative instinct (although in a much inferior degree when compared with its origin); and power to become *gradually Material*. Its first step towards materiality, acccording to Moses and the most ancient writers, seems to have been to generate *Vapour,* Humidity and Water. This then, naturally and orderly, produced a Chaos, wherein the unmoved tranquil Fire or the first principle of Light, Heat, and Fire, was dormant in Water, in a state of inaction, until God moved that first principle electrically out of the Chaos and it was manifested in Light; leaving a sufficient quantity in the Chaos for its motion, condensation, and insipissation into elementary bodies, *Water* and *Earth,* as well as atmosphere *Air,* which had a greater affinity for Water, and Water predominated in it; but as it gradually disengaged itself from it, Fire became predominant.

Thus the manifested Light retained the generative power of producing humidity, of fermenting and acidulating that Humidity, it thus continued to corporify itself gradually and became an incorporified Spititus Mundi, and by intermediate means, impregnates the passive elements, Water and Earth, with its vivifying principle, the *Universal Fire.*

This most subtle principle is full of Life and Action, for this reason we call it the first agent, the Male Germ, the Soul, a Subtle Art, a Subtle Water, and a Volatile Earth.

As soon as Air becomes impregnated and animated with the first principle, it communicates immediately with Water and Earth, to impregnate them. This communication is done instantaneously as the elements are prepared gradually to meet and intermix with each other, by a continual circulation.

Our atmosphere is continually loaded with Vapours, Exhalations and Clouds. As soon as these vapours become condensed into rain, dew, snow, or hail, and fall down, the volatilisation of Water and Earth, and are ready to meet those which come down, so that there can never be a want of the generation of such vapours, which when they are sufficiently dilated or extended constitute one *Common Air.* This is more or less pure accordingly as it is animated by the universal fire, in its first form of incorporeal Nitre.

The Heavens (the Ether beyond the atmosphere filled with the universal Cold Fire manifested in Light) receives the ascending Vapours, which as they recede or ascend from the atmosphere becoming more subtile and spiritual until they actually return to their first universal State of Ether.

The atmospheric Air continually receives the volatised Water, and succeeding Vapours, until it is saturated or overloaded, when the superfluous Humidity is forced down again in dew, rain, or snow. This Fire and Air come down into the Waters and impregnate them; the waters depose their thickest part and give it to the Earth; the earth thereby becomes overloaded with superfluity of earth, and Water is again volatised and ascends as vapour.power of ascending and descending God has implanted in the Universal Fire, as the great and only agent in Nature, which causes the perpetual circulation.

The lover of Natural Knowledge may clearly learn how the effluvium of one Element becomes the food and nourishment of another. The same takes place with all animated Nature; a tree loses its leaves during the winter, the leaves fall to the ground, where they putrify and become humidity, which penetrates to the roots and feeds the tree again. Observe this well and you will fully comprehend the *Superius* and *Inferius* of Hermes, and our CATENA HOMERI or Platonic Ring. Thus you see a continual transmutation of Matter or change of Modification. Yet the inward Fire of Nature always remains the same as it was in the beginning. All things were water at first, and return again. Apply this throughout our Book, which is no small step towards our Art.

Chapter Seven
Of the Atmosphere or Air and its influence

Air is the second principle after the separation of the Chaos and is the vehicle of the first i.e., Fire. We mean here genuine and animated Air. This we call Male - *Male* germ, and first operator in all things.

The Heavens, or Fire, is the Anima and Life, whilst the Air or extended rarefied Humdity, is the Spirit, and receptacle of the Soul and principle of Life. Consequently, animated Air ought to be named, *Spiritus Vitalis macrocosmi;* or the Vital Spirit of the Earth, which we inhabit.

Air is a most subtle humid vapour or rarefied water, wherein Fire swells abundantly. This is more corporeal than the Ether beyond the Atmosphere, which Ether is totally unfit for inspiration, it being too subtle to fill the air-vesicles in the lungs of animals; Air, being the genuine medium between Fire and Water - as it partakes of both, is therefore capable of receibing the subtle celestial fiery influences as wellas the sublimated vapours from below, and by a continual circulation, these vapours are converted into Air, and by a similar process this Air becomes animated by Fire, and as soon as it becomes saturated, the superfluous humidity is condensed and comes down in the character of *Animated Water*, such as Dew, Rain, Hail and Snow. By this, you see the atmospheric Air is the first medium to unite *Fire* with *Water* and *Earth,* and without it the heavens could not communicate with Water and Earth.

This Air becomes Water, and the thicker the water gets, the better it mixes with the earth, as on the contrary, the Earth by subtilization by means of water is again converted to Air. Thus nature operates perpetually producing changes by *intermediate* elements and not from one extreme to the other. When they unite in vapours, they fabricate the universal Germ of the World, which is partly dissolved in Dew and Rain, and partly remains in the Air, for the purposes of Animation; the atmospheric animated Waters fall upon the Earth, as the receptacle of all celestial vitures or influences, and thus fertilise it, for the growth and nourishment of animals, vegetables and Minerals.

The Earth itself is a condensed or fixed Heaven, and *Heaven* for Fire is a Volatised Earth, Air is a rarefied Water, and water is condensed Air.

We have to note here that one Element differs from the other only in this, that one is *Volatile*, one is *Fixed*, one is *Fluid,* and the other is *Coagulated*, this *arises from their Subdivision amongst themselves,* and yet every one is, and remains inherently the *same (viz), Primea Materia,* or Universal Fire.

The Air may be called the Kidneys of the Macrocosm, because in the Air, is chiefly found the Conflux of all Radical, Substantial, Macrocosmical Fluids, and the pure extract or essence of the World is absorbed thereby. And in the Air, the *ancient primordial chaos* is daily and hourly generating, destroying, and regenerating all natural things.

What is Dew, Rain, Snow or Hail, but a *regenerated Chaos*, out of which Animals, Vegetables and Minerals receive part of their vivifying principles and nourishment. And all this is generated in the *Air.*

Chapter Eight
Of Water and its Effluvium

Water and Earth have an affinity for each other, so have Fire and Air, they all have a varied affinity and are necessary to each other. Earth requires Water, Fire requires Air. Air without, or deprived of Fire, becomes putrid Humidity. And Water without Animated Air becomes Mud, and Earth. Water is a condensed Air and a fluid earth.

Water is the third principle, but the first *passive* Element. The Female Germ and menstrum of the Microcosm, which conveys food and nourishment to all sublunary creatures, and is with the Earth of all things.

As soon as Water becomes Air, and this Air converted into Dew or Rain, they fall to the Earth, and mix with the grosser Water and Air, and begin to ferment by means of the primogenial implanted *Spirit* or *Fire.* And one element begins to unite and operate upon the other until they have produced their fruit from convenient matrices.

Here the Artist may learn Wisdom from Nature, and follow her if he wants to learn how the principles are mixed together. Let him look for a medium of union which is easy to be found; and if one medium is not enough, let him employ two, and if both are inadequate let him employ three, but homogenials, as Minerals agree or have affinity with Minerals, and Vegetables agree with both Animals and minerals, and stand between the Animal and Mineral Kingdoms as reconcilers between them.

Minerals are fixed Vegetables; Vegetables are volatile Minerals, and fixed Animals, and Animals are volatile Vegetables, thus one Kingdom is transmutable into other in regard to its internal qualities.

Animals use vegetables for food, and by their inward nature change them into flesh and blood. When Animals die and are buried underground, they in due time decompose, and liberate the mineral Vapours in the soil, which are taken up by the fibrous roots of the plant, and along with the minimal decomposition propagate and nourish the vegetable. Thus do the Animal and Mineral produce the Vegetable.

Vegetables again when they putrify, assume a Nitrous Saline Nature, which disolved by Rain, and carried down through the pores into the Earth, or the Sea, from whence it ascends again as a *mineral vapour.* Thus vegetables are changed into Minerals, or animals, but more frequently into animals.

This is the true *Pythagorean Metempsychosis. Heaven,* or *Fire,* and *Air* are the *Male Germ,* Water is the *Female Germ* and Menstrum. The Earth is the Womb or Matrix, wherein the two first, by means of the third, operate every generation.

Chapter Nine
On Earth and its Effluvium

Earth is the Fourth and last Principle of Chaos. It is the second passive element, the matrix and Mother of all sublunary creatures. Earth is a coagulated fixed Heaven, a coagulated fixed Water and condensed Air, the cntre and receptacle of all the heavenly influences, and the Universal Germ, which takes *here* a body as well as in the *Ocean.*

Heaven, or the universal principle in Light (Fire), by its extreme subility is of all elements the most active and omnipresent. Its motion is imperceptable naturally, although visible in Light. This *Universal Fire* is perpetually active, pervading all things, and is the original Cause of all *Motion* and *Nature.* It moves the most subtle Air on the outward superfices of the Atmospheres of the opaque celestial bodies. The outward subtile Air moves the denser regions of clouds and vapours within, and this active vibration is gradually reduced in motion as it nears the body of the planet. Every subject under the Sun, although invisibly small, contains Life or Fire, and of course, the four Elements known to us as Fire, Water, Earth and Air. Now if every subject contains the universal Fire, so every subject has a motion, either visible or invisible. This Heaven or Universal Fire never rests, but is ever animating the atoms of the Elements and manifesting itself in invisible influences, strange virtues and powers.

For instance a plant-root, or mineral torn from the spot where it grew, would gradually appear to die. But the Universal Fire within it would soon show its virtue, if that plant or mineral is rendered medicinal.

The *Fire or Spirit* is diffused throughout the whole system of Nature. The meanest drop of Water, or smallest grain of Sand or Earth, is filled with this Universal Spirit.

Observe that the whole difference of things consist only in Volatility or Fixity; that is: these cause the different modulations of matter; the whole *scope of nature is to corporify and fix Heaven,* so that it may manifest itself and *evolve* through the *Elements,* and so it acts upon the elements by affinity and antipathy, dividing and subdividing according to the freedom of its motion. Thus do all the manifested forms of Nature appear, each containing more or less of the Elements, some watery, some airy, some fiery, and some earthy, but all actuated by the *One Universal Fire,* which manifests itself as a Life Principle.

We have explained to you how vapours are converted into Air, and Air into water; we will now examine the nature of these vapours.

We have told you that there rests in the centre of the Earth, a latent Heat, which we believe to be most active in the centre by reason of its swift motion. This heat causes a continual transpiration and sublimation of vapours, such vapours are Dews and Fogs. These vapours are twofold and fourfold; two because they contain Water and Earth; fourfold, because they contain the four Elements. I call these vapours Watery and earthy, because they contain those two elements volatised and subtilized and converted into Air (or Heaven), and if they ascend, they are further subtilized.

That such vapours have been Water will be easily admitted, but that they contain a subtilized earth, may be doubted; but note that

I have said before, that one element is the conductor of the other: and that they dissolve and subtilize each other.

Fire dissolves and subtilizes Air, by consuming its superfluous humidity; Air dissolves and subtilizes Water, by means of the Fire contained in it. Water dissolves and subtilizes the earth: by means of the animated Air, which it contains, as water would be dead without it. *Vice versa,* the earth condenses Water; Water condenses the Air; by depriving of its animated or predominant Fire. Air condenses and corporifies Fire, by which means the Air becomes animated and becomes *Mundi Volatilis incorporeus.*

You are to note that Nature has its *degrees of volatility* and *Fixity,* as for instance: that part of Fire which mixes with the Atmosphere, is not so pure and subtile as that which is at a remote distance; in the same manner, the highest atmospheric air is purer, colder and drier than that which we breathe. The superficies of the water is lighter, more ariel and more subtle than the thick slimy ground waters which settle on stones, etc., covering them with slime or subtle mud.

The earth has its degrees of Subtility and Fixity, such as watery juices, sulphurs, coal, minerals and gems of a wonderful fixity.

The volatile subtile earth, in particular its *Virgin earth, viz,* its salt is more easily dissolved by water, than a pebble or sand. So is the volatile water more easily converted into dense or lower Air than common Water.

If you understood us correctly, we show you here the first beginning of nature and the *True First Matter.* As the *Four Elements* proceed from the primordial vapour, they are forced to generate continually such vapours, embodying their own principles. These are converted by Nature into a Chaotic Water, and return to the Earth again in showers of rain. In this Chaotic water is invisibly contained the *universal germ of all things.*

Now we have treated of the regeneration of the Chaos or Universal vapour. We shall further show its power and virtue, so that you may touch and see it.

Chapter 6

Secret Teachings of the Zelator Grade

The Complete Explanation
Of The 1=10 Grade Of Zelator

The Exordium

This explanation of the 1=10 grade is allied to the Z1 and Z3 papers. This was written by Mathers and handed out at Theoricus Adeptus Minor level. I would ask the reader to compare this with the Felkin paper handed out with the 1=10 ritual. This is published in the Z-5, Secret Teachings of the Golden Dawn, Book 2 the Zelator ritual, pages 93-108. In its own way I think that paper is just as thorough as the Mathers paper (but seen from a different perspective) and it was given out when you went through the grade.

The Theoricus Adeptus Minor must remember that, in the Grades of the Outer as they are now presented, there are shown to him in symbol, the path which he must traverse in his search for the Higher Divine Knowledge. Not until he has actually passed through this Veil and attained to the Inner, does he enter on that Path; but before he does, so the symbols must be awakened in the Astral, and he must have as it were, a map, registered on his consciousness of the way he has to traverse, lest he lose himself and fall, as many have done, into the Abyss of error and delusion. There may be many methods of awakening the Symbols and preparing the aspirant to enter the path of Wisdom. The ceremonies of the Outer, as now used, are found to be well adapted to this time and race. Yet there are other methods, as for example that of a special oral instruction by an Adept or Guru. Moreover there are differences in Ritual, not only at different periods, but at the same period in different countries. Let none therefore deem that a ritual differing to which he is accustomed is necessarily wrong, or on the other hand is superior to that which he knoweth.

Now, in order that ye may clearly understand the symbology of your progress, it is founded on the Arrangement of the Sephiroth on the Tree of Life, and their meaning as set forth in the Sepher Yetzirah. Recall, therefore, the Attribution of the various grades to the Sephiroth on the Tree. In each grade, the Arrangement of the Temple and its Officers is symbolic of the Sephira to which it is attributed, and the explanation thereof is given to the Adeptus Minor as he passes through the various stages up to the Grade of Adept Adeptus Minor, when he is fitted to become an Adeptus Major. In the 0-0 Grade, as ye have already learned, the Arrangement of the Temple gives, as it were, a general scheme, being modelled on the Egyptian Hall of the Dual Manifestation of Truth, all of which is explained, and the symbology of the Furniture and Emblems on the Hall, the Robes and Regalia of the Officers and their Thrones, and the Visible and Invisible Stations, etc., are described in the Mss. of the ZAM Grade, known as 'Z 1'.

In the 1=10 Grade, the Arrangement of the Temple and its officers is symbolic of the Sephira Malkuth, The Kingdom, to which this Grade is attributed. The Aspirant unto the Higher Mysteries must now understand that in the course of his training, his symbolic Ascent of the Mystic Mountain of Abiegnus, he must enter into and conquer, and possess in turn, each of the Four Elements; and this he must first do in the Microcosm of his own body, in order that his magical power he might be hereafter able to dominate the Macrocosm or Greater World which is outside of him. Therefore, as he passes thriugh the Grades of the Outer, the nature of these Elements is shown to him in symbol, to the intent that, when he cometh actually as an Adeptus Minor to attempt to know and conquer them, he may not come to the task unprepared. Through the Grades of Adeptus Minor, all the symbolism which he has hereto been shown, will be explained, and the various magical Formulae derived therefrom will be set forth. he will thus understand from the first Initiation into our Order, up to its highest Grade, the system of teaching is absolutely continuous. Now, as the student in the West, in the regular place of the door, Thou art in Darkness, but thou art entering into Thy Kingdom, i.e. that of Malkuth. though thou standest in darkness, having but just emerged from the Outer and Uninitiated World, thou seest the Light before thee, for thou art entering Malkuth as an accepted Aspirant after Occult Wisdom.

Now to thy right as thou standest, is the Pillar of Mercy, and to thy left the Pillar of Severity, and the influence of these descend on the Sephira Malkuth. Whence to the North be all the symbols of cold and darkness, and to the South, be all the symbols of warmth and of Light, and on the centre straight before thee, is the straight Path directly on to the Higher. Here then are the inlfuences of the Central Pillar, through which the Glory of Kether, by the mediation of Tiphareth descendeth by means of Yesod to illume Malkuth, that the King entering his Kingdom may attain his Crown. On the North are the banners of the West and the Black Pillar, and in the centre the Cubical Altar of the Universe. But between the Aspirant and the Altar there lies the symbolic gateway of the Occult Sciences, the two Pillars of Hermes and Solomon, whose symbolism has already been explained.

Symbolically the door is in the West, and to the Adeptus Minor there will appear, as he stands at the door, a triangle of blackness bounded by two lines from North West and South West corners, emerging down the centre of the Hall; down the edges of this Triangle, and about half way to its apex stand the Pillars forming, as in the 0=0 a Gateway. As seen through this gateway is the Cubical Altar of the Universe whose symbolism was explained in the ZAM Grade. Only in the Hall of the Neophytes, as arranged for the 0=0 Grade, it occupieth the place of Malkuth on the Tree, but now the entire hall representeth Malkuth, and the Cubical Altar is, as it were, the synthesis of that Sephira, symbolising everything that can possibly be perceived, conceived or apprehended by man in his physical body, and this indeed is but a small part of the Sephirah of Malkuth.

Firstly is the Cubical Altar in the centre, as the heart of Malkuth, from the two opposite corners there will appear to the Adeptus

Minor, two other converging lines dividing the Hall into two triangles, whereof on the North, is as the Northern side of the Altar, of a Russett colour, that of the South of Olive, while the Western Triangle behind the Altar is Citrine.

The nature of these colours and the manner which they arrise was shown in the Minutus Mundus Five Fundamental colours MS.

But note further, an in addition, that is Russet of the North side of the Hall, there be two parts red to one yellow to one of blue. On this North side of Malkuth there first manifested Adam, when, as it is said Elohim created ETH HA-ADAM that is to say, the Red One. The red clay they were initiated by the Breath of God, and therefore in the Northern part is placed the Enochian Tablet of Earth - the Great Watch Tower of the North. A long account of the Enochian tablets is followed here, but it is now deferred until the Aspirant understands the Arrangement of the Temple and meaning of the Ritual. It is therefore issued as a supplementary MS on the Tablets.

Of the Altar

Seeing in this Grade only, the Sephira of Malkuth is shown, the emblems of the Rose, the Red lamp, and the Bread and Salt, emblems of the sacrifice of Osiris Onophris, are not openly displayed, yet they are, as it were, hidden , and implied in the arms of the Red Cross which is now placed within the White Triangle of the Three Supernals, as though the Crucified one, not only only brought down and manifested unto the Outer Order this sacred sublime symbol, but Himself placed therein the Symbol of Self Sacrifice, showing that thus only can the Divine Triad of Light be brought into action in Matter. And, above the White Triangle is a Lamp, not as in the 0=0 Grade allied unto the element of Air, but as revealing the source of Light, for it shineth upon the White Triangle even as the one effulgent Light of the Three Supernals shineth on and bring into action the Divine Triangle into Matter.

Now as the Aspirant entereth into this Grade into the Sephira Malkuth, and so commenceth to comprehend the Tree of Life, and he hath learned that the ten squares composing the Cubical Altar of the Universe representing for him in one connection the Ten Sephiroth, so doth he at the same see the diagram of the Kerubim and the Flaming Sword, and these Kerubim are Metatron and

Sandalphon, and the Flaming Sword united the Sephiroth and keeps the way of the Tree of Life. Great and terrible are the mysteries connected with these Kerubic Guradians with the Flaming Sword, and which will gradually be unfolded to the student, as he gains fuller knowledge of the Sephiroth and the Tree; at present, he stands at the entrance of the Sephira Malkuth, he can but recognise the fearful weapon gurading the path of Occult Progress, but not barring this way, but rather as keeping him on the right track so that he may progress without danger. For the First Adam was cast out of Eden, and God placed the Kerubim and the Flaming Sword to keep the path, but the Second Adam opened the way.

Of this East Wall of the Temple

The eastern side of the Sephirah Malkuth is the part whence the paths that lead to the other Sephiroth emerge. Bewteen this wall and the place of the Altar is the lightest and most brilliant part of the Sephira. On the wall are symbolically Three Portals. These gateways are of Supreme importance, for by them alone canst thou advance to the Higher. Yet in this Grade they are but Gateways, and not until the Grade of Practicus Adeptus Minor when thou comest to tranverse the path of, canst thou be shown the full symbology of the Path. The Aspirant sees only gateways, he knows not whither they lead. To the Adeptus Minor, their symbology and form is that of vast Egyptian Pylons which is a narrow way where by a Giant Guardian keeps watch.

Of The Stations Of The Officers

The Theoricus Adeptus Minor should remember the symbolism of the Chiefs and Officers and their robes and insignia as detailed in the Z.1 and Z.3 for their symbology is the same. Only in their stations are they different.

The Throne Of The Hierophant

This is in the 0=0 Grade at the East of the Temple, but not on the Outer Side of the Veil of Paroketh, but rather in front of the Path of Tau, that he may receive through the Portal thereof the influences of the Three Supernals translated by the mediation of Tiphareth and conveyed through Yesod, that Path which is called

Administrative Intelligence and thus in a measure he manifesteth openly unto the Outer, the hidden form of a Giant Guardian of the Portal. And his throne is between the Banner of the East, which directly deriveth the influence of the Pillar of Mercy, and the Banner of the West, whose influence is from the Pillar of Severity. He is the inductor into the Sacred Mysteries, who on the material plane (the Sephira Malkuth) keepeth the way of Tau, whereby alone the Aspirant can emerge from the limitations, cares and sorrows of the world, and he must judge faithfully those who are fit. Wherefore must he hold the just balance between Mercy and Severity, and hence his Throne is placed between the Banners of the West and East. (East and West)

Of The Throne Of The Hiereus

This is placed to the North of the Hall, level with the Altar and in front of the Tablet or Great Watch Tower of the North, whence he partaketh of the symbolism of the Great Kings, seniors and Chiefs of the Earth; and in front of the Tablet standeth the forms of the Mighty Lord of Earth whose influence the Hiereus receiveth and transmuteth unto the temple. The Hiereus, who is a terrible avenging God at the confines of matter, is to protect the realm of the Kingdom of Malkuth from the terrible demons whose habitation is beyond the confines of matter and beyond the Great Watchtower of the North. For rightly did the Norse and Teutonic races place their Hell in the Northern regions of snow and ice, knowing well as they did the demons, whoe house was in Niflhelm or Nifelheim, the abode of Loki and his evil progeny, a dark abode far from the sun its gates open to the scathing North. The throne of the Hiereus, then, is placed in the eternal affirmation against the Evil Ones.

Of The Throne Of The Hegemon

In the 0=0 ceremony the Temple represents the lower portion of the Sephira of the Tree of Life as far as Parkoreth, the Veil of the Temple being the subsidiary Sephiroth: Malkuth, Yesod, Hod and Netzach, in Malkuth of Assiah. On such arrangement the Seat of the Hegmon between the Pillars was the point of intersection of the lowest reciprocal Path with that of Samekh. In this grade of the 1=10 however, the gateway between the Pillars stands open, and the Hegemon or Reconciler sits in the South, receiving the influence of Mercy, as the Hiereus of the North receiveth the influence of the Pillar of Severity. Therefore doth Hegemon, complete with the Hierophant and Hiereus the establishment in the Temple of the Triangle of Light, although the banner of the West draws down pure Light as the Hiereus draws intense Darkness.

The Throne Of The Inferior Officers

The Kerux, as the Guardian of the inner side of the door hath his Station in the centre of the Western end of the Temple where the Door is symbolically placed. Stolisties and Dadouchous have their Stations to the North West and South East of the Black and White Pillars respectively, and remember that they represent the Urim and Thummim of the Hebrews, wherein is contained and concealed a powerful and important formula to be presently set forth. The Officers, their robes and insignia are the same as in the 0=0 Grade.

Of The Invisible Stations

In my 1=10 book you will note on page 32, a list of God Forms which show a different placement on the Temple floor. Sandalphon being to the East of the Altar, and in the Mathers paper he is in the West. The God forms from the Element Grades came from a paper by Moina Mathers, copied by Jack Taylor from a copy given to him by Mrs. Felkin in the 1930's. This copy I am told was brought back to New Zealand by Euan Campbell, in the 1930's, a Whare Ra member who was friendly with Langford Garstin. Prior to this the New Zealand Order had its own set of God forms, by either Doctor or Mrs. Felkin. Another New Zealand collector, Tony Fuller, showed me a few years ago a set of original diagrams of God-forms (through the papers of Frank Salt, a former Hierophant of the New Zealand Temple) which seem to be a mixture of both the Moina Mathers paper and the early Whare Ra versions. He was aware of Campbell's notebook on these God-forms which I had been shown by Campbell's widow in the early 1980's, which tallied with Taylor's copy as given in the Llewellyn book. The reference to energy patterns on the floor in the form of the hexagram are better shown in the Moina's paper than those given by her husband. This God form paper was started in the 1890's and had a later date of 1921 on it. It appears she revamped the God-forms for the elemental grades and changed things considerably in the 1=10 placement of the Invisible Stations. Mathers must have gone along with some of this because I was recently shown a partial copy of an AO document (dated 1915) for the God-forms which is identical to one section of the 2=9 God-forms of Moina's paper. Since this paper came from England and not from New Zealand, it appears that Moina's god-form papers were in use in the AO in the Practicus Adeptus Minor level. I have no answer to this puzzle, but have found that the later papers of Moina Mathers and the God-forms appear more consistent than the Felkin association. It was known that Moina changed a few things and perhaps this was her contribution. PZ

The Station of ADONAI HA ARETZ

Chief of these is Adonai ha Aretz, the Soul of the Earth, to whom this grade is especially attributed. His station is in the East of the Temple, brooding over and dominating all the extent of Malkuth. Recall the special method of Vibrating his name, and the appearance and colouring of the vast elementary figure and endeavour to see Him, the whole of the Eastern side of Malkuth. His head reacheth into the Zenith, clouds and lightnings are around the Cross, the wings stretch North and South, unto the limits of the Universe, and the feet are upon Hades Nadir, and the reflection of the green robe is in the citrine of Malkuth, vastly feminine, and partly masculine, is the Figure described in the teaching of ZAM.

The Station Of The King Of Earth
IC ZOD HE CHAL

This is immediately in front of the Great Tablet of Earth, in the form of a Kingly figure, as of an old but vigorous man, wearing a gold cross, dark robe over his left shoulder and arm, the right shoulder and arms bare, having a golden sceptre in his right hand. His station is between the Tablet and the Lamp and Salt, wherefore there should always be a space here. The Tablet may be hung or fastened on the wall, and the Lamp and Salt should be on a small table, symbolically representing the Altar of the North before it.

The Section Of The Bride Of The Qabalistic Queen

H-KALAH : Malkah the Bride, has her station opposite the King of Earth and in the South, halfway between the level of the Pillars and the Altar. She receiveth the influences of EDELPARNA, The Great King of the South, Which tampereth into the gracious Light by the sweetness of her own nature, but this Grade neither Edelparna nor the Watch Tower of the South is shown, but only his influence felt through Malkah, yet sweet and gracious though it be, the children of Man cannot endure the Blinding Light thereof. Now these three (ADONAI HA ARETZ, IC ZOD HEH CHAL, EDELPRANA) form a Triad which invisibly informeth, influence and acts through the Visible Officers, Vis. the Hierophant, Hiereus and Hegemon, if one of these be a Theoricus Adeptus Minor , he should, in the 1= 10 ceremony put on the appropriate form, otherwise he will put on the same form as in the 0=0.

The Station Of The Four Archangels

These stand in the Four Quarters of the Temple

RAPHAEL to the East:
MICHAEL to the South:
GABRIEL to the West:
AURIEL to the North:

The Adeptus Minor sees these in their appropriate colours, robes and insignia as above and beyond the God-forms of the Invisible Stations.

The Stations Of Sandalphon, Metatron And Samael

The station of Sandalphon is to the East of the Altar, and forming, as it were, a subsidary triangle. And Samael in this Grade answers to the Evil persona of the 0=0 and Metatron to the Light Divine.

The Symbolism Of The Opening Ceremony Of The 1=10 Grade Of Zelator

The material affirmation of the Kerux that the Temple is properly guarded preceedes the consecration and purification by Fire and Water, which marks the limitation of the place as it were, exorcises and protects the entrance of all evil Astrally. Stolisties and Dadouchous sprinkle and cense to the East only. For the Great form of ADONAI HA ARETZ dominating Malkuth to the East Himself reacheth the limtations and taketh the elements of Fire and water cleanseth the Temple. As it is said 'whomsoever I shall cleanse needeth not save to wash his feet'. In reliance of the power of ADONI HA ARETZ, Dadouchos and Stolistes, from the level of the Pillars, which is the level of the feet, cense and sprinkle but once. The Hegemon then affirms the attributions of this Grade to the Element of Earth, immediately following the Adoration of the Lord King of Earth and the recital of his Titles and Attributions to him of the three Sephiroth of Malkuth, Gedulah and Geburah, as in the Ritual of the Penatgram.

Concerning the name ADONAI

This is the plural noun, derived from the singular ADON, meaning 'Lord' and 'Master'. The plural by Hebrew usage, being intensive and signifying not 'Lord' but 'The Lord', the Great Lord. In vibrating, great care must be taken by the Theoricus Adeptus Minor to use the proper sound and place the accent right, for the vibrating formula will be of a greater power to him than to the ZAM.

Now the word ADONAI may mean either the 'Supreme Lord' or it may mean 'Lords', and in the latter sense it is used in Genesis 18.2., when Abraham addressed the two angels whom he took for men. The difference lies in the pronouncing, for when the word ADONAI signifieth the Supreme Lord, it is applied to God. It is written in pointed Hebrew, that is A-do nah-oe, or by some Jews: A-do-nan-oe. In the Synagogues it is pronounced ADONAI (Ad - dow- nou-ee) and it is pointed thus in the scriptures and in the dictionary of Genesis. The final Yod is not plural, its origin is doubtful. It may be a personal pronoun or it may derived from an adjective. The plural of Adonai, in the sense of Lords or Masters is regular ADNUM(F), or as in the case of Lot and the two angels (Genesis 11) in the script ADNI is two yods points with Oh. But when it meaneth merely 'my Lords', it is written ADNI. In the former the initial is short, but distinctly marked, pointed as above ADNI or would be pronounced Adow-nai, and in the latter, it is barely heard at all. In both, the second syllable 'do' is a marked long O, like the English word No. Some Jews pronounce it 'dow', like the English 'now'. In the former, the third syllable is a strongly accented 'nah' (or now), followed by a long but unaccounted 'ee'. Four syllables in all. In the latter the third syllable becomes almost a diphthong, something like the English affirmation 'Aye', and this is only a word of three syllables. There is no diphthong in Hebrew, but a short and slipped 'e' follows the 'a', giving almost the same sound.

And in vibrating this Name, thou shalt give careful heed thereto. What then is this ADONAI? This Hebrew name signifies a 'Lord' or 'Master', correctly a Divine Ruler. Astronomically the Sun. The same root form appears in the name of the Supreme God of many races and in various God names and words derived therefrom. The Syrian 'Adwis' (Adonio) is a well known example. As in the name chosen by the Pharaoh known as Akhenaton, the Glory of Aten or Adan, or the sun's disk. So that the intensive plural means God of Gods, and was the title by which YHVH named Himself (see Jeremiah 3v17. ADONOI HO ORST) then as the partciluar aspect of the Infinite God is in relation to this Earth, or to the material universe. And since every aspect was of the infinite and must be itself infinite so must this be an infinite and Omnipotent God. And seeing that 'in Him we live and move and have our being' and our lives are sparks of His Ineffable Radiance, so we have within us the magic power, as has been taught to the ZAM to put on the form of Adonai even as we put on other God-forms of lesser Gods, and to speak in the name of Adonai.

Now here is hidden a magical formula of enormous power, whereby indeed the Adept who can use it properly, can accomplish whatever he will. For to employ rightly this great name Adonai, is to connect all nature and the forces thereof.

The Rose Of Sharon And The Lily Of The Valley

Much has been written about this title, and the Rose of Sharon has been supposed to be the wild narcissus of the fileds, on the ground that the name ChBTzLT was supposed to be derived from BTzL, the Chaldee however, renders it JAICHAH, which signifies a rose, and the two roots Chobah 'to hide' and Tzel 'to shade' meaning thus the rose which is veiled or hidden. Some of the early Rosicrucians, for the same reason, used the rose in their Ceremonies, from a tradition that the angel Ave had covered this rose with a veil of moss. The Lily of the Valley is not the flower we know by that name. It is a six petalled lily, as is shown by the Hebrew name ShUShN from a root meaning six, and therefore referred to the Hexagram. Father Sineret, the learned Jesuit, conjectures it to have been the Persian or Crown Imperial Lily. The full meaning is 'the Hexagram or Signet Star' of Tiphareth, shadowed or hidden under the symbol of the Mystic Rose. (This is the Adoration of the Children of Men dwelling on the Earth. They see ADONAI HA ARETZ as the manifestation to them in the Root of Adonai, i.e. of God the Vast One, the Infinite and Omnipotent. Therefore they all face East).

The Kerux now calls upon the earth to adore Adonai. The earth was the manifestation of Adonai in the King of Earth IC ZOD HEH CHAL, and the Great Northern Watchtower. Therefore, before this Tablet, he sprinkles Salt, symbol of Earth in its twofold nature as a sacrifice (symbolically sacrificing or making tidy the earth). The Officers then, as taking on the personality of Earth, go to the North, which is the sacred quarter of Earth, and the Hierophant makes it with his sceptre the Invoking Pentagram of Earth, and the Hierophant narrates the Creation of Adam, for in the Northern Quarter, the Red one first appeared, and here was divided the human creation, for previously they were all but one, but where the North created ETH HA ADAM, the Adamic race were divided from the Elementals as has been partially set forth by Theophrastus Paracelsus. The Hierophant, therefore, here speaks in the name of ADONAI as the King of the Earth, and in the Name of Kalah, the Queen, and calls on Elementals to arise. And while the Hierophant sees the Insignia of the other officers, and the meaning of the Signs, of the Name and letters whereby he commandeth the Elemental Spirits of Earth, these shall all be set forth in the MS. on the Four Elemental Tablets. The battery of knocks follows, these being ten, which is the material number of the 1=10 Grade.

As in the 0=0 Grade, the Candidate is waiting in the care of the Sentinael, and the Hegemon is sent to superintend his preparation. All that was said to the ZAM may be now considered as repeated here. The Candidate at his entrance, carried in his right hand the Fylfot Cross or Swastika, the Talisman of the Jains, which was partially explained to the ZAM when the insignia of the Dadouchos was described, in addition to what was said, the square of 25 squares whence the Fylfot is derived, is the Kamae or magic square of Mars, and so belongeth because by the Sword of Mars must the more intractable Elements of Earth be overcome and made subject to the Light. The earth is composed of the four elements and therefore the zodiac signs of their triplicity are fitly placed on the squares of the Cross, thus indicating at the outset how the Sword through the Fylfot Cross dominated the four elements and forces them to assume that form, and by this, may the candidate enter safely into the Sephira of Malkuth.

Here Follows The Discourse Of The Swastika

To render this explanation more simply, this discourse is now a separate MS. and with regard to the Kamea or Magic Square of Mars this is only indicated in the squares taken from it to form the Fylfot. But in the Grade of Theoricus, Practicus and Philosophus in the Outer, the kameas of the Planets are shown and and therein forms part of the teaching of the Adeptus Minor.

The Candidate being now brought in, the Signs and Tokens of a Neophyte are repeated in order that in symbols they mey be impressed upon his Sphere of Sensation, and the Hierophant once more affirms that nothing can be done in the Plane of Earth and in the Sephirah Malkuth, save by the aid of ADONAI, and the candidate renews his pledge to the 1=10 grade. The sacrifice of salt follows, and here note that sacrifice means 'making holy', and the signification of this is that the Candidate will henceforth will endeavour to make holy the material Earth. And as the Adeptus Minor will knoweth,the primary signification of the word 'earth' being his own material body, the Microcosm and Macrocosm, so he pledges himself now to make his material body holy.

Kneeling between the Pillars, he hears from the Hierophant what is his task in the future viz to analyse and comprehend the nature of Light that ws revealed to him in the 0=0 Grade. The ZAM who attained to ThAM can see how he has been lead to do so. For in the 0=0 Grade, as he has been said, he was shown generally the lower portion of the subsidiary Tree in Malkuth. It is this, on its symbology, which is the material vehicle for the Light he has to analyse. Successively then in the 1=10, 2 =9, 3= 8 and 4= 7 Grades he is shown the symbology of the Sephiroth belonging to the First Order and the paths uniting them, but without any explanation, and various other teaching is given him, fragmentary and disconnected in appearance, but essential for his future progress. In the Portal, the whole Tree in its relation to the Orders and Grades is shown. This constitutes the analysis which the Hierophant adjures him to make. In the 5=6, commencing his work as a ZAM he begins to comprehend. And now, comprehending thus for the ThAM he prepares actually to enter the Immeasurable Region. The Hierophant then expounds to him how Tetragrammaton and Elohim formed the Tree of Knowledge of Good and Evil, which is in Malkuth.

Concerning Tetragrammaton

The Great name YHVH rendered 'Jehovah', or 'Jahweh' or 'Yahweh', is never pronounced by a Jew, it is said that the true pronunciation is a secret revealed only to the High Priest and pronounced by him once a year when quite alone and in the Holy of Holies. When a Jew meets with this word YHVH, if it refers to

God as the Supreme he pronounces it ADONAI, and in writing uses the same points. But if it refers to God in the work of creation he pronounces it ELOHIM, the masculine plural form from a feminine singular Eloah. The whole implies the united active and passive essences. This the first stage of Creation is from the Eternal Mother, but when the creature is produced, its form may be manifold, hence the aparant creative energy is plural and positive. As title ELOHIM is referred to Binah, the Supernal Mother, and as Binah leads to the Seven Succedent Emanations, no Elohim has been said to represent a sevenfold power of God-head. So about Malkuth are Seven Columns, and our Splendours which surround it, concerning which there is more to be said hereafter, but first must the Paths of Good and Evil and the Straight and Narrow way between them must be mastered, and these are terminated by the Invisible Stations of Metatron and Sandalphon.

How the teaching of the Hierophant is here directed to show the tendency of the natural man and the Obstacles in his Path; how he may conquer and attain, when guided by the Light of the Occult Wisdom. The Natural man seeking for knowledge, seeks it by natural means, by physical investigation of phenomena by his five senses, and this is called the Path of Evil, not because it in itself is wrong, but because, being natural and finite, it can by no means attain to the Hidden Knowledge which is Divine. 'Canst thou by seeking find Gods?' So says the Great Archangel SAMAEL. The wicked and rebellious man who, that is, without Divine Guidance, attempts by his own reason and observations to probe the Vision of the Ages, gazes at the Face of Nature and finds therein, naught but terror and obscurity. So are they who say that nature is cruel and blind, they who would cast out nature as Evil, for these shall not attain to the Hidden Knowledge. But he who brought in the Name of ADONAI may be not rejected. The Natural Man failing to attain the Hidden Knowledge by natural means turns in reaction to entirely spiritual, for which, however, he is yet unprepared.

The Candidate, therefore, by direction of the Hierophant, now attempts to enter the Path of Good - that is, seeking entirely by material means - only to be barred by the Angel Metatron. Not as yet canst thou bear the dazzling radiance of that Light. Now therefore, he is directed to the straight and narrow Path, inclining neither to the right hand nor the left. Here both Samael and Metatron would bar his way, but the Hierophant intreposing, admits him. During this part of the Ceremony, the Hiereus advances to the Invisible station of Metatron, and finally the Hierophant to the Invisible Station of Sandalphon, and thus, the Oficers who first formed in relation to the Candidate - the Triangle of Fire, now form the Triangle of the Star. From this he learns that not by material science alone, can progress be made toward the Hidden Knowledge, but that in every occult and magical formula there must be a material basis, and in all material and scientific work there must be occult power, whether recognised or not.

From this ceremony of the Three Paths is derived a formula whereby the Adeptus Minor, putting the Tree upon himself may be able to attain the Hidden Knowledge when he wills. This belonging to the Higher Clairvoyance, which is the subject of a specific treatise. The Candidate therefore, by direction of the Hierophant, now attempts to enter the path of Good - that is seeking entirely by material means.

The Candidate is now brought to the diagram of the Kerubim and the Flaming Sword, concerning which it is written in the Book of Formation, in the 6th paragraph:- 'The ten Ineffable Sephiroth have the appearance of the Lightning Flash, their origin is unseen and no end is perceived. The Word is in them as they run forth and as they return, they speak as from the whirlwind and returning, fall prostrate in adoration before the Throne.' The Hebrew word for 'Lightning Flash' is BRQ , some times translated as 'Scintillating Flame' . It is the same word as the name of that as Barak who fought with Deborah against Sisera. Compare the Persian Barcas.

The secret Sign of the Grade, that of the interposer, is now given, in addition to the explanation given in the 1=10 of the Outer. This is the position of affirmation in the taking of the oath adopted by many nations, and ye calleth upon ADONAI to witness that the candidate now entereth the straight and narrow Path, and affirming both the material and spiritual, it affirmeth the Truth of the Incarnation. And the fuller and further meaning of this sign and its connection with Quesheth the Bow shall be expounded in the second part hereof, which dealeth with the second portion of the ritual.

End of Part One.

MS referred to:

1. Magical formula on Grade
2. On Enochian Tablets
3. On Urim and Thummim
4. On Elementals
5. On Swastika (2)
6. On Kameas and Planets
7. On Higher Clairvoyance

Second portion

Concerning The Secret And Mysteries Of This Grade

To the Aspirant in the Outer these appear to be merely certain arbitrary signs whereby a Zelator may be tested, and whereby he may prove his membership of the Grade. They do, however, veil and imply certain magical formulae, the nature of which is shown to the Theoricus Adeptus Minor, and the full method of working is given in the Practicus Adeptus Minor along with other Mighty Formulae) which are communicated to these Grades. Now, as in the 0=0 Grade of Neophyte, these have a three-fold interpretation, vis.

1. The apparent meaning
2. The Spiritual or Mystical reference.
3. Practical interpretation

Let the ThAM therefore, read again, and consider what was written in Ritual - Concerning the Signs of the Neophyte, and in Light thereof, consider what follows as to the Signs of the Zelator of the 1=10 Grade in the Outer.

The Step

1. The apparent meaning is the completion of the notion of entering the gateway of Occult Science - bringing into action the power of Nepthys, to indicate consummation of that whereof a beginning has been made, - thus actual entry into the Portal.

2. The Mystical and Spiritual meaning is the actual stamping down of the Evil Persona. The beginning of their action is on the side of Chesed, but the completion is on the side of Geburah, for the negative must ever precede positive, as it is written: Darkness was on the face of the deep for this is the establishment of the Negative: And the Spirit of the Ruach Elohim moved on the face of the waters. And this established the Positive, the action is complete. It beginneth with Self sacrifice and is consumated in Victory over the Enemy, as in the Supreme example did the Crucified One attain through Self Sacrifice and finally put all the enemies under his feet.

3. The Practical Application. It represents the completion of the Magical Force, and let the Adept who have given the Step, as described in the ritual of the ZAM, imagine himself colossal, and stamping on the Earth till it rocks beneath him, understand now that, on doing he scatters the Powers of Unbalanced Forces, but now this Second Step with the Right Foot entering the Portal, he makes firm the ground whereon before he shook down all that was unstable wherefore is the step of ELOHIM the Creator.

The Sign

1. The Apparent meaning. This is the Interposition of the Hierophant, or, according to another interpretation, the Affirmation of the Faith of the Zelator.

2. The Mystical or Spiritual reference. It represents the hand stretching up towards Kether, to attract and draw down the Light from the Higher

3. Practical Application. In this Grade, thou seest before thee the Three Portals, the letters of which form the word Quesheth the Bow, the Rainbow of Promise, which is the Key of Colour. Therefore, having taken the Step as before described, cast down and subdued the Powers of Unbalanced Force, and entered the Threshold endued with Magical Power to create, thou stretcheth forward thine hand as though to touch the Bow. For, in this Grade, thou art to analyse and comprehend that Light. But, when the Light emergeth from Kether, it is White, undifferentiated and incomprehensible, but it now shineth before thee as Quesheth the Bow, and the mysteries of Colour may be revealed unto thee: For colours are Forces, and the child of the Children of the Forces art

thou. But the Adeptus Major, giving this Sign, giveth it with the left hand, and with the hand closed, for he graspeth the Bow. Now, when thou attempteth any Magical work, especially on the Astral Plane, thou wilt do well to commence with this formula, putting on the God-form appropriate to the work thou art engaged in, and taking the two steps as directed, with a full consciousness of their meaning and practical application, and simultaneously thou shalt endeavour to see before thee the Bow, and stretch thy right hand to touch and bring down into consciousness the Key of colour wherewith thou shalt work.

The Grip

1. Apparent meaning. As in the 0=0 Grade, the Grip or Token representeth the seeking for guidance in darkness, and after seeking in vain, at length finding it, so this 1=10 grade of Zelator, the candidate having entered on the Occult Path, grasps a guiding hand.

2. Mystical or Spiritual reference. It showeth that the firm grip which can be relied on must formulate the sacred and sublime symbol, the Triangle, which is the only firm and rigid figure that can be formed of straight lines: Two contending forces, and One which unites them eternally. Thus it giveth us the means of knowing, even in the darkness of material ignorance, whether the hand that grasps ours and professes to lead us be the true guide that shall lead us upwards . For any hand that formulateth not the triangle is the hand of an imposter and not of an Initiate. Thus we may test the spirits who profess to guide us and reveal to us the mysteries. For, if they confess not the mystery of the 'Tria Juncts In Uno', they are not of God, neither know God. And herewith, all the position of the fingers, refers to the Ten Sephiroth (which then together form VYLAH, AaYLAH or ADM ALAH) Adam Auilah-the Heavenly Man or Primordial Being, and this inculcateth that one alone can never formulate the Heavenly Man, for only by the grip of brotherly love can this be attained. If, then, with the Sacred Symbol of the Triangle, the grip of brotherly love is exchanged, mutually joined to formulate the Ten Sephiroth, then there is guidance in Darkness.

3. Practical Application. Before beginning any practical work let all the Adepti taking part therein exchange the grip, endevouring at

the same time to realise the Mystical or Spiritual reference, and silently anew to pledge themselves, to Unity and Harmony in working, and to Devotion to the Great Work: which is so to purify and exalt their spiritual nature that, with the Divine Aid, They may at length attain to be more than human. That is to say, may formulate in themselves the ADAM OILAH.

The Grand Word

ADONAI HA ARETZ: The meaning of ADONAI has already been expounded. The Grand Word of this Grade sheweth and affirmation that ADONAI, the Lord, who is Lord of all the Universe, is Lord of this material World.

The Mystic Number

The Mystic Number of this Grade is 55. This is formed according to a well known Qabalistic process, known to the Pythagoreans, as the formulation of the Triangular or Perfect numbers, formed by the addition of the units or digits from unity I or 1, consecutively up to the number concerned, e.g. that, in this instance, of the 10 Sephira of Malkuth: 1+2+3+4+5+6+7+8+9+10 55, counting downwards from Kether, the Mystic Number of which is 1, through Chokmah, the number of which is 1+2 3, Binah, 1+2+3 6, and Chesed 1+2+3+4 10, and so on. The Password is derived therefrom, and Mystic number 55 is Nun Heh, Nun 50, Heh 5 55 (Note: this is a Mystic Password of the 1=10 Grade, and must not be confused with the general password of the Order, which is changed at the Equinox, as is expounded in the ritual Z)

The Secrets and Mysteries of this Grade, therefore, as it were, recapitulate and affirm the advance which the Candidate has made in the Path of Occult learning, thus:

He has shaken down the material edifices of Unbalanced Forces, wherein , as in a prison house, the children of earth are held bound: and he has entered with a firm tread on the Path of Divine Wisdom. He has stretched forth a hand for guidance, and has received an answering brotherly grasp, that is its grip gives him the Sign whereby, he may know that it is leading of God: and it leadeth him to the fulfilment of his Aspirations to become more than human, a Heavenly Man. He affirmeth that, as the Lord of all is Lord of the

Earth, so even in this material body, can he follow the Path that leadeth to Righteousness, and he affirmeth the Great Mystery of the Divine Incarnation...For every Spirit that confesseth Jesus Christ is to come in the Flesh is of God. Therefore we call on ADONAI HA ARETZ. And, knowing all these great mysteries, let them be unto us an Ornament, as it is said, even Nun Heh. The Theoricus Adeptus Minor should constanly recur the mysteries of the Grade, for they are not idle, meaningless forms, but contain within themselves the Key to all his Advancement, for unless he advance in this spirit, then will his learning and knowledge be in vain and he will never make any true progress. The sash of the Zelator recapitulates these ideas, and the Theoricus Adeptus Minor should endeavour to sum up and concentrate in his mind what is here said of the Secrets and Mysteries of the sash of the Zelator, and to sum up all that has hitherto been taught to him.

The Portals

Having thus far expounded the nature of this Grade, the Hierophant now calls the attention of the Candidate to the Three Portals before him in the East, concerning which a MS has been put forward by our G.H.Frater Sub.Spe, entitled "Paths and the Portals". The Hierophant calls his attention to the similarity of the symbols on the Altar, the Red Cross within the White Triangle, to the design emblazoned upon the Banner of the West, this Symbol he bears upon his breast whenever he wears the characteristic sash of the Zelator, and the same symbol should be constantly present on the aura of the ThAM upon his breast, and should always be visible to the clairvoyant as the Sign and Token that he has received into his nature this knowledge of the Light of Life. His attention is then called by the Hierophant to the Great Watch Tower or terrestrial tablet of the Earth in the North. A MS entitled Clavicula Enochian in addition to, and in continuation of, the MS already studied by the ZAM. The Hierophant next takes the Fylfot Cross or Swastika from the Kerux, and briefly indicates the attribution of its 17 squares. Two MS on the Swastika are issued to the Grade of ThAM and its symbology and uses, therefore, need not further be alluded to here. And the formula which is veiled and implied in these Signs is the subject of a separate MS but the full method of the working thereof is not shown until the aspirant hath reached the Grade of Practicus Adeptus Minor, being of a high and important nature and by no means to be placed in the power of any who have not undergone long and arduous training.

Summary Of The First Point

Now, observe that his first or introductory part of the 1=10 ceremony bringeth the Aspirant into the Sephira Malkuth, in the centre whereof, at the edge of Darkness and the Beginning of Light, he sees before him the Cubical Altar of the physical Universe, thriugh the Gateway of the two Pillars, and, beyond the Glorious Figure of the Lord of the Earth. Three Paths conduct to the Hidden Knowledge, and he is shewn by the straight and narrow Pathway in the centre is the only safe and practical one. Thus he is brought to the Cubical Altar, where the Hierophant as expounder of the mysteries, sets aside the Opposers, who would block his Path, and expound to him the Secret Signs. No explanation is then given him of these. Not until he becometh, by his perseverence and zeal, ThAM, doth he know of the formula hidden therein, and some of the secret Signs and Sigils which control the powerful spirit of the Earth, will be shewn him. He is now admitted unto this Sephira but the nature and the mysteries thereof have yet to be shewn him. For this purpose, a Light rearrangement of the Temple is needed, in order that certain symbols may be shewn in their proper place. The Zelator, therefore, is directed to quit the temple for a short space, in order that the full nature of the Sephira to which he is admitted may be shewn to him. In the First Part he is, as it were made free of the Sephira. He is now to analyse and comprehend the nature thereof.

Part Three

Second Part Of 1=10 Ritual

The position of the furniture of the temple remaineth as it were before, the stations of the Officers alone being altered, and the two diagrams are being placed North and South, and the diagram of the Kerubim and Flaming Sword being removed form the altar. Now, as the Aspirant entereth,he is told that the temple now symbolises the Holy Place of the Jewish Tabernacle, and having entered, he is informed what lieth outside. This Sephira, Malkuth, belongeth essentially to the lowest of the Four Worlds of the Sepher Yetzirah, that is, to the Assiatic World, the World of Action, whereto belongeth Olam ha Qlippoth, the Worlds of Shells, which is the World of Matter made up of the grosser elements of the other three worlds. The evil spirits are called Shells, in the Qabalah. They are grossest and most material of all forms. Their ten degrees answer to the ten Sephiroth, their darkness and impurity increasing with every step. They are the Evil and Averse Sephiroth. The first two are, it is said, nothing but absence of visible form and of organisation: the third is gross darkness; and below this, are the Seven Hells. Yet as Christ entered the abode of Qlippoth, hence it is clear that they may possibly be redeemed. Outside, then, of the Holy Place, was the altar of Burnt Offering, whereon animals which were considered to be symbolic of the Qlippoth were sacrificed, or we should say, were made holy. Being made holy, the Qlippoth can enter into the Holy Place and take part in the economy of Malkuth, the Kingdom. Thus, we have seen Samael taking part in the reception of the candidate into the Sephira, and called there the Great Archangel. Yet it is Samael the Prince of the Qlippoth, and, by the Qabalistic writers, it is said to be synonymous with Satan. So we see, in the Book of Job, when the Sons of God came and presented themselves, Satan came and presented himself, and was given a commission by God Himself. For the most part, the making holy was accomplished by passing through the Gates of Daath. As it is said in the Precepts of Alchemy, in the prosecution of the Great Work (that is to say Transmutation) First there arises the Crow (that is to say the Blackness of Death, and Putrefaction). And it is said Except a corn of wheat fall into the ground and die, it abideth alone. Hence, in the symbology wherein, animals are taken to represent the Qlippoth, and must be the animals who die on the Altar of Burnt Offering. This then, stood without the Holy Place, being, as it were, the gate of the Qlippoth. But this is not shewn to the Aspirant, nor is he given any definite teaching concerning the Qlippoth, for this belongeth not to his present Grade, but shall be given to him hereafter, if he perseveres. Only here, he should note that, even for the Qlippoth, is there a hope and possibility of entering into the Kingdom; and he should learn, therefore, not to be uncharitable towards any; and to be humble; for not be his merits is he called within.

Of the Laver

This, was outside of the Holy Place, and concerning this nothing is told to the Aspirant, save that the Priests washed their hands therein before they entered the Holy Place. All, therefore, must be consecrated or made holy, before they can enter. Evil, as symbolised by the Qlippoth must be purged by Fire and passed through the Gates of Death. Even the Priests themselves must be purified with Water. And, from the Union of Fire and Water, ariseth the most heat of Generation - or of Regeneration, whence cometh, as it is said, a death unto sin, and a New Birth unto Righteousness. Symbolic of these two cleansings, the Aspirant is therefore now consecrated with Fire and purified with Water by the Dadouchos and Stolistes respectively, and this is done in Silence, because as hath been said, the Altar of Burnt Offering and the Laver of Water are without the Holy place, and the full teachings therein belong to a Higher Grade.

The Entry Into The Holy Place

Being now placed just without the Symbolic Gateway to the West of the Pillars, the Aspirant is challenged by the Hiereus. He now sees that the places of the Officers are different. The Hiereus, who formerly was seated to the North and guarded the Path of Evil. Moving up into the Invisible Station of Samael, is now stationed to the West of the Pillars, guarding the Holy Place against the Kingdom of the Qlippoth: and the Hegemon to the East of the Pillars, in the character both of reconciler or Guide, is placed midway between the Gateway and the Cubical Altar of the Universe. But before the Aspirant can pass through the Pillars, the Hiereus bars the way with his sword, and demands from him the Signs of the Neophyte to mark that none from the Outer and Uninitiated may enter the Holy Place, which is the special dwelling of ADONAI HA ARETZ; and with regard to these, the ThAM should now read over again the description and explanation of these Signs, as given in Ritual Z. And these not merely prove to the Hiereus that he has been duly initiated into the Mysteries of the 0=0 Grade of Neophyte, but they constitute a formula whereby entrances may be obtained to any Secret Shrine or Temple of Qablistic or Rosicrucian Mysteries. And, notwithstanding that, as hath been said, in Ritual Z the full understanding of the formula drawn from these Signs cometh later, (being, first expounded as a working formula to the Grade of Practicus Adeptus Minor), yet the mere giving of them with the knowledge now posessed by the Aspirant, will suffice in many instances, and will be, among other matters, of great use, in case of any difficulty in a Tattva or in any of the Enochian Planes.

Having passed from between the Pillars, he is challenged by the Hegemon, as guardian of the Holy Place, to give the Sign and Grip of the Zelator - continuing and completeing, as it were, the Signs of a Neophyte, and thus demonstrating his right hand to be there in the Path of Occult Knowledge, and know the Secrets and Mysteries thereof.

The Table Of Shewbread

The Hegemon, as the Reconciler and Guide, leads the Aspirant Zelator to the Northern part of the Hall. Now, this shewbread is a sacred symbol. The principle reference of it is to the Soul of the Initiate, the Human Soul, the consecrated Hostia or Bread of the sacrament. For among the religious symbols of immemorial antiquity, handed down from Ages forgotten, have been those connected with the growth of Corn, Bread or cakes. The word 'schulchan' (Hbr), translated table, means literally a flat surface upon which something, e.g. the offering, may be set forth (from shalach, to send forth, to set forth) and SER translated crown, means rather a rim.). Prominent among the sacred Symbols of Mysteries, was katlathos(Grk), consecrated basket of cakes, and like other accessories of the Tabernacle, it was frequently covered with a blue veil. The Cakes themselves were termed challeth(Hbr), plural of challah, so called they were perforated from challah, pierced or wounded. Probably the first two syllables of the Greek word kalzthos, and its roots are derived from these Hebrew words.

The North is a Region of Cold and Darkness, as the station of the Sun below the Horizon. Wherefore, is the Table of Shewbread placed in that quarter, as alluding to the Sowing, Death and Resurrection of the Corn, and its Transmutation into a form of Host, and its connection with the 12 tribes of the Signs of the Zodiac. So was there interwoven into its symbolism the ideas of a certain rescuing power to aid the human race as these Tribes had been, as it were, rescued and aided to escape from a condition of bondage.

And this set forth in separate MS entitled *(The section concerning the Diagram of the Table of Consecrated Bread and the Exemplification of the Twelve Signs of the Zodiac.PZ).* For the sake of clarity this is omitted here.

Of The Seven Branched Candlestick

The South side of the Holy Place is the region of Heat and Light. Appropriately, then, as it is in the Place of the Symbolic Lightbearer, and here, accordingly, was placed the seven Branched Candlestick. Why then, was the number seven? Because all the Heat and Light cometh from the Sun upon the Earth, as it were, the product or essence of the Solar prana, the which, as thou shouldest well know by this time, O Aspirant to our Mysteries, who hast attined unto the Grade of ThAM, is divided into Seven Tattvas of our Eastern Brethren (of which five are known to the Lower Grades of the Order), and these seven correspond unto certain manifestations of the number seven, as the Seven notes of the Musical Scale, which are largely the subject of the first MS on the subject of the seven Branched Candlestick which originally followed here, but is now issued as a separate teaching. The seven colours of the Spectrum, and the Seven Planets, the symbology of which is woven into that of the seven sides of the Mystic Vault of the Adepts are the subject of the ZAM teaching which should be studied by the ThAM at this point.

And the practical application there contained in a MS on the Ritual of the Heptagram, wherein is fully set forth the connection the connection of the symbol of the Light Bearer with the Tarot cards, and its magical uses. Now, the Hegemon, fitly expoundeth the Mystery of the Host and Sacramental Bread, symbolising and representing the Soul of Man, so doth the Hiereus, who is the Mighty and Avenging Guardian of the Sacred Mysteries fitly expounds the mysteries of Fire and Heat, as set forth in the diagram of the Seven Branched Candlestick and in the Signet Star of the Heptagram. For the Fire without is the unbalanced Fire of Hell, which is destruction, ruin and desolation, but the Fire within is the life-giving Light and warmth of the Sun of Righteousness, and the Hiereus, throned upon Matter and robed in Darkness, divideth the one from the other.

Reception At The Altar

The Aspirant Zelator, having now received (albeit only in elementary form), the Mysteries of the Twelve and the Seven, the Hierophant as Expounder of the Mysteries, himself descends from his throne, and conducts him to the Altar, and it is fitting that, at this stage, no lower officer than the Hierophant should bring him the knowledge, the meaning of our Altar. Observe carefully O ThAM, that our Cubical Altar is alluded to in the address of the Hierophant, under two symbolic figures. It is the Altar of Incense which stood in the Holy Place, before the Veil, which separated it from the Holiest of Holies and being in the form of a double cube, it symbolically represents the ten Sephiroth. Consider then what I meant by these figures and numbers in order that thou mayest apprehend these great mysteries, and first of, the Sephiroth.

The Altar Typifying The Ten Sephiroth

The Qabalistic knowledge of the ten Sephiroth, so far as is necessary for the comprehension of the symbology of the Altar, is already familiar to the ThAM. This only needs to be recapitulated here. The Sephiroth are the most abstract possible comceptions of the Nature and attributions of God, and are usually thought of as numbers. Now, as there are nine digits, after which the series ends, and we recur to the unity of ten, and begin again, so is Malkuth said to be repetition of Kether, and Kether is said to contain Malkuth, the upper surface of the altar is attributed to Kether, and the bottom to Malkuth. Now, when the Aspirant Zelator enters the Hall, the lowest surface of the altar is, to its position, invisible to him; but all the other surface squares, nine in number, may be seen. He has been instructed to "Quit the material and seek the Spiritual", that is to say, he must lose sight of, or pay no attention to, the outward and material aspect of things, but must fix his mind entirely of the spiritual truths and the realities that lie behind. As it is said to him at this point, if this cubical altar were raised above his head, he would see only the bottom square - the others, from their position would be invisible to him. Now this is precisely the position of the outer and uninitiated man, as he stands as it were, outside the door and gazes on the face of nature. He may know that, behind the seeming, there lieth the Concealed Form of the majesty of God, yet, being uninitiated, he cannot see it. This is to be earnestly kept in mind in all magical formulae derived from the ritual of this grade.

Concerning The Altar Of Incense

Although the Altar is alluded to as the Altar of Incense, the incense which was burned on the Altar of Incense that stood before the Veil in the Holy Place, was of a special kind, and was regarded as so Holy that imitation of it was prohibited under severe penalties. It was compounded of four sweet odours: Sammin, symbolic of the Four Elements, namely nataph, stakte (mor and smurna) myrh: shaceleth or onyx-onycha, chalnonah-galbanum; and libinah, or libanos (hence olibanum), Pure Frankincense, pounded together in equal weights (Exodus 54). Take unto thee sweet spices, stakte, and onyona, and galbanum: these sweet spices with our frankincense:of each shall be a light weight. Then, the four elements whereunto, as it is said ELOHIM has distributed that Universe which he called into manifestation, were symbolically burnt, and, in so burning, were united into a sweet smelling savour, and thus the four again became one, and in that unity ascended to the Throne of the Lord of the Universe, like a prayer, or, as certain of the old Qabalists have said: carrying with it to the Most High the prayers of the Faithful. Then the symbolism of this burning of Incense is that the separation of the Elements, which is their manifestation must be destroyed, in order that their unity may be manifested; in other words, only through the Gate of Death can the At-one-ment be accomplished. And this burning was upon the Altar over-laid with plates of gold, gold being alchemically all the elements brought to their highest perfection. This this gives us then, the ADM AILH (sic. note. I am inclined to think that the root of this word must be AaLH to ascend, to be exalted, and by various other meanings - upper, higher, supreme, etc). Perhaps the word here should be with the letter Aayn(Aain), the heavenly or Archetypal Man, typified by the two Sephiroth, brought about to his highest, and most divine perfection. Then through the Gate of Death, blending the Four Elements, till in transcendental unity they pass out of manifestation, going up as a sweet savour to remain unmanifest, in the essence of God.

(Further note by FFJ. Carnegie Dickson, *(made sometime after 1937 and before 1949. PZ)* AaLH and AILH all signify burnt offering, because of their ascending up to heaven. The Altar of Incense of the Hebrews thus typified (though they knew it not by reason of their stiff necked obstinancy and rebellion), the Death of the Crucified One and the resulting perfection of His nature through suffering and Atonement. He wrought for the World and His Ascension to remain in the Eternal Hypostatic with His Father).

Albeit, our Altar is black, for black is the absence of colour, is the hue of Putrifaction and Death, the Crow of the Alchemists. For in all the grades of the Outer Order, the Aspirant has not yet symbolically passed through the Gates of Death. He is therefore adjured to learn to separate the pure from the impure, and until he passes through Paroketh - the Veil which was broke or divided the Holy Place from the Holies of Holies, which must be rent asunder from top to bottom, on the agony of death, the Altar doth appear to him as black.

It is by the science of alchemy that this knowledge is obtained, and this separation is accomplished, for, whereas the lowest square of the altar denotes Earth, the top which is Kether the Crown, supports the other Three Elements, the symbols of which are the three Mother letters. Thus, as it is said, Kether is repeated in Malkuth and Malkuth is repeated in Kether, the Unity is reaffirmed in Malkuth, the Three Elements are concentrated and combined in the fourth. And this mystery is declared in the Great Name of Tetragrammaton YHVH which is really the name of the Three Letters, for the final, he recapitulates and summarises the symbolic meaning of the other three, and the Heh(F) which is the aspirate, is a symbol of the breath of God, and the breath of man. Wherefore is the breath of the Macroprosopus, which is in Malkuth. And the breath of Life, and here again it is manifest that, it is the Macrocosm, so it is the Microcosm, As it is above, so it is below, was written on the Emerald tablet of Hermes. If then, O Zelator Aspirant, thou wilt analyse and comprehend the Earth, so that, by the sublime science of Alchemy thou mayest transmute it to pure spiritual Gold, thou must consider the Three Elements of Air, Fire and Water, the natures of which are blended therein, and the nature whereof the symbols of the Three Mother Letters, Aleph, Mem and Shin.

Three Mother Letters

In the letter Aleph there lieth a great mystery, for the form of the letter itself correspondeth to the Three Letters, namely Vau, Daleth Yod *(the Vau is the oblique central and shape, the Daleth is the upper right part of the letter and the Yod is the lower left PZ).* And these three, written thus, give the name of the letter Yod which is 10, and thus Aleph representeth the first of the ten Sephiroth, both Kether and Malkuth. Moreover Daleth 4, Vau 6, and Yod 10, and 4+6+10 20, being repetition of 2. Hence, as it is said 'The unit became the Duad manifest itself, and from the body of man was taken the woman in order of manifestation (bring about manifestation), and Lo! the two were one.'

Of The Grade Title And Symbolism

In recognition of his advances, there is now conferred upon the Zelator a Title and Symbol, and the Title is Pereclinus de Faustis. And it is stated in this Mss. that this title meaning literally 'snatched from the jaws' (Note: by FFJ. I have always had difficulty in interpreting this Title Faustis in Latin means happy or fortunate and Faustitae means good luck, happiness or the Goddess thereof. One would infer that Pereclinus might be derived from the Greek word, but there is no adjective or substantive pereklivos (GRK) given in Liddell and Scott, the nearest word to it being toperikiivos, a couch - or round table - from periklpuo (perecline), to slope away or decline (of the sun) and the perclines, sloping on all sides - which does not seem helpful, from which is derived the geological term pereclinal, meaning (of strats), sloping in all directions. In making this investigation, one is of course, struck with the resemblance of this word to the word, peregrinus, a traveller or pilgrim, one who passes per, through, and ager, a field or country, - to travel abroad in strange lands, and figuratively, to sojourn in the flesh - peregrination. In Astrology, peregrins signifies the wandering of a planet in some part of the Zodiac in which it has no essential dignity. The interpretation 'wandering far from land of the happy' suggests itself a possibility. I fail to see how the rendering of 'snatched from the jaws', given in this is obtained, F.F.J.) ... 'snatched from the jaws', which title is borne by all the Zelators, but the full meaning of this title, along with the other titles conferred in the various grades of the Outer, is expounded unto the adept when he reaches the grade of 6=5 or Adeptus Major. And the symbol for that is ARETZ, the earth, unto which element this Grade is attributed. And the meaning and purpose of the Symbol is that, in all Magical Operations, connected with this Grade, the Theoricus Adeptus Minor must take as a foundation his own earth. That is to say, his physical body. Therefore are the magical operations of this Grade ceremonial and dependent on a material basis and on accurate ceremonial. Therefore are they greatly in error who say 'only the spirit matters', for these would deny the incarnation of Our Lord in Material Body, 'beloved, believe not every spirit, but try the spirits, whether they are of God, because many false prophets are gone out into the world. Hereby know ye the Spirit of God: every spirit that confesseth Jesus Christ is come into the flesh of God: and every spirit that confesseth not that Jesus Christ is come in the flesh is not of God: and this is the spirit of Antichrist, whereof ye have heard that it should come; and even now already is it in the world (1.John.1) (next line unintelligible and is not taken from John 1. 1-3 as indicated).

And the necessity of the Physical basis is the foundation of the sacramental system of ceremonial magic, as taught in our Order, and will further be enlarged on in the Mss 'On Magical Operations derived from the 1=10 ritual', which will be handed to the Theoricus Adeptus Minor when he has studied what has herein been set down, and has proved his knowledge thereof. There followeth a brief account of the Sephirah Malkuth. This Sephirah and the Tenth Path of the Sephire Yetsirah, the 'Resplendant Intelligence' is a subject of a Mss. of the Practicus Adeptus Minor Grade and need not be here further enlarged.

Then follows the reading by the Hierophant of the list of subjects to be studied by the Zelator or Zelator student in the 1=10 grade. This should never be omitted from the ceremony for it intended to mark on the aura of the Aspirant the most elementary forms of certain symbols, 15 in number, and corresponding to the sacred name of YOD HEH, and, in this connection, let him remember that the ordonary number 15 is never written by the orthodox Jew by these sacred letters, but as Teth Vau. These symbols he will learn to formulate vivify, and their use in ceremonial magick will be taught to him as he advances in his knowledge of our sacred science.

The Closing

Seeing now that in the Opening, the Elemental Spirits of Earth were invoked, and that they have been present throughout the ceremony, and sharing in the mysteries, they must now be dismissed. But, before doing seeing that in the Holy Place, though present and partaking in the Mysteries, they are dumb in the persona of the Adept and initiated Sons of Adam, the Hierophant, must himself be their mouthpiece, and, as it were, in their name recite a prayer to the world of the Universe who is ADONAI HA ARETZ. The temple is then closed with the Lesser Banishing Ritual of the Pentagram, and with a battery of Knocks.

The THEORICUS ADEPTUS MINOR should make himself familiar with this explanation for it is the basis of the Magical ceremonies which are founded on this ritual, Moreover, it should demonstrate to him the absolute continuity and consecutiveness of the Official Teaching of the Order. Of necessity, the elementary knowledge of a great number of subjects has to be given in the early grades, but the student has now arrived at the point, where each of all of these are combined and continued in the great mass of teaching bequeathed to us by our Founder, CRC. (End of the Mss)

Addendum by F.F.J

As noted under the title of the Mss. at the beginning, the Chiefs of the Isis - Urania and Amen Ra temples of the original GD issued this teaching to members who attained the grade of THEORICUS ADEPTUS MINOR. As their direct successor, and as the now Senior Chief of the Amoun Temple et Aureae Crucis connected therewith, I issue it by permission to senior members who have attained the 6= 5 of Adeptus Major, though, for historical reasons, I have left the original references to the subgrades of the Adeptus Minor text. Fortes Fortuna Juvat 7=4.

The Stella Matutina did away with the subgrades of the 5= 6 and some of the original Adeptus Major papers became 6=5 study course. Mrs Felkin did write a commentary for the Elemental grades but these were appended to the Elemental rituals. This MS was originally a "Theoricus Adeptus Minor" teaching of the Isis - Urania and Amon Ra temples of the "G.D". It is the equivlent of the Z 1. Explanations of the 0=0 Ritual, issued, not as routine, but by Permission, to the Zelator Adeptus Minor when he was considered by the Chiefs ready to benefit by it. This 1=10 Ritual now becomes a 6=5 Teaching. FFJ (Carnegie Dickson) .

Practicus Adeptus Minor Study.

Not counting the diagrams of the God-forms, there are approximately 15 diagrams associated to this grade. Some were handed in later knowledge lectures and others were given during the ritual. A lecture associated to a diagram sometimes not only explains the diagram's intrinsic meanings but opens the way for additional areas of study- that the diagram represents. The colours associated to the diagram come from the Four Colour Scales, and by doing research into the diagrams the use of the colours become apparent. The Seven Infernal Mansions and the Four Seas are an example of how one aspect of the Princess scale of colours can be explored. When I went through this level there was virtually nothing for me to go on save what was in the rituals and the diagrams. I kept coming back to Taylor and got more enigmatic answers and more questions than I had intended. Taylor pushed me in this area relentlessly and told me that there was a path there and that if I was half as good as I thought I was then I should be able to find it!

My original studies for this level were skeletonic notes to the diagrams of the 2=9. Slowly things did start to become much clearer and eventually I did workup of each diagram and submitted them for Taylor's approval. Much of these original workups were included in the *Golden Dawn Ritual and Commentaries* book that I self published. It was not only the diagrams that I had to work on, I had to continuously work on the energy currents (shown by the Admission badge outlines for each Path and Sephiroth) and we had to find out what was happening at each point in each ceremony. At this juncture, my studies in the Kabbalistic Soul showed that it was simply not detailed enough to any real indepth research to the level we wanted to take it. The framework chosen for most of this was the Subtle Bodies and Chakras. It was a favourite of Taylor's, and of mine, after my Tantric studies in India in the 1960's. When the work began on this aspect of study things opened up quickly and some of my original research was published in the *Kabbalah of the Golden Dawn*.

Except where documented differently, all of the diagrams and associated lectures here are my own work. I had seen enough of what Mathers did for the Theoricus Adeptus Minor grade to know the general direction he was headed, and I used that as a template to construct the following lectures. Overall I have not given ALL the diagram explanations for this level, but have given enough of them to get individuals started who have seen the direction I have travelled, and who want to go in that direction themselves. Since temples are now pretty much going their own way for these levels, I anticipate some may want to use what I have done for some sort of yardstick to go by. There is nothing out of the ordinary in these lectures that any serious Kabbalistic student could not duplicate and extrapolate. This is why they are being published, as I would hate to think that in ten or twenty years time when I meet my maker, that my unpublished papers would be thrown out on the rubbish tip by some well meaning friend trying to manage my affairs. I have taken the attitude Regardie did, and that is if only one book survived then you have done your job!

Frankly, there is a lot of scope to improve on what I have done, and for those temples actively working the levels of the 5=6 I hope this example will help them in their own individual studies. There is another part of me that wants to show Golden Dawn students what they are missing without continual research into existing material. I was going to include a brief analysis of the Tarot card 'Judgement' at this point, but decided against it. The manner in which I broke down the 'Universe' card can be easily extrapolated to the 'Judgement ' key. Or some may wish to go their own way.

Chapter 7

Practicus Adeptus Minor

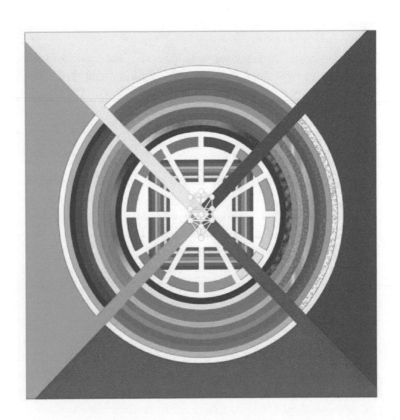

The Garden Of Eden
For The
Practicus Adeptus Minor Grade
By Pat Zalewski

The Garden of Eden diagram in many respects is yet another abstract version of Key 21. The Tree represents the central figure of the card, the twelve gates are clearly shown for the first time, each Gate consists of seven concentric squares. The four streams are analogous to the four kerubic emblems in each corner of the card. The surrounding wall then becomes a void, for beyond that there is no meaning other than space.

It must be remembered that it took a great deal of time and trouble to make the Garden of Eden, and the first attempt was not successful and the vessels, prototypes of man were destroyed. The Central Tree as we see it now, is a rectified Tree, for the first Tree had no connection to Malkuth, though the foundation was laid, the Kingdom was not reached. In the original tree the paths were different as well. When the vessels (prototype man) were broken, different forms of energy was needed and an additional Sephiroth of Malkuth was joined to the Tree. If you study the diagram of the tree and see the lines running under it from the four streams, you then see some of the old energy patterns of the Paths of the Tree. By studying the Tree in this diagram, you will see the four streams converging at Daath, for in this original paradise this was the point where the Tree of Knowledge met with the other Tree of Good and Evil.

There are number of references to revelations in trying to explain aspects of this diagram and its relationship to Key 21 in particular. Mathers tells us bluntly, in the 2=9 ritual, that Key 21 is the 'Bride of the Apocalypse' which gives a huge hint of what he was thinking when he constructed the rituals. This refers directly to both chapter 21 and 22 which describes this diagram and Key 21.

Paradisical Wall

The outer or largest of the concentric circles is titled 'Adam Qadmah Sthimah'. This is the 'Concealed Primordial Man'. There is some confusion as to what ring is closest to the centre, because the Outer Ring appears to the Outer Limits, which is a paradox, for the Outer Ring describes the highest manifestation or energy that makes up the wall. The lowest ring is closest to the Chaotic State which is earth. Simply imagine a circular drum with 11 levels (with Eden being on the uppermost level of the drum). The highest circle of this drum, or wall, is the least contaminated, while the lowest, where it joins the outside world is the one that will crumble first. In essence, we are working backwards from the Light towards the Darkness, as we study each of these rings.

This upper circle is the recipient between energies of Kether and the Ain Soph Aur. It is called the Arik Anpin - The Macroprosopus. Here we have ended the energies of the first Adam Kadmon, which was shown as a huge face, the Macrocosm (this is not to be confused with Metatron who was sometimes called the 'Lesser YHVH') but this is the figure that was concealed and the only reference to it is through Knowledge. In terms of the Neophyte ritual, this is represented in the final part of the ceremony, the Adoration and the Eucharist is partaken. Here one has communion with the Concealed or Higher Self, which is perceived as the Body of Osiris. In the Egyptian Book of the Dead, this scene is shown by the plates of Osiris-Ani in Adoration before the God Kephera, going by in his Solar Barque. The next plate showing both Tem and the Lion in the barque, is the bridge forward into the Inner gates of Eden itself. The Solar Image behind Tem showing the power of the Hidden or Concealed manifestation.

The second concentric circle is the production or doubling of the first, but to a lesser extent. It is the knowledge of the Separation in the unification of the word YHVH. On arrival at this circle one will find that the aspiration and belief structure exist, but on a much higher level than before. It is a complete re-adjustment of what one has learnt. This is the formation of the ABBA and AIMA, in the Partsufim context of the Tree. In the Book of the Dead this shown by the two Pillars and the Two Hawks. One Hawk represents RA, while the other is OSIRIS. It shows the two levels of learning, through sacrifice.

The third circle represents a place for the mundane Sephiroth to form. This is done through the entrance-way of Daath, the non existant Sephirah. It is the ZAUR ANPIN and relates to the letter Vau, and incorporates the six Sephiroth below Daath. In the Book of the Dead, this is analogous to the plate showing the 7 Gods, which relates to the seven Officers of the Neophyte ceremony (excluding the Sentinel).

The fourth circle is being represented by the letter Heh-KALLAH THE BRIDE. For the Son is of a Higher form and when he mates with Kallah, a lower form, then a hybrid is produced. The fourth circle shows the energy of the Son coming down to communicate with that of the Bride. It is the concept of the Sons of Light mating with the daughters of men. This is the subtle action of those Chiefs on the dais during the ritual. In the Book of the Dead, it shown by the Four Canopic gods and their power over the different parts of the body and soul of the candidate.

The fifth circle is the space of Tehiru (contracted primordial space) which represents the ultimate freedom from the letter Heh. This surrounds all spheres below the first Adam, up to the point where the Ain Soph Aur begins. Before the Ain Soph Aur can manifest in space, in which it has to manifest, it must be restricted so that it knows what it boundaries are, before the triple manifestation can begin. Tehiru is a necessary space between Primordial man as seen from the Partsufim concept, to the development of the Ain Soph Aur and the ten Sephiroth. In the Book of the Dead this shows the Death and rebirth through the funeral plate, with Ra holding the twin Ankhs, emerging from the pastos. This shows Osiris, as Ra, partaking of himself. In the Neophyte ceremony, it is the taking of a new name, the motto.

The sixth circle relates to the entranceway to the World of Tohu(Chaos) where the complete ten Sephiroth are mapped out in their primordial (but unmanifested) State. To some extent, it is like the Primea Materia of the Atziluthic Emanations, before they have a chance to fully form. It is said to be like a Sephiroth with a bright glow emananting from it. The glow of Light showed that it was weak, and the receptive of the vessels or Sephiroth could not hold the Light. They were incomplete, the missing element is said by some to be the absence of Malkuth, for their energies had to have receptive principle for their positive emanations (Daath was considered a Sephiroth at this point hence the the number ten). In the Book of the Dead, this is shown by the plate that has the eye of Ra-As Osiris over the funeral building, and effect of Sunrise. In the Neophyte ceremony this is related to the circumambulation of the Candidate.

In the seventh circle the establishment of the vessels or Ten Sephiroth this energy started to manifest on the Worlds of Briah, Yetsirah and Assiah. In the past, a finite part of this energy existed on the lower planes in semi-shaped forms that we call Elementals and Devas. Now, for the first time it tried to anchor in Yetsirah, with a form that was too dense for that world to hold. With the result that as it reached the lowest, Yesod, it began to crack, as those did above it. Each Sephiroth was crushed into each other as the powerful force of light drew the Sephiroth back into each other. A line was drawn at Daath, the entranceway to Briah, and it ceased to be a Sepherah. As a point of entranceway it was closed, and all that remained was a shadow of its previous self. The top three Sephiroth continued to function and had to rethink their organisation. In the Book of the Dead, this shows the reception at the two pools of Truth, before the Higher Initiation can occur. Within the Neophyte ceremony this is the entranceway to the land of the Dead, the West.

In the eighth circle the Sephirah of Kether decided to withdraw the paths that would normally go through Daath and re-route them through Tiphareth, so that the Dew (Emanation of Light) could exist below the Supernal and keep the original Shells (Sephiroth) energy to each other, as well as re-arranging some of the positions of the Paths. This was necessary, as the Path of Qoph (back of head –of Kether) which originally emanated from Kether, was out of sequence in the formulation of the Letters. The letters had to be arranged in descending order. The Paths of Aleph and Beth remained in their original positions. All the other Paths that lead directly to Daath changed, for the power of Daath was lowered to Tiphareth. Once the letters of the Hebrew alphabet were correctly arranged, then the formation of the Tree into Assiah was complete.

In the Book of the Dead, it is the plate of Osiris changing himself into the form of the Benu Bird. It is the speech of the Hierophant and placing the Candidate between the Pillars or Entranceway to the temple.

In the ninth circle Chokmah and Binah suffered slightly from the cracking of the Sephiroth in much the same way of that which occurs in wheat or barley. This is because the paths from these two Sephiroth went directly into the next world of Briah. They tried to sustain the shells below them with their energy and did not cut it off until they realised they needed all of this energy or Light to sustain themselves. In the Book of the Dead it is shown in the funeral bier of Ani, guarded by Anubis. The Order has the circumambulation of the Candidate as he walks the narrow Pathway between Light and Darkness.

In the tenth circle the World of Assiah found itself with some of the fragments of the previously shattered Sephiroth, these were corrupted by the density of matter and formed the Qlippoth, which mirrored the Worlds above them. It is from this, that the Root of Evil came into Assiah, for the Light was not directed - but badly deflected. For this began the concept of the Free Will of Assiah. In the Book of the Dead, this is the choosing of the Candidates, and the Golden Dawn it is the same message. It is the World of the opening of the Great Abyss, from which Evil can come out of the Pit.

The Paradisical Wall in many ways resembles the Mountain of Initiation, which was first shown in the Portal Ceremony.

Twelve Gates

Within the next component of the diagram we are shown the Twelve Gates. These are referred to in Revelations Ch. 22:

> *And had a wall great and high, and had twelve gates, and at the twelve gates, twelve angels, and the names written thereon, which are the names of the twelve tribes of the children of Israel... In the midst of the street of it, and upon either side of the river, was there the Tree of Life, which bare twelve manner of fruits, and yielded her fruit each month...*

The Twelve manner of Fruit described above are related to the twelve main components of the physical body, each placed under a heading of a Zodiac Sign, hence the reference to the monthly changes. It is a concept of cyclic renewal, immortality. It refers to the birth, through the process of reincarnation, typified by the different lifetimes through the cyclic zodiac. These are shown as the Twelve Names that are borne upon the Banners of the Enochian Tablets.

Seven Squares

These are the Seven Abodes of Assiah, the Material World. The Seven Squares are linked to the Holy City. Again Revelations takes up the theme:

> ...And he carried me away in the spirit to a great and high mountain, and he shewed me that Great City, the Holy Jerusalem, descending out of heaven from God...

The 2=9 ritual tells us that they are linked to the Seven Churches, which are the seven major glands of the Endocrine system, the physical basis of the Seven Chakras (I have alluded to this slightly in an earlier chapter and will not repeat it here, though it was part of this original lecture and is covered enough in the explanation of the 'Universe Key" more) for inside the **Paradisical Wall**, all the chakras are balanced together in harmony, in the Perfected Man.

Four Rivers

> And he shewed me a pure river of water of Life, clear as crystal, proceeding out of the throne of God and of the Lamb...

Rev. 22.1

These are the elements in their corporeal forms and represent the vital components of matter. These relate to the World of Assiah, for the Garden of Eden has its location when the Tree of Life appended Malkuth under Yesod, for Malkuth is the Kingdom. The elements are represented in Revelations as the Four Beasts, which in turn relate to the four lower centres or Chakras. It is these

Creatures that have the earthly pull and when the Temptation has risen above it, it is the Four Rivers that counterbalance things - as they must flow through Daath. In Key 21, the Four Kerubics represent the Four Beasts, the forces which man must overcome if he is to enter Eden.

Colouring Of The Diagram

The first ten concentric circles are in the colours of the Sephiroth in each of the Four Trees. The Four Rivers separate the Circle into the four directions - the same as in the Temple. The east represents the King Scale, the West the Queen Scale, the Prince Scale the South, and the North the Princess Scale. The outside circle represents the Kether broken down into the four worlds. The next nine circles (going towards the centre) represent the remaining nine Sephiroth. The 11th circle is coloured black, representing the base and most corrupted part of the Wall. The background from this point on, in the centre of the circle is white for purity of Spirit. The 12 broken circles are in the colours of the signs of the Zodiac in the paths of the King Scale.

The inner wall of seven layers is in the colours of the numbers on the grade sashes in the Outer and Inner Orders. The Four Rivers are in the colours of the elements, Green here is instead of black for earth. Green stands for Growth and Black for restriction. They are placed in the position of the Kerubs as depicted in Key 21. The Rivers are analagous to the Kerubs, which actually crosses the broken circle Sign of Leo, the starting point in the Golden Dawn Zodiac. The Tree at the centre is coloured a brilliant white.

The Infernal Habitations
By Pat Zalewski

This is a study of the Dark side of the Tree and is a reversal of the Partsufim Theory. Personally I have always thought its strength was in an alchemical analogy. You have the seven stage corrupted system in the Material Base, which has to be purified before any Transmutation can take place on the Higher levels. While I have found a study of this diagram intriguing, the symbolism is hopelessly out of date with the modern psyche. PZ

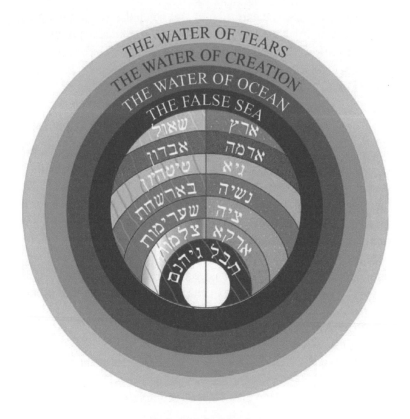

Infernal habitations

The basis for this diagram is contained in the Zohar, part One, folio
45a-47b. It tells us the Infernal Habitations were created at the
same time the world was created. To understand this correctly, we
have to look at the first verse of Genesis: 'In the beginning, God
created the heaven and the earth'. Unfortunately this translation is
not entirely accurate. It should read 'In the beginning, God created
et the heaven and et the earth.' The Zohar informs us that et (or
eth) the particle, shows the Upper and Lower Worlds were created
at the same time due to the fact that et is made up of the first and
last letter of the Hebrew Alaphabet (some translators have inserted
the last et to read ve-et). The inference being the first thing God
created was the Alphabet, inferred by et, which is in line with the
theory of the Sepher Yetsirah.

If we examine the Second day of Creation, we will find: 'And God saw the Light was good, and he divided the Light from the Darkness.' In the initial created Light, there were negative or mirror elements that God separated from the Light and he placed in darkness in the negative regions, which he called the Infernal Habitations. This division was brought about by the breaking of the vessels in the Partsufim, the first experiment. For the fragments of the original vessels of the Partsufim were made or separated into the Infernal Regions. God realised that he could not support the Dark or Negative forces with his Divine Light. By separating the two, he gave man, the Second Adam, a choice of which to choose from.

Waters of Tears

'Let there a firmament in the midst of the waters.' This implies that the Upper and Lower divisions of the waters. The lower region of the waters is called 'Waters of Tears', for the waters that descended to the lower regions do so in the form of tear drops and as such represents the Yod force. The words 'Waters' is used in this particular instance because it describes the basic essence of all life. The Hebrew word for water is Maim, and we reminded of the 12 key of the Tarot, the Hanged Man. Here we have the pictorial imagery of a individual trapped in the cave of Mem. He is trapped by virtue of the shape of the letter, which enclosed the life around it. More importantly we must consider the Hanged man a necessary evil. The indivudal must go through enforced suffering (through entrapment) to reconcile the error of his ways. The Hanged Man shows by his illumination though suffering, that Light, will eventually come to the Lower regions, but only through trial and error. In almost every respect, the Hanged Man, represents the first Waters of the Lower regions, and is brought about by Sorrow. For the Shekinah left the First Adam after he was destroyed and it is the tears of the First Adam, for his plight, and the Second Adam from the Separation of his imperfect brother. The Water of Tears actually created the boundaries of the Lower regions, the initial impetus and mirror image of the Yod Force, Emanation, Nearness or Intimacy.

206 INNER ORDER TEACHINGS OF THE GOLDEN DAWN

Waters of Creation

While the Water of Tears was actually formed as part of the original Light, The Waters of Creation were generated from the Water of Tears and represents the first birth state in the Infernal Habitations. This represents the mirror image of the HEH state which corresponds to that realm of creation. The tears have now generated into what some have called the Shells, and they are formed in close lines with that of the world above, but have been allowed to follow their own actions. They are much the children of their own world, which is in the evolutionary state. The Shells are often allied with the Edomite Kings and their destruction. The 17ᵗʰ Key, The Blasted Tower, shows the destruction of the Shells and their expulsion from the realms of Light. The Waters of Creation were aided by one of the Shells, or imperfect vessels that was not destroyed with the rest. His name is Hadar, the last King, and he, along with his wife, Mehithabeel, escaped to the Lower Regions and brought the Imperfect Light and the power to procerate with them. In the diagram of Eden before the Fall, Hadar is the lowest King with half his body submerged in Malkuth.

Waters of Ocean

The Water of Ocean relates to the VAU potency, corresponding to the upper world realm of Formation .Here both Good and Evil cohabitate together in the form of living creatures. The entire concept is not unlike this world, for the Water of Ocean refers to the Mental World and the effect on group activities. In reflections to this world one could say it relates to Politics. Where Good and Evil meet in the Never Ending Seas and try and control the masses. We are told that the serpent issues forth and that relates to speech overwhelming the masses. This is a karmic pool where every creature can transcend or remain stagnant. The Waters of an ocean have tides which ebb and flow like all forms of life, whether good or evil.

The False Sea

The False Sea is analogous with the HEH (Final) and the Material World, and the falsity of matter over Spirit. This is typified by the 15th Tarot Key of the 'Devil'. It is the point where the illusion that matter and its material base is the highest point of existence with an obvious lack of the Spiritual concept. A closer study of the 15th Key will show that any Spiritual direction is materialisation as the guiding Light. The emotions brought into play here as they reflect an individual's wants and desires, taking a self centred approach. We must remember that the Shells of the Qlippoth were discarded and roamed the Earths as monsters, shown by the figure sitting on the Altar of Materialism in the 15th Key.

The Seven Earths

The Seven Earths are reflections of the Seven Upper Sephiroth (Malkuth to Chesed) that were in the Garden of Eden, in the Pre Adamic state, when the Kings of Edom ruled. They are transpersonal states of awareness, and mirro the the Upper Tree by the power and knowledge brought to them through Edomite King Hadar, who escaped to the Lower regions fearing the destruction of his race. Some have stated that the earths relate to the material side of man's nature, his passions and desires, when they are left untempered. Other relates them to different time periods. They start in Thebal, and work to Arctz in the outer layers. It should be remembered that the Lower Tree does not start with Kether. Since it is a reversal of polarities, it starts with Malkuth and a true reverse image of the Upper Tree. Schaya states in his *Universal meaning of the Kabbalah*

"When the Kabbalah shows the lower earths to be imperfect modes of participation in the human state, it thereby emphasises the perfection of the latter; the human state is thus seen to be the culmination of a long cyclic and hierarchical dvelopment of previous and present terrestrial states. Each earth has four levels within it, which are impressions from the four worlds."

1. THEBAL

This Earth has the title of 'Mitred Earth and Water', is the one that overlaps with our Material World of Malkuth. This world is much denser than Malkuth, as we understand it, for in it are concepts of a fixed nature that will not change. It is from this that the essence of materialism travels through the Triple gateway to our Malkuth. Through his former power, the Edomite King Hadar, uses his influence in Malkuth to make it like his version of Eden, which he left behind. Hadar has the ability to co-exist in our Malkuth, as well as the one he created when he fled the Upper Tree. The Greek counterpart of Hadar is Hades ('unseen') – King of the Underworld. His Kingdom is Hades and he is mentioned in the Odyssey, Illiad, and Theogony. In Hades you have all the attributes of Hadar. Hadar has a value of 209 and relates to some words of similar value, AGRH 'profit', which shows that any work undertaken in the Kingdom of Hadar will be rewarded. It is linked to other Hebrew words such as 'dispersed' and 'oppressed'. One shows that anything gained will be lost and that the whole process begins over again. In this instance, Thebel, through the influence of Hadar, relates to an addiction of the senses, for Malkuth is the Kingdom and rewarder of Kether.

2. AREQ

This level is simply titled 'earth' and is the mirror image of the Sephirah of Yesod. The ruling Edomite King in this area was Baal-hannan. This earth is rich and has water. The difference between it and the world above it is the density of Areqa. It is the world of dreams and illusions, where the unreal meet and try for solidarity and find that materialisation has nothing to offer them. It's water content is quite considerable and it is the earth of swamp and marsh. The swamp gasses form the beings that inhabit this level. It is the earth of refelection, for the images that come from the world above are like dreams. This earth is a residue of the continuous buildup of Astral negativity of the first world, and acts like a filter to Thebel, by clearing it of the dregs. Thebel has an element of Light (from Hadar) and this shines in reflection to Areqa, like moonlight on a dark night. In Areqa there are four phases that have carried over from Malkuth, and are loosely connected to the four elements. The first level is the reflection of Fire, and is fast, and constitutes action - quick action and a basic dissatisfaction with the Self. The next level brings about a false state of fulfillment with life as we understand it, but this will later change. The next level shows change and a shifting of purpose. The last phase shows the completion of a sense of purpose but this is done on the inner levels of development with a lack of recognition of the spiritual origins of the creative urges Areqa brings. There is no conscious understanding of what is happening other than instinctive urges.

3. TZIAH

This earth has the title of 'Sandy Desert', and is devoid of water - apart from the occasional oasis. One of the main experiences of this earth is its isolation. The Edomite King who once ruled this region was called Saul. This is an earth that absorbs every thing brought into it and gives little back. In it, there is a certain lack of direction, or of time. This earth does not retain any form of water or nourishment. One of its main functions is to stagnate and not to change, and that is the level of consciousness that all who enter here must endure. Where Hod shows Splendour, this land shows desolation. The water or nourishment, from Areqa has filtered into this land, but the land has not held it and the water has passed through it to the world below. This is much like the state of awareness shown by this earth, which is a clinical attachment of the Self (by not holding onto things) from the day to day problems by dealing in the abstract. The four urges or levels of the previous earths comply here as well. The first level shows one's thoughts and desires are influenced by ones aspirations. The next level shows communications influenced by the deepest subconscious predispositions. The third level shows the emphasis on the abstract concepts while the last level shows our thoughts are influenced by practical necessity.

4. NESCHIAH

This earth has the tile 'Pasture or Meadowland'. It is well fertilised, and nourishment from the heat of Tziah and the water that passed through it into Neschiah have made it a fertile land. The Edomite King who reigned here was King Samlah. The title of Netzach is

Victory, and in many respects this is strongly related here, for the real question is, is this fertile land put to any practical use? It is an easy land to co-exist in, and does not require much effort on the part of the individual who travels through it, for it relies on luck and its geographical bountiness, yet it is a state that it is not worked for, and one can easily turn into lethargy. The first level of influence is subtlety of expression, a laid back approach to one's emotional expression. The second level shows a constant need for reassurance and closeness. The third level relates to their emotional and spiritual needs to be reciprocated, and the fourth level deals with the need to have material ties, unless it is on a level that can be taken left on a moment's notice.

5. GIA

This earth has the title of 'Undulating ground'. It is a mirror of the Sephirah on the Upper Tree to Tiphareth, the vital central component of the Tree. The Edomite King who once ruled this land was Haded. The deep rifts and valleys of this earth relate to entering a far deeper level that has been encounted so far. In modern terminology it is like encountering an area of tectonic activity. It is a treacherous area that can have individuals fall into, if they are not careful. It is a time that anyone who travels to this earth will undergo extreme stress. Gia is an area of earth that is less cramped in space than those above it. It opens up into new layers of activity. It is the experience of moving into the Macrocosm. An area of Self Sacrifice, and where the old values will be left behind, for taking on the 'big picture' and understanding its measure. The first level of this earth relates to shedding one's past experience and accepting a new type of responsibility. The second level shows a major emotional upheaval as one's previous beliefs are shattered. The third level shows the intense intellectual awareness that one has to deal with, while the final level shows the new practicalities one has to deal with, for the old ones are not enough.

6. ADAMAH

The title of this earth is 'Reddish Mould'. The Edomite king who reigned here was called Husham. This is an earth where heat and dryness are common place. It is not a desert, but a land that has not had much nourishment into it. It is an earth of raw essentials where everything has to be forged. This is the area of Golem making. We must consider that this earth is but one step away from its final goal as a homogeneous element in the earth below. It is an earth that is constantly transmuting itself through conjunctions and separations, for this is part of its alchemical makeup. The constant factor applied here is heat, sometimes gentle, sometimes harsh. The first level of this earth shows the direct application of energy applied to a situation through the concept of power and initative. The next level shows the self assertion of one's ideas before they have a chance to be fully crystallised. The next level shows expression of a direct action through ideas, while the last level shows the need (and patience) to express concepts through application. The tendency in this earth will be to leave things unfinished.

7. ARETZ

The title of the earth is 'Dry and crumbling' and the Edomite King who ruled here was called Jobab. This is the last of the Seven Earths and is the reflected side of Chesed. We have here in this earth the abstract concept taken to the extreme before it transmutes on even to more deeper levels. The light of the previous Edomite Kings shine reflected into this earth but the light will not extend deeper and hence there is a type of enclosure here that is extremely difficult to get through. The first level shows the development of a new type of philosophy, idea or concept. The second shows the emotional connection needed to bring this about. The third the intellectual dogma one adheres to while the final level shows the plan coming into action through the day to practicalities of the situation.

Seven Infernal Habitations

The names, or titles, of these Habitations are the names of Guardians of each gateway that leads to each earth. The individual will have to experience what each angel (or demon - depending on your standpoint) will make one undergo before entrance to each of the Seven Earths. The Seventh Earth is by way of a reversal, for the last earth turns inward, and reverses itself yet again like a chain link, and as such, the last Infernal Habitation leads back towards the way of the Light, for all negative experiences have been experienced and the Soul now turns its way upwards.

1. GEHINNON

Gehinnon is the gateway to Thebal. The word Gehinnon, is an amalgamation of the two Hebrew words 'ge-Hinnom'. The word 'ge' translates as 'proud'. The valley of the Hinnom was a place of sacrifice to the old Gods 'Baal' and 'Molech'. It was later formed into a rubbish tip. Although this is sometimes translated in the English 'Hell', it is a gross misconception, for the word is analogous to the Underworld of Greek mythology. The meaning however is clear. To experience Gehinnon one must sacrifice (or lose) one's own children. The abstract concept behind this is that we give up our heritage, for without children there is no one left to carry on our name. It is the final destination that shows no renewal for those who enter. The entrance gate of Hell is represented in the dark side of the 32nd path, and the 21st Key of the Tarot - the Universe, which is associated with Saturn, which in turn leads to the Underworld of the Hades. This is the case of a radical transformation and the world as we knew it is left behind.

2. SHAARI MOTH

This is the gateway to Areqa. The title 'Gates of Death' shows one entering the region from which all the old concepts and ideals have been shattered. The title of this guardian shows that one is in the Underworld, but has not had a chance to go to the level we are supposed to go after the death experience. The Limbo state is closely allied with the Judgement of Osiris in the Egyptian Book of the Dead, where the deceased has a chance to reflect upon the experience of the life one has just left. It is the Judgement Hall of the Dead where one goes before sentence is carried out. This is reflected in the 20th Key Judgement. In this Key, Hell is on one side of the card (the fiery land) while the other side shows the redemptive waters. Here the myths of Pluto are carried through

3. TEZELMOTH

This guardian is called 'Shadow of Death'. It is the knowledge that death is oncoming and there is nothing one can do about it. This relates to those who have had a terminal illness of those under sentence of death. It is an area that shows no escape and that an individual must complete his or her task in an incarnation as best they possibly can. The 19th Key of the Tarot refers to the Sun. Its darker side shows a restriction of the boundaries where its normal side shows that those boundaries are transcended. The restricted boundaries show that the individual will have to live under a handicap of some magnitude before the incarnation is completed.

4. BAR SHASKETH

This guardian is called 'Pit of Destruction' . Psalms 40:1-2 state:

> *I waited patiently for the Lord; he turned to me*
> *and heard my cry. He then lifted me out of the slimy*
> *Pit and out of the mud and mire; he set my feet on*
> *a rock and gave me a firm place to stand.*

It shows the emergence of an individual, where he has deliberately made his last incarnation a mess and must live for time in the 'Pit of Destruction'. This is the darkest side of the 18th Tarot Key of the Moon. The Pit of Destruction in this instance is the pool that gives life to the crayfish. It relates to the individual trying to get out of the hole that he or she has dug for himself and this can be done, by taking a hard path of existence. It is to experience life and all its hardships head on with no backtracking. The Lunar influence is shown by its negative side, typified by the Goddess Lilith.

5. TITAHION

This is the guardian called 'Clay of Death'. This is the worship of the false God, usually in the form of clay idol. Psalms 40:3-4 tell us how to avert problems faced here. It shows misguided forms of worship and placing our trust in those who cannot help us. A good example of this is the darker nature of Key 17, which shows the waters being drawn from the River of Life, the Nile. The Nile was a form of worship as a living entity and not as a manifestation of YHVH. The Nile was a destructive force at certain times of the year (when the Sun entered Scorpio) and it flooded, causing death with the clay or mud covering and destroying the crops which caused death and destruction for the population who ran out of food.

6. ABADDON

The title of this guardian is called 'Perdition' or spiritual death. This guardian was called the Dark Angel of death and destruction. The name Abaddon means 'Destroyer" The 16th Key of the Tarot is associated in connection with this angel. This shows the wrath of YHVH by his destruction of the Edomite Kings and their subjects. The experience here is one of constant warring and a lack of peace, The individual will be constantly at war with the self and others around him.

7. SHOEL

The title of this guardian is 'Depths of the Earth'. The 15th Tarot Key best illustrates this concept. We have here a situation in which the individual is trapped in the desires of his own materialistic nature. There is no further death he can sink to. As such, the next cyclic step is upward, and the individual will have the chance to transcend this earth, for here is the opening to Malkuth.

Colouring

Nearly all the colours are taken from the lowest and darkest Princess Scale. The exceptions are the four colours of the Outer concentric circles. They are (from outside the circle inwards) Citrine, Olive, Russet and Black. The Seven Earths are coloured in the following colours:

Thebel:	Black rayed with Olive, Bright Yellow.
Areqa:	Citrine flecked Azure
Tziah:	Yellow Brown flecked White
Neschiah:	Olive flecked Gold
Gia:	Gold Amber
Adamah:	Red flecked Blackish red
Aretz:	Deep Azure flecked Yellow

These colours are taken from the Sephiroth of the Princess Scale. Starting with Malkuth as Thebel and working up to Aretz as Chesed.

The Infernal habitation are taken from the paths. Each path relating to a planet from the same scales.

Gehinon:	Black rayed Blue
Shaari Moth:	Silver rayed Sky Blue
Tzelmoth:	Light Indigo rayed Violet
Bar Shasketh:	Bright rose rayed Pale Green
Titahion:	Amber rayed Red

Chapter 8

Alchemy and the Tarot
By Pat Zalewski

Abaddon:	Bright Red rayed Azure or Emerald
Shoel:	Bright Blue Rayed Yellow

The letters are all white which shows the initial power of reflection of the former Edomite Kings.

In my book *Kabbalah of the Golden Dawn*, I outlined a scheme of applying the letters of the Hebrew alphabet to the 3, 7 and 12 stages systems of Alchemy. In the *Magical Tarot of the Golden Dawn* this theme was explained further, in relationship to the individual cards. This paper goes even further than the published explanations in both books and looks more at the alchemical symbology of the meaning of the drawings of the cards. The whole system is based on the Sepher Yetsirah and not on the direct connection to the Sephiroth. This association can be applied from a practical viewpoint working directly on the experiment - whether animal, vegetable or mineral. The cards become a meditational tool for looking deeper into each phase of the experiment and should be handy during each phase of operation from making of a simple tincture or essence in the Herbal Kingdom, to mineral work and beyond it. The steps here are not mere psychological representations, but are closely allied with each practical step. For those familiar with the works of Frater Albertus and his Paracelsus group and the French based 'Philosophers of Nature Course', these cards may be a helping hand in opening to discovering new doorways. For those of you familiar with the alchemical symbology or shorthand for each of these steps one cannot help but wonder at many of the drawings for each level being apparent in each card. For example, the arrow in the Tower being the same as the symbol for Calcination, the cross in a circle in the Wheel of Fortune, clearly outlining wheel for Sublimation, the hat symbol and altar for Distillation etc. All of this depends on the particular alchemical shorthand for each step, which was created by the alchemist in question. Fred Gettings has done some excellent work in his *Dictionary of Symbols* which includes many ancient alchemical scripts, and I suggest the readers study this work in detail. A special thanks to Richard Dudschus for allowing me to use his drawings of the Trumps, something we both worked on many years together.

Alchemy as seen from the Golden Dawn Perspective is sketchy at best. In the book *Sword of Wisdom*, by Ethel Colquhoun, she mentions that Mathers wrote a book on 'Splendor Solis'. What it contained is anyone's guess, if it did exist though she did make the point that Mathers related it to the 22 trumps. This was the only hint I have seen making the analogy with the trumps and alchemy. Adam McLean and myself looked for years for an example of this work, and so far nothing has turned up. I must admit though that if I had not done any practical alchemy then I would not have been able to propose the Alchemical associations to the Tarot Trumps. One question often asked of me is 'Did Mathers intend this?'. My answer is 'Probably not'. Mathers conceptionalised many general theories, most of them on an unconscious level. Yet when seen from a slightly different viewpoint, as given here, they stand up to some detailed analysis. This is because I have used the Trumps as a template system which coincides neatly with the alchemcial steps.

The Fool, Judgement and the Hanged Man represents the Three Alchemical stages of Separaration, Purification and Cohobation. which in broad terms covers the whole alchemical spectrum. By using the analogy of the Elements, of Air, Fire and Water, we begin to see the wide scope of development they encompass. The next level is applied to the 7 Planets and are more refined, and the third level is applied to the Zodiac Signs which is refined even more further. The drawing of the colour scales on the Pastos shows this development in terms we can see at a glance of how the system works from the 3-7-12 levels of Alchemy.

The Fool
'Separation'

There are three separate components in this Key, the Tree, the Child and the Wolf. The central figure of the child represents the Spiritus Mercurius, it is the ever moving principle, like Quicksilver. This is shown by the Shape of the child which resembles the Fylfot/ Hermetic Cross - the whirling principle of nature. The wolf shows the Sulphur side of this Key, the volatile kept under control, shown by its docile appearance and the leash in the child's hands. The

Tree itself represents the Salt or Earthy nature of the Triad. The archetypal imagery of the child abondoned in the woods represents the chaotic state that that these three components are formed from. All the three principles are linked by the child – as Mercury, controlling the volatile state of the experiment before the Salts can be formed.

The use of the term Separation has a wide meaning when placed in its alchemcial consideration. In this particular instance it has grouped together a number of alchemical steps. The Separation process is not Chaotic, but within certain fixed guidelines of the experiment, with each never truly separate from each other. The Separation process must be handled carefully, for the whole concept of the Separation is not one of destruction by renewal. For each separate component part is strengthened together to form a stronger whole before the ultimate aim of the experiment can be completed. This Key can reveal how this is accomplished.

If you place the Separation process in practical terms, in say the Vegetable Kingdom, the rectified or tried alcohol is poured into a glass jar partly filled with fresh herbs or plants. This is the stage of Separation that is called Maceration, as the alcohol causes the oil to Separate from the main body of the plant and float to the top. After a period of time, the alcohol, that contains the Sulphur (oil) is then drained off into a Distillations apparatus; then the Distillation takes place, thus further separating the alcohol (Mercury) from the oil (Sulphur).

A closer look at the tree in the card shows that it represents the physical nature, the blossoms are analagous to the 6 Chakras (the seventh being the head and above, its not always counted as a Chakra as such in Tibetan literature) or driving forces of nature that guide the Adept in the experiment. These blossoms are linked to the first Days of Creation, for that is what Alchemy is about. The alchemist, like the figure in the card, must rely on his or her higher nature to guide him in a choatic state so that some semblance of order is achieved. Before this Higher Guidance can be accomplished, the dark or volatile nature must be held in check first. The 36 leaves on the Tree represents the decantes of the

Zodiac and as such alludes to the time element in nature, for every thing has its correct time, shown by the leaves on the Tree being placed higher in card than that of the figure. Each blossom has four divisions - which in turn relates to the four balanced elements holding the power of the chakras in check.

Judgement
'Purification'

When you study this key, you will note that the human figures at the base of the card are on both volcanic and land (Fire) and in the sea (Water). Both these elements have to be experienced first before the Purification process is complete. The central figure stands in the Sign of the Theoricus – Air Grade. This shows that before the process of Purification with Fire and Water occurs when their Airy or Volatile nature must be transformed as well. This is done through the concept of heat, shown by the triangle in the centre of the Key and placed over the lower figures. From a practical viewpoint, Purification occurs when the plant which has the alcohol drained from it is calcined into a white powder over a direct heat source. This is where the Sulphur evaporates into a hard substance is then calcined as above.

The figures are four in number as as such represent the Partsufim theory: The male is the Fire or Volcanic force (ABBA) while the Child is a combination of both and anarogenous (Zauir Anpin) and the two figures in Water are Feminine (AIMA and KALALAH). These are the four Figures of the Partsufim which show the changes from the Macrocosm to the Microcosm.

The Hebrew letter Shin joins with Fire and Water to produce Air. Shin, represnets a hissing sound, which represents the volatile air as it passes through the laboratory equipment. Shin represents the ancient hieroglyph of teeth, the breaking down of food. Here it works the same principle by breaking matter down so that the more difficult stages of digestion can be completed.

The angel above, blows on the trumpet from which issues Seven Yods or musical notes. These represent the various vibrational levels that occur during the experiment that the alchemist must undergo and deal with the experiment before the Purification process is completed. Around the Angel is a rainbow, the Cauda Pavonis or Peacock's tail (this occurs in the mineral world and not the Herbal. Its location at the top of the Key relates to the Higher Mineral World). Where the seven rainbow colours are visible, the flag with the cross on it represents the fixed nature of the experiment. The twin serpents in the rainbow show the dual nature of the experiment of both the Alchemist and the process he works on, for both energies must be released together for the experiment to succeed. The twin serpents represent the Uraeus staff of Hermes that controls the difficult stages of the experiment. They are the serpents of Good and Evil, both will have to be experienced before this stage of the experiment is perfected.

Hanged Man
'Cohobation'

This is the process uniting the Sulphur, Salt and Mercury through the watery process of Cohobation – series of successive Distillations where the three principles of Sulphur Salt and Mercury are united together in a much stronger form than before. The shape of the cave in this Key is the letter Mem. Mem is a feminine letter by nature and indicative towards the birth and rebirth principle. This is shown by the cross above the downward pointing triangle, which is one level of the form of the Hanged Man. In the 3=8 Water Grade of Philosophus we are told of this symbol:

> *The Cross above the Triangle represents the power the Spirit of Life rising above the triangle of the Waters and reflecting the trine therein, as further marked by the lamps at the angles. While the Cup of water placed at the junction of the Cross and Triangle represent the maternal letter Mem.*

The figure shows the combined nature of Sulphur (the legs and lower torso) the salt (upper chest and neck) and Mercury (the arms and head). The three symbols herein are reversed in this Key. Yet another outline of this figure is the LVX symbol-showing that if the body is purified enough the Light will enter - resulting in a baptism or Spiritual rebirth. All Three principles are now trapped, shown by the bound figure. The open cove around it show the tide which ebbs and flows (raises and lowers) which is analogous to a series of successive Distillations.

Key 12 is placed formly on the Pillar of Severity and shows that any karmic lessons learnt will be harsh tones as opposed to the Wheel of Fortune on the opposite side of the Tree, on the Pillar of Mercy, who has an easy time of it. Within the framework of Key 12, it shows that the experiment will not succeed until the realisation process has been accomplished. Like the experiment itself, the goal will only be achieved if repeated mistakes are learnt. In the

Adeptus Major ritual of Mathers, we are told that the Hanged Man represents the barque of Osiris and relates not only to timing (hours of the day and night) but also to the principle of going through the various levels of heaven. It is the Rebirth principle and the transmutation of matter (life to the dying) accomplished by Cohobation.

Blasted Tower
'Calcination'

This is the start of the seven stage process – a further refinement of the previous three stage system. This Key represents the Calcination Process. The heating of the Material Base (not the liquid) until the impurities have been removed. The colouring process involves the Blackening, Whitening, the Yellowing and the Reddening (a simple practical experiment is the use of calcined herbs and all these colours will appear in sequence). This Calcining process goes beyond the herbal Kingdom to the Mineral, with exactly the same results. If you look closely at the Tower in this key, you will see that it resembles an alchemist's anthor or oven. The base of the Tower is made up of rocks, this relates to the raw mincral state that has to be transmuted in the anthor. On the Tower itself, you will see there are three degrees of heat that have to be applied to reach the goal of the experiment. This is shown as the three openings in the Tower. On the right and left hand side of the Tree respectively are the twin Trees of Good and Evil. The Left hand side of the Tree has eleven Sephiroth - the impure Qlipothic or Black Tree, and the right hand side is the tree of perfection-being the ten white Sephiroth. The famous Splendour Solis manuscript talks about this:

> *The heat cleans that which is unclean… it throws off the mineral impurities and bad odours and renews the elixir*

The two falling bodies shows the Separation process of the experiment. Originally these two bodies were part of the Material Base because they have not been perfected but have been expelled. There is strong analogy here with the destruction of the Edomite Kings and the Adam and Eve of the Garden of Eden. Each figure thus represents the failed experiments of man on earth. It is a warning to the alchemists that too much applied heat will ruin the experiments for the bodics arc prccious and will spoil easily.

The Crown (representing the King) is the pinnacle of the experiment and here it is split or separated for the Tower by the power of the Lightning Flash. The flash symbolises the releasing of the Crown which has been imprisoning the King. This is through Mars, the God of war, for that is the only way a release will come - through violent action. The Calcination process covers the steps of Reverberation (Aries), Exaltation (Leo) and Fixation (Taurus).

Wheel Of Fortune
'Sublimation'

Key 10 represents the cyclic Sublimation process. This is when the liquid matter is placed in a container (usually a glass with a long neck above it) over a heat source. The vapour or essence then extracted for the matter, as the most air rises up towards the top of the neck of the flask, from which it originally came. This essence is strengthened before it returns to the matter below it, so that the vitalisation process gradually increases the potency of the matter and changes its composition.

When we view Key 10, the central hub of the wheel is related to the Sun, a source of heat that turns the wheel around. The twelve spokes of the wheel represent the length of time necessary for the experiment to work successfully. The 12 cycles relate to the twelve zodiac signs and the 12 months of the year, a complete circle. The rim of the wheel is shaped in the form of a circle – without beginning and without end . This is similar to the Ain Soph Aur – Limitless Light - that must be brought into manifestation before Kether gives birth.

The sphinx at the top of the card shows the ever changing presence of the transmutation process - nothing is static. It is the transmutation of the four elements in their densist nature. In some cards the sword is placed in the paws of the Sphinx which is to show the Airy nature of the Sublimation process. The positioning of the Sphinx at the top of the card in Felkin cum Westcott arrangement version has the same meaning as with one with a sword. The Ape at the base of the card is analogous with the Spirit Mercurius, which relates to the Higher nature of the alchemist performing the experiment. He has to judge the correct dosage and proportion and perform much the same function as the Ape in the Judgement Hall in the Book of the Dead, when he places a feather on the scales to see if they balance correctly. Sublimation incorporates the Dissolution – Subtilise; Resolution (Virgo), Exaltation (Leo), Cohabation – Imbibition (Libra), Fixation (Taurus) and the Conjunction – Impregnation; Integration; Extraction (Pisces).

Empress
'Solution'

Key 3 referes to the stage called Solution. This is when the matter is dissolved in liquid (usually by its own vitrolic essence) as a direct result of the previous step of Sublimation. The Solution is a stage where the first real potentising begins. It is a state of Potentia – the Gestation period before everything is about to begin. It is an important intermediate stage of the experiment. This whole concept is borne out by the title of the Empress as the Pregnant Lady and shows her prebirth state. Daleth, the Hebrew letter associated with this card shows the indivisible state and is often linked with the breast, hence a form of nourishment for all who seek it. The Splendour Solis (figure 13) states that this is the concept that 'a heavy body cannot be made light without the help of a Light Body.'

The closed curtains at the back of the Empress reinforces the state of Potentia, has not yet given birth or revealed her true nature and hence they remained closed until the that time comes. The dove shows the impregnation has occurred (because it is flying upwards and has finshed its task). It shows the airy volatility of the experiment. The arms of the throne are in the shape of a lion's paws and hints at the power behind her, which is the emergence of the Green Lion. This is the power behind the throne that has not yet come through, but is forming, hence its potential state that is about to give birth. During the gestation period represented by this Key, the Empress is pregnant with twins, one volatile and the other fixed. The volatile aspect is the Green Lion who devours (absorbs) her twin once she is born. The Queen holds the symbol of copper above her womb, for that is the element she will work through. The sceptre she holds shows her power is absolute and cannot be transformed. The Solution incorporates the steps of Cohobation (Libra). Fixation (Taurus), Circulation (Cancer) and Digestion (Scorpio).

High Priestess
'Putrefaction'

Many would be surprised to see Putrefaction placed here, though if the true nature of the luna influence, which is one representation of this card, when it is understood it will be no surprise. With the waxing and waning of the Moon we have the life and death cycle. The effect of luna light on the alteration and decomposition of certain minerals is well known (polarised luna light will blunt a sharpened razor blade exposed to it overnight). The word Putrefaction relates to the Decomposition factor which is part of the Transmutation process which in turn relates to the elixir of life within the cup. Putrefaction is to a certain extent part of the Dissolution process where great care must be taken so that the matter being dissolved (under moist heat) must be stopped at a certain point in the experiment. This is when the separation has occurred, for at this critical level, an entirely new substance has been formed or transmuted. It is one of the most important steps in the alchemical operation. Its Separation process is of the celestial essences from the elements. The Cup the High Priestess is being offered to be drunk - which is the act of Dissolution and Separation. The steps within Putrefaction are Separation: Filtration and Distribution (Gemini), Circulation (Cancer) and Digestion; Fermentation: Corruption (Scorpio).

<h2 style="text-align:center">The Magician
'Distillation'</h2>

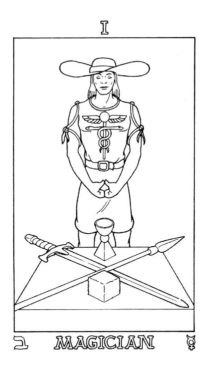

This key relates to the Distillation process. This is analogous to the the Separation of Spirit, through vapour, from matter, through a Distillation apparatus, with a receptacle at the end to catch the liquid. It is separation of the volatile from the non-volatile. It differs from the previous step of Sublimation because the vapour is not returned to the matter, which in effect has changed composition.

The altar of the Magician represents the material base or matter used in the experiment. The shape of the cube relates to the three dimensions of space which corresponds with the three main directions of Distillation:

1.   Upward or Ascending Distillation.
2.   Downwards or Descending Distillation.
3.   Lateral Distillation.

On top of the cube are the Four Talismans of Ireland that represent the Holy Name YHVH. These relates to the four degrees of heat:

Yod   -   Low
Heh   -   Moderate
Vau   -   Moderately High
Heh (F) -   High

The altar represents the concept of Distillation that changes the gross thick bodies into a thinner liquid substance, or Separation of the pure licquor from the impure feaces. The symbol on the breast of the magician is the Caduceus (the Spirit Mercurius) . This is Distillations of the Spiritual and essential humidity, or the phlematic from the spiritual. The magus is the phlematic and the caduceus is the spiritual. The hat worn by the Magician is the highest symbol in this Key and is the shape of the ouroboros, or figure 8 on its side. This is a symbol for infinity and shows Distillations of the hidden part of the things by heat, first going into vapour then being condensed again by cold. The steps of Distillations include Distribution; Separation; Filtration (Gemini), Digestion (Scorpio), Elevation (Sagittarius), Cibation (Capricorn) and Congelation (Aquarius).

The Universe
'Coagulation'

This key refers to the alchemical step of Coagulation. This occurs when all parts of the experiment are reunited and brought back together, as solid or thicker substance when the liquid has evaporated. There are four forms of Coagulation, two by heat and two by cold, so that one is permanent and the other is transitory. As we review this from an alchemical viewpoint, we find that the Four Kerubs represent the four divisions of Coagulation. The woman at the centre of the Key shows that she is the archeus of the earth, who controls the experiment. For Paracelsus tells us that no phlegm can be Coagulated unless it was part of a corporeal matter, and this is what the figure in the seven pointed star tell us, for every thing she controls must be formed through a seven stage system

The seven points of the Heptagram relates to the seven minerals, while the Luna crescent shows that Luna rules the experiment. In the Mss 'Splendor Solis' (5th treatise, part 1. Cap11.) how this is accomplished is revealed.:

> *...Coagulation, which is turning water again into the corpus of matter, meaning thereby that the sulphur, which was before, was dissolved by the Living Silva, absorbs the same and draws it into oneself.*

The hidden reference to Sulphur is shown in the cross legs of the figure, and we are reminded of the triangle above the cross. The twelve zodiac signs are the twelve stages of the experiment, the seven must be experienced first before the twelve can be entered into. A complete cycle of the experiment, for the figure is transformed into the spirit of Mercury, shown in the outline of the figure.

The Sun
'Tincture/Lapidication'

This key represents the final state of the experiment when the liquid Tincture or the hard Stone, whichever is the end result is ready. The bottom of this Key shows an equal balance of Water and earth. This relates to both the hard and liquid approach. The boy is standing on the earth, which shows the dry approach, while the girl is standing in the water showing the liquid approach. Both these children are borne out of the elements, yet they are linked together with their potency of power. The Wall behind them is the framework of the experiment taken over a complete cycle of time. Above the heads of the twins are seven Yods. Each Yod represents a vibration and must be multiplied seven times its own number to produce additional quantities. The Sun above them is the core essence of the Tincture/Stone, and it is this power that is harnessed. The 12 rays around the Sun show the 12 steps and the Yods above the twins show the seven stage system. The end results for both is found in this Key. The three stage system is shown by the sunflowers. So all the three, seven and twelve stage systems end with this key. Around the Sun is the 36 pointed circle showing the decantes of the Zodiac which relates to the time factor. In Splendour Solis Figure 22, it says:

> *The reason why all natural things are put together in one body is that there may be a united composition.*

The Emperor
'Reverberation'
IV

ת   EMPEROR   ♈

This is the start of the 12 stage system, which is a further expansion of the above Seven stage one.

Reverberation is the second stage of Calcination. It continues the Calcination process where the Blasted Tower leaves off. The initial burning has now finished and a more refined process of direct heat alternating with Reverberation and Repercussion of the salts into a fine clay. This is needed to take the experiment through to the Yellowing and final stage of the process being the Reddening. Within the Reverberation process there are three different concepts.

> The First is through ignition.
> The Second is Closed Reverberation in a sealed furnace with graduated heat
> The Third is Open Reverberation and it used for hard bodies that are not easily dissolved.

The orb held by the Emperor is the symbol for Antinomy, the Divine ore that makes up the body or Primea Materia for the Philosophers' Stone. The symbol of Aries represents both the creative and destructive cycles. Aries represents the season of Spring in the Northern Hemisphere. In Nature this represents a fast growth period where the vital fluid rises through the stems of vegetation. It is the process of generation shown by the ram's horns.

The Hierophant
'Fixation'

This key represents what some call Fixation The stabilising of a volatile substance until it is no longer volatile and remains permanent in the fire, to which it is gradually accustomed. Usually this is done by introducing a fixed substance to the work. The association to the strength of Taurus, the first of the fixed Zodiac signs is a good one, for that is its alchemical nature. When explaining the concept of reverberation in natural terms we have the heating of the ground to release growth. In this stage, the various nutrients of the soil in the forms of trace elements are then absorbed by the plant so that the vegetation becomes established with its surroundings. The growth period here is a lot slower than the preceding sign. The sap of the plants and the dew are rich in nutrients. The signs of the Bull of both sides of the throne of the Hierophant relate to the salts of the experiment. The scroll in the form of a square is also a symbol of the salt.

The two Taurean symbols show that two lots of salt will be combined to form a third (shown by the square above them) the fixed nature of this part of the experiment. The closed curtains behind the Hierophant relates to the nature of the substance which has not yet been revealed. The papal cross worn by the Hierophant shows that the sanction of the experiment through Holy orders. This is the symbol of ritualistic dogma and control, but in its higher form relates to the blessing from the Spiritual, something the experiment would not be continued successfully without.

The Lovers
'Separation'

VI

LOVERS

The use of the Separation process here, instead of the Conjunction, is a Golden Dawn innovation, by the application of the Perseus myth. The Soul or Spirit (as Andromeda) is freed from the Material Base. The watery solution has freed its Spirit by the Airy (sword of Perseus) nature of the rising vapours. The liquid matter (the sea) has acted a catalyst in removing the Spiritual nature from its Material Base. The monster in this instance is the overuse of the powers of the solvent before it has the chance to devour the Spirit so the timing of the release is essential, as shown by the zodiac points on the shield of Perseus - the Liberator. The dregs or impurities (the stone) are left behind. Persues and Andromeda show the Masculine and Feminine in balance. By its nature the Sign of Gemini shows the duality of nature and the Separation process is firmly entrenched in this concept. It is the Sun's Exaltation and as such a type of rebirth or birth state. It is last month of Spring growth where the vegetation has grown to its maximum height.

The Chariot
'Circulation'

This Key represents the Alchemical state of Circulation. This is where through applied heat, the liquid in an apparatus is circulated continuously until a state of Exaltation occurs. This Circulation inlcudes the Sublimation Process, where the liquid is heated to a gaseous state. It then cools at the top of the Circulation vessel and returns the liquid to liquid once again. When we view this Key we find that the Chariot rises through the heavens, through the vapour clouds, which the driver, as the Spirit, directs the horses to travel. The white horse shows the purity aspects while the black horse shows the base matter returns to the liquid and does not rise again. The eagle between them refers to the Sublimation process as the method of transforming the Black state to the White state. The wheels of the chariot denote the cyclic nature of the process.

This key represents the Sign of Cancer, a water sign, its place in the Northern Hemisphere is as the Sun reaches its Summer Solstice, where the planets reach their natural zenith and consolidate. It is a gestation period, not unlike the actions of a crab burrowing in the sand. Every type of vegetation is revitalised with rising sap, which in turn is linked to the Circulation process. The Lunar influence of death and rebirth, rise and fall is a governing aspect of Cancer and is shown in the crescent shape of the horns on the driver of the chariot.

Strength
'Exaltation/Solution'

This Key represents the state of Exaltation. It is reached through the rising vitality and virtue of the matter to a higher spiritual level through a transmutation process which involves dissolving it to a high degree. This, to a certain extent, is part of the Sublimation process. Mathers directly referred to this card as the 'Green Lion' (in the Convoluted Forces paper) which is a name for a solvent that dissolves a stronger substance into it by absorption. This is shown in the Key by the apparent weaker Green Lion – as the woman, who is indicated by her passive receptive nature controls the stronger Red Lion beside her, by sapping its strength. In this instance superior strength will not work through any method of confrontation. The Green Lion wears down the superior strength of the Red Lion and absorbs it until it is no more. It is the essence of the alchemical sex act, where the passive love of the Green Lion overcomes the active force of the Red Lion.

Leo is a Fire Sign in the heart of Summer. It has now reached its peak of growth. It shows the ripening process of the fruit and berries and repesents the ripening process at its best. It is the first stage of the Putrefaction of the solution or elixir.

The Hermit
'Dissolution'

This key represents the Dissolution process, which is part of the stage of Putrefaction where a solid substance is reduced to a liquid, stopping at the first phase of the operation. This is Dissolution, for it changes the gross to the subtle, the fixed to the volatile. Here the Hermit has dissolved himself of material possessions and seeks the volatile nature of his spirit as his guide. The Hermit represents the month of Virgo, the last gasp of summer where the harvesting begins before the vegetation starts to dry out. This is the time of full maturity for vegetation. There is a certain sterility about the ground, which needs replenishing, before anything else can grow in it. This too, is shown in the Key, by the desert like surroundings.

The Hermit shows the arrival of the visible Spiritual nature, for he is the voice of the spirit that will guide the operator through the experiment. This is shown by the Light of the Lamp to guide the seeker in finding the Hidden Knowledge that he holds out to anyone who follows his principles and will reap their own rewards.

Justice
'Imbibition/Cohobation'

This key represents the state of Imbibition/ Cohobation. This is where a series of successive Distillations take place where the volatile substance is repeatedly poured back over the the dried matter.. This process loosens any structure of the matter, taking with it during Distillations, the soluble from the insoluble and leaving the insoluble fixed. By this process things become their opposite – sour becoming sweet, sharp becoming soft. The second stage with Cohobation is Imbibition. Mercury and Sulphur are combined as a liquid to and are joined gradually to the body, the salts, where they are re-absorbed and retreat into the body. This washes the body with frequent lustrations until it is wholly coagulated within and unable to rise but remains fixed.

The Left and Right Pillars in this key represent Fire and Water. The central figure between them is Air, which is signified by the upright sword. The Fire transmutes (by sword-vapour) and is carefully measured against the quantity of matter (in the scales) when it becomes a measured liquid. The checked floor represents the material base whose essence must rise up the tube of the vessel by Fire which is then transmuted to Air and then to Water - basic Distillation. The whole process is then started again. The fox being held under foot represents the capturing of the elusive quality of the essence that has escaped from the Material base (the floor). After every Distillation, the Material Base changes in potency, shown by the colours of the floor. At this point of the experiment it is when the liquid drips back down the water Pillar (the tube). You will note that the sword is held in Geburah but has its point in Binah, showing the guidance of Divine Wisdom. The scales are in Chesed while the heart of the figure is in Tiphareth, with the head in Daath.

Libra represents the season of Autumn and a change or balance from Summer to Winter. The sap falls back in the vegetation and the leaves fall off the trees. It is a time of regeneration.

Death
'Digestion'
XIII

♐   DEATH   ♏

This Key shows the alchemical state of Digestion. This is where the mild heat is applied over a long period of time, to the matter, which gives up its vital essence. This process is called Masceration. It is where the gross elements become lighter, as the essence is removed and Separation occurs. The flesh on the ground shows the first part of the Separation process, where the dregs have been removed and these will sooon dissolve. This is the Nigredo or Blackening, the final part of the Putrefaction process. The scythe shows this separation and implies it is rhythmic. The snake above is the escaping spiritor source of wisdom of the material base, and the eagle above it relates to its etheric nature (the vapour at the top of the vessel). The lunar symbolism relates to the the length of time for this process to take place (usually one Lunar month of thirty days) that the digestive process needs to be effective.

In nature, this relates to the month of Scorpio and the action of the Autumn rains on the vegetation rotting on the ground, which is then absorbed by the solid for its nutrients. It is the destructive quality of the water brings this about. This is give a rebirth for the next generation of vegetation to grow in place of the old.

Temperance
'Elevation'

This Key represents the Elevation process of Alchemy. It is where the spiritual or ethereal essence is removed from the corporeal or gross, the volatile from the fixed (such as vapour), through the process of fire or heat. The first version of this Key seems to relate more directly here with the figure over the heated cauldron. The second version is more subtle, and as Mathers notes 'more restricted' in meaning. However with the water jugs being poured , the volcanic fire in the background make it plain that the Elevation process is not a dry one, or humid (as in the first version of this Key), but is more liquid in orientation and is more closely allied with (though not identical to) higher forms of the Distillation process.

The backdrop of this Key is water and fiery earth. Their essences or higher natures are shown in the jugs held by the angel, who reunites them together. What is not shown in this Key, but is assumed, is that the angel will keep pouring one jug into the other, over a period of time, which is not just simply the fiery essence being poured into the watery. The cross on the breast of the angel shows that eventually the fixation process will occur with this movement, shown by the bi-sexual nature of the angel. The wings show the volatile or airy nature behind the experiment. The 6 pointed star (with the dot in the middle) over the head of the angel, shows the Elevation process is gone over 7 times.

Sagittarius shows a fall in Temperature. The previous work of Dissolution is carried on a more ethereal level.

The Devil
'Cibation'

This Key symbolises the alchemical step of Cibation. Cibation is the concept of wetting or feeding dry matter. It is part of the integration process where it has impregnated itself. Its own liquid has been dropped into its own dried matter, and this way it feeds itself by eating its own flesh (sometimes called the peacock's flesh). This is eating its own tail, which is called the Uroboros. The metamorphosis that takes place is associated to this Key in a sense that it is self renewal, but limited to a situation where one part of life sustains the others. Hence the limitation, shown by the two figures in chains which restricts them. The horn held upright by the Devll is full of water, while the others hand holds fire. The water drips down from the horn into the matter below (sometimes called the Bituminous matter – depending on what one is aiming at in the experiment). The figures below are the fixed Mercury and Sulphur while the altar is the salts. Above the figure the upright pentagram relates to the unfixed Mercury and Sulphur.

The Cibation process will saturate the stone until it can take no more of its own blood (liquid). Capricorn is the month where there is separation among the elements in the soil due to the breaking down and combustion of the two previous signs. It is a slow assimilation porcess of receiving the nutrients and as such is a time of assimilation and preparation.

The Star
'Congelation'

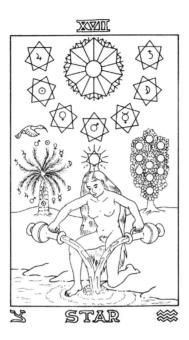

The alchemical state that Key 17 represents is Congelation. This is where an object is thickened or gelled, and is likened to ice over water, for within it, it contains a fluid substance. When the surface is broken the essence flows out. This is analogous to this Key, where the hard surface of the Star is shown above each small star and relates to one of the seven metals and the liquification of the matter is shown below, by the ethereal forces flowing from the urns into the river. Sirius is the Star of Summer, though it is placed here in mid winter, and relates to the heat of summer being applied to the metals to liquify them. The seven pointed star above the female figure shows the seven stages of Congelation before it becomes effective. The Tree of Knowledge shows the way the experiment is carried out and the Tree of Life on the right hand side relates to the degrees of each stage. Aquarius is a air sign at the heart of winter when the ethereal forces work through the water or rains to nourish the sleeping roots and vegetation into wakefullness.

The Moon
'Conjunction/Impregnation'

This alchemical state is called the Conjunction/Impregnation. This relates to the bringing together of the separated parts of the experiment into a homogeneous commodity. It is the final step in which all the component parts of the matter that have been separated and strengthened individually are placed back together again. The Green Lion becomes White, so that the white may become Red. The impregnation is shown by the crayfish emerging from the pool, the point of conception. On either side of the path are two dogs, they will try and pull the crayfish off the path so that they can devour it. They are the solvents of the experiments. The twin towers show the two extremes of heat needed. The path of the crayfish passes between both. The seven Yods shows the seven vibrations needed before the crayfish reaches the lunar state of the Solution. The Crayfish is hard and has to be reduced to a Solution before use, shown by the Luna tears of Diana that fall upon it. For the crayfish travels the Path and is bathed in the white Luna influence. Pisces shows the nourishing of the hidden seeds in the soil, it is the growth period before birth through the virginal milk.

Chapter 9

The Moon and the Tarot

The Lunar Diagram On The Tree Of Life
By Pat Zalewski

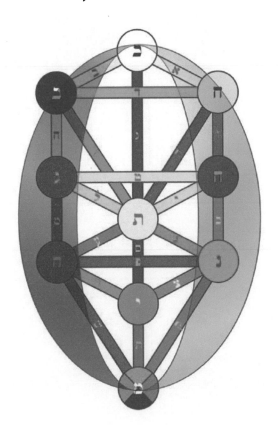

The symbol of the two opposing Moons on the Tree of life, is a variation on the Vesica Pisces (Fish Bladder). Its symbolism has dominated ecclesiastical architecture in mediaeval times. Although it is considered a Christian symbol, its origins go back much further and was known in both Egyptian and Babylonian times. The Vesica, as the diagram shows, is formed by the intersection of the arcs of two equal circles, and it contains a double equilateral triangle, the figure of the Rhombus. The proportions of breadth to length, of the Rhombus or Vesica are as one root of three. This relates back to the Kabbalistic Supernal. It must be considered that the Vesica Pisces symbol, when applied vertically, is the basis and formation of the ten spheres of the Kabbalaistic Tree of Life.

Light

In Isaiah 30:26, we are told *the light of the Moon shall be the Light.* The inoperative word here being Light, it is precisely this that this diagram refers to. The Light of the Sun in Tiphareth is reflected by the Luna influence in Yesod, through the Middle Pillar. This Light is the Astral Light, which the candidate will first encounter in Yesod. It will appear to come in small glimpses for long periods and there will be nothing seen at all. The twin crescents show both the waxing and waning of the Light, which is appropriate for this diagram:

The Astral Light warns us of a coming influence by its action on the more or less sensible. Instantaneous sympathies, electric loves, are explosions of the Astral Light, which are exactly and mathematically demonstrable as the discharge of strong magnetic batteries.

The right side of this diagram is white while the left side is black. The Light and Darkness are personified by the feminine Eve and Lilith. Eve is the Pillar of Mercy of the Tree, while Lilith is the Pillar of Severity. Yet both are the same aspects of the other. The Darkness typifies the decreasing Lunar Light. Eve is life, mother of all, while Lilith is death the baby killer.

Note: the Sephiroth of Malkuth and Kether is split into two parts to accommodate the arcs. The right side of the Tree repesents the new Moon. The first 45 degrees are from Malkuth to Netzach.

This is the slightly Chaotic state where the impulse governs our actions. It is a struggle for growth, where the Lunar Light has warmed our spiritual growth in a predestined direction, like the rising of sap in vegetation during the period of Spring growth. This is allied to the birth of Eve, from Adam's rib, and the rise above the material (by virtue of the Garden of Eden, the idyllic garden of material and spiritual harmony) nature shows the link with the Light of Divine guidance.

The Crescent Moon is associated from Netzach to Chesed - 45 to 90 degrees

This is the struggle to establish a spiritual sense of self awareness by the study of the harmonious aspects surrounding one. Eve here, starts to see the different levels with the Garden of Eden, and undergoes a structured form of change.

The First Quarter of the Moon is from 90 to 135 degrees, from Chesed to Chokmah

This is where one becomes fixed on personal growth at almost any expense. This is Eve starting to question their reasons for being placed in the Garden in the first place. It is a time of accepting growth structures and various archetypes as guiding forces to us. As a result of this, a whole sense of awareness opens up.

The Gibbous Moon is from Chokmah to Kether - 135 to 180 degrees

The full Moon peaks at the righthand portion of Kether. It is the point where the Light is at its strongest and its magical and magnetic point of that, works close to illumination or fulfillment. Here Eve finds a way or method to be the equal of her creator. She has found a way to access the deepest recesses of herself, so that she can gain more, and become totally independent from her creator. It is a point of theory that has not quite actualised the practical experience of independence.

The Full Moon from Kether to Binah - 180 to 225 degrees

This is the portion where the Light from the Garden of Eden is shut out and Eve now becomes Lillith, who was the first wife of Adam. From this, it shows one learning from one's past mistakes. It is Lilith who as acted instinctively as a form of self- preservation, and must develop her own concepts and teachings, for the teachings of the Garden of Eden are now denied to her. Kether, the Crown, is lost to her and now she continues for the Understanding in Binah. She must bring forth new methods of learning that relates to the hostile environment she has landed herself in. She wishes to become Queen of her surroundings and tries to subjugate all wild species to her whim.

> *God formed Lilith, the first woman, just as He had formed Adam, except that he used filth and impure sediment instead of dust and earth. Adam and Lillith never found peace together. She disagreed with him in many matters, and refused to lie beneath him in sexual intercourse, basing her claim for equality on the fact that each had been created form earth. When Lilith saw that Adam would overpower her, she uttered the ineffable name of God and flew up into the air of the world, she dwelt in a cave in the desert on the shores of the Red Sea. There she enegaged in unbridled promiscuity, consorted with lascivious, and gave birth to hundreds of Lilim or demonic babies daily'*
> (Otzar Midrash J.D. Esienstein,1915)

She has a clarity of purpose and direction that she learnt in the Garden of Eden and will apply these principles in the chaotic state, but under her own management of ideas.

The Disseminating Moon - from Chokmah to Geburah, 225 to 270 degrees

The Understanding of Binah is now forsaken as her easy going structure, or set of ideals are now turned into a fanatical set of dogmatic belefs or structures. It shows the Martian nature of Geburah in action as its title of Severity depicts. Geburah's other title of *Pachad* or *Fear* is represented here. Lilith brings forth fear and superstition to control her environment . The legend of Lilith the Child killer is shown here as well:

> *From the moment she came forth, she went up and down to the Cheribum who have* little faces of tender children *and desired to cleave unto them and be one of them, and was laothe to depart from them (Zohar 18B...) Then the Holy One, Blessed be he, brought her out from the depths of the sea and gave her power over all those children, the* little faces *of the sons of men, who are liable to punishment for the sins of their fathers (Zohar 19B).*

From Geburah to Hod - 270 to 315 degrees

This is the crisis state from the Severity of Geburah which has changed to the Splendour of Hod. Change has occurred, as the Severity of the previous phase could not last any longer. It is in the state of reformation. Lilith has now accepted the change and realises her status.

> *(God the) King has dismissed the Shekinah and put the handmaiden Lilith in her place. This handmaid, Lilith, will one day rule over the Holy land below as the Shekinah once ruled over it, but the Holy one, Blessed be He, will one day restore the Matrona to her place, and who shall rejoice like the King and the Matrona? The King, because he has returned to her and parted from the handmaid, and Shekinah because she will be once more united to the King... '(Zohar 3, 69a-b).*

Balsamic Moon, from Hod to Malkuth, 315 to 360 degrees

The old ways here are being put aside as the new period of Light is entered into. The Splendour of Hod is left behind as the new Kingdom is reached, learnt upon the lessons of the old. It is the provision for the future, a seed state of awareness that tries to recapture the lessons given out in the Garden of Eden. Lilith now starts to leave the Ego behind as she tries to emulate Eve, in the pure state of the garden through her intercourse with Adam.

> ...She is dressed in scarlet and adorned with forty ornaments less one. Yon fool goes astray after her and drinks form the cup of wine and commits with her fornications and strays after her. What does she thereapon do? She leaves him asleep on the couch, flies up to heaven and denounces him, takes her leave and descends. That fool awakens and deems so he can make sport with her as before, but she removes her ornaments and turns into a menacing figure. She stands before him clothed in garments of flaming fire and making the body and soul tremble, full of frightening eyes, in her hand a sword dripping bitter drops. And she kills that fool and casts him into Gehenna' (Zohar 1 148a-b Sitre Torah).

The above quotation shows the descent into matter through intercourse and the rising of the Kundaline. For as she enters Malkuth through Kether, the Sword or Lightning Flash is recalled. The Middle Pillar is brought into question, for there are two levels to it, one higher and the other lower. The Sephiroth has both a positive and negative effect, the Lunar diagram surrounding this reminds us of this.

When applying this diagram of Tree of Life, and the twin Lunar arcs to alchemy, the alchemist Smith is worth quoting:

> The Great Work consists of stupendous double movement. The first of these, the regimen of Lunar, the effects of the descent (or death) of the body

and the ascent (rebirth) of the Soul; this simultaneous event corresponds to the raising up of the Spirit, celebrated in the union of the Above and the Below. The second regimen of Sol (Shown by central Pillar in the middle of the Luna arcs P.Z) effects the fixing of the Soul and volatisation of the body, which corresponds to the drawing down of the spirit, celebrated in the marriage of Heaven and Earth. The work is One Thing: if it separates Soul and Body, Spirit and Matter, it is only that they be more joyfully and completely united, making the heavenly spirit corporeal... the earthy body spiritual and glorified.

The Lunar Arcs and the Triple Goddess of the Neophyte Ceremony.

When you examine the Luna diagram carefully, you will find that both sides represent two drawn bows. The right one for just and righteous causes and the left one for wanton destruction. The Mathers description of the 'High Priestess Trump', in his 'Seven Branch Candlestick' paper, shows a figure holding a bow across her lap, as does Crowley's. The bow can be used for good or evil, and as such, gives the freedom of choice to the user. The twin arcs in this diagram relate to the 3 Coptic God forms of the Neophyte grade.

1. Thmaa Est, as the central figure.
2. Thma Aesch, on the Pillar of Severity.
3. Thmaa Ett, on the Pillar of Mercy.

All three God forms are different aspects of the function of the Hegemon during the Neophyte ritual. In her central position between the pillars, she must control the forces around her. If the energy in the temple is weak, she must draw the energy from the dais behind her, and distribute it between the pillars evenly. She must push the energy currents beyond the pillars, and when this is done through her function of Thma Aesch, from the Pillar of Severity she derives her strength. If the energies are too strong and unbalanced, she then draws from the power of Thmaa Ett and the Pillar of Mercy, to bring these energies down towards a more balanced level before the third God form of Thmaa Est comes into play, and regulates all the energy currents as the Guardian of the Portal.

The triple Goddess effect is shown in many forms of Diana – as the young virgin, shown by the right hand crescent Moon. This is symbolic of Spring growth, untouched by man's sorrows. This takes us to the height of Summer. Between Summer and Autumn, the full Moon shows motherhood, giving birth to the darkening Light – the old crone. As the maiden she is Athene and Artemis, both showing the attributes of maidenhood. Athene relates to nature and is in harmony with growth of the seasons. Artemis though is more closer to Kether, while Athene is more closer to Malkuth. In Malkuth she has sprung fully formed from her father Zeus (Kether):

'For Kether is Malkuth and Malkuth is Kether' says the 'Convoluted Forces' paper. Athene is the start of the Lunar current in Malkuth. In many respects she is the principle of rebirth yet she is fully formed, being part of the four elements.

Going up the Tree to Netzach, the Sephirah of Victory, she represents the warrior goddess. As sge approaches Chesed (going straight up the Pillar of Mercy) she begins to merge with Artemis, the virgin huntress, for the Mercy of Chesed and the Wisdom of Chokmah. On arriving at Kether we have the Mother Demeter. On the left hand side of the Tree is the decline of Light. This can be likened to Persephone and her period with Hades, in the Underworld, where she is denied Light until she reaches Malkuth again where she then springs forth as Athene.

In the Neophyte ritual, the Kabbalistic layout of the Temple floor, the Hegemon sits on the path associated with Samekh, which in turn relates to the zodiac sign of Sagittarius, the Sign of the arrow. She sits in the front of Yesod and the Invisible station of Apophis. Her link to the Lunar influence of Yesod is obvious and it is she who controls the gateway to Yesod. If she relaxes her guard, the doorway to Aphosis will open, and the negative energies will enter the temple. Being constantly of guard, she is the Goddess Maat, Guardian of the Hall of Truth, where everything, including the scales of balance, is under her control. She controls the Path of Peh, Mars coming across her and these energies she must control as well. As controller of the gateway of Yesod, she shows that the astral lunar current – a gate of the mind, will be subjected to pulls in many directions. The brightness of Kether reflecting through Tiphareth and into Yesod, shows the distortion that occurs in reflected Light and how careful one must be. If you look closer at the Lunar diagram you will see a sacred cross at the centre of the arcs (Atah, Malkuth, ve Gedulah ve Geburah – The Kabbalah Cross). This is the Calvary Cross which she wears.

When studying some of the hidden symbolism of the Princess Cards, the Lunar crescents and cross are shown in them. This relates to the four gates of each arc of the diagram. For each Princess will be rotated around by the eight quarters of the Moon. Each Lunar Phase will in turn alter the meaning slightly of each card. Each quarter will be considered the influence of each trump as it rolls over them. Hidden in each of the eight lunar gates is the 8 spoked wheel, the symbol of Spirit. For this is a true reflection of the Spirit of Kether being reflected by the spirit of Tiphareth.

Chapter 10

The Caduceus

This paper was given in part, 'Golden Dawn Rituals and Commentaries' as an explanation of the Chief Adept's Wand, pages 454-456 (in an abridged format). This is the FULL paper, which is quite substantial, and not only looks at the Wand of the Chief Adept, is now produced for the first time. Though most the paper is my own work, I did take the liberty of adding some components of an early Stella Matutina paper on the officers.

Egyptian Symbolism

The early Egyptian Symbolism of the Caduceus represents the Goddess Maat, through the Uraeus serpents and the Solar Disk. Uraeus worship (in the form of the Goddess Uatchet) was prominent in the Lower Kingdom, it was the vulture in the form of the Goddess Nekhebet. The early topography shows the vulture above the serpent, yet both of them represent Egypt as a united Kingdom. Maat was the goddess of Truth and Justice, the weigher of the scales in the afterlife, with the feather of rectification. There is a strong association between Maat and Ra, the Sun God, for both ruled from a higher power and gave order and justice to the world, for it was Maat who regulated the rising of the Sun God Ra. In the pre Osirian time, over a lengthy period, time, one god became leader and an extension of the other in attributes, for the Sun, the visible ruler of us all.

It is relevant here to study the connection between Maat and Thoth, for Maat was considered the feminine counterpart of Thoth, for it was these two that stood each side of the Sun God on his boat. The solar Disk surmounted on the top of the Caduceus is analagous with the boat of Ra with Thoth and Maat, shown by the wings, on each side of the Disk. In the papyrus of Ani, Thoth and Maat stood each side of Horus and helped him to steer a straight course across the sky.

The serpents who sat on the forehead of Ra spat venom at his enemies and were protectors of Nu, the Sky God. They represent both birth and death. The winged solar disk surmounted by the two serpents, is a potent creation symbol. The staff itself can be found in associationwith Sesta (Thoth's other feminine manifestation). It represents the life force in transmission between the two spheres of Life and Death, it represents time.

The Caduceus and the Kerux

There is more than one type of Caduceus. The difference being the number of times the snakes or serpents cross. In this Caduceus, in its Astral form, they cross at Malkuth, Yesod and Daath. The first cross is at the base of Malkuth, and you will note that the serpents come from the lower roots of the Tree of Life. This is the initial; joining at ther lowest point of Creation, the Material World. Here the positive and negative potencies are brought together for a cross fertilisation through the framework of the four elements. Through the analogy of the actions of the Kerux during ritual, the joining or crossing process can be studied. To bring the two serpents together, the actions are the Kerux and his duties in the Neophyte ceremony. This is cemented in the 1 =10 ceremony and in the 2= 9 ceremony. The first crossing of the serpents occurs in Yesod (the initial cross in Malkuth is more of a fertilisation process that starts the serpents to rise.) As such, the Caduceus is used as an Admission badge for the 2= 9 Badge for the entry into Yesod. After the 2= 9 ritual, the role of Kerux is not needed until the 8= 3, when he is transformed into the function of another Officer.

Out of the seven Officers in the Neophyte ceremony, it is the Kerux that holds a position of particular significance. The Sentinel, being outside the Portal of the Hall is in some respects apart from the main Officers. There are three triads. The Triad of the Three

Chiefs, the next is the Hierophant, Hiereus and Hegemon. Of these, it may be observed that they jointly take part in every Outer Order Initiation (up to the 4=7 level). The last triad is that of the Kerux, Stolisties and Dadouchos, and of these, the Kerux is the Chief. The Kerux of course, continues his duties as far as the 2= 9, which symbolises the entry into Yesod, which shows that he can rise no higher than that level. Since Yesod is symbolised by the element of Air, which is analogous of the symbolism of the intellect, is not needed, as the true initiation opens up within the self because Air (Ruach-Breath-Spiritus: in its Hebrew, English and Latin context) is linked to Spirit. It is the joint link of Spirit and Intellect where the rational process is let go for the higher unrevealed purpose. It is the Hegemon, symbolising Aspiration and Intuition (something felt rather than seen) who takes over for the Kerux as guide for the candidate. For the Intellect is limited, and such limitation is placed upon him as he stands in the Path of Tau and the earthy part of Yesod, the lowest portion of the Ruach.

In 1=10, the Kerux admits the candidate to the Portal of Wisdom (his stations being West and North) and in the 2=9 fuller explanations are given of the lamen of the Kerux. The Kerux, in Yesod, reflection Air from Tiphareth and Kether while the Moon of Yesod reflects the Sun in Tiphareth. The Kerux is Mercury, the Child of Jupiter, hermes son of Zeus, Ruler of the firmament of Air, the guide who leads the souls of Dead to their abode in Hades. The analogy here is to the Kerux guiding the Candidate through the Path of Tau, through the Astral Plane, form the material World of Malkuth to the Yetsirahic world of Yesod. His position in the Hexagram formation (as the officer stands before the Earth Tablet in the 1=10 ceremony) shows he is a mirror of the Hierophant (directly above him) which links the material to the spiritual, which is shown as the central portion of his lamen, joining Kether to Malkuth. Hence his seat is in the West in the 0=0 ceremony and in part of the 1=10, and when he sits in the North at the conclusion of the 1=10 and 2=9 ceremonies, it is to be observed that the triangle of Air when reversed or reflected becomes the triangle of earth. The Kerux leads the procession in the pathway of the Sun, and proclaims the commands of the Hierophant. He is, as it were 'The mouth of the King, and his feet' he is the connecting link between Metatron and Sandalphon.

The relationship between the Kerux and the Hiereus is a curious one and full of hidden symbolism. The Kerux, in the 1=10 sits in the West (in the first part) in the place of Hiereus. Since the Hiereus is the protector against evil in the temple, like the Sun setting in the West standing against the Darkness the Kerux is a Guradian, as stated in the 2=9. The link here is with Anubis and the Charon/Hermes archetype who lead the departed souls to judgement as well as reward, for the dead always had money placed on eyelids to pay the ferryman Charon. In both the afterlife and in initiation, the twin serpents of Good and Evil will try and take the Soul away from its true course - which the guide will always prevent. For these are representative of the rising serpents of the caduceus. Man cannot take the light without experiencing the dark, hence both of these serpents are necessary evils that the soul will encounter to build up its strength and true direction.

In the 2=9 Air Grade of Theoricus, the second crossing of the serpents on the caduceus is shown, and this exchange can be best symbolised by the Greek letter He, Eta, that was written in the Temple of Delphi, which was considered the navel of the material world. The He is the Truth, while the two E's compounded should be written so that both face inwards towards each other and joined together so that they resemble the letter H, a symbol of perfection. This symbol represents the crossing of the serpents through Yesod. The Hebraic value of Heh is five, and shows that there are five values assosiated to it (The Greek kabbalah has 8, *Mercury*, associated to Eta, and the full name Eta has a value of 309 and relates to the Greek name of the Moon).

1. Physical nature and its passions
2. Desire nature or emotion
3. Intellect or reason
4. Intuition or Inspiration
5. Will

In Man, Passion, Intellect and reason are positive, while Emotion and intuition are said to exist negatively. In women, this is said to be the reverse. Hermes was considered to be a type of man, Aphrodite a type of woman, the union of the two in one male and one female, the hermaphrodite being the completion of the Greek Eta, joining the male E to the female E, forming jointly the letter H.

Hebraic Association of the Wand of the Kerux and the hidden Caduceus symbolism

The Hebrew association of the letters Shin, Aleph and Mem are mentioned in the 2=9 ritual as being associated to the caduceus (the wand of the Kerux in those three colours). The Bahir tells us that the letter Mem, both male and female (Mem final being exclusively male). There is some confusion of the association of Water to Mem and then placed in Malkuth (it is carried with the Blue pointed end pointing downwards and representing the earthy nature of Malkuth.) If we study the 12th Tarot Key, the Hanged Man, which is associated with Mem, then a glimmer of understanding of this principle becomes apparent. Here the water of Mem surrounds the Man so that he can go through a state of Baptism. He must suffer first before the realisation comes. Because Mem is placed in Earth (the human body being made up of mostly water) man must suffer though his earthly nature until he becomes more spiritually aware. This is accomplished through the transformation of the Nephesch (symbolised by Mem) into Ruach (Aleph – Air) which is the grip position of the wand of the Kerux.

The shape of Aleph is the shape of stance of the child in Key 0 (the Fool) which is the same shape as the Hermetic Cross, which is an Admission badge into the 1=10 Grade into Malkuth. The Fool represents the Terrestrial Eden that Man has been expelled from and that which he desires to reunite again with, hence Aleph is the gateway to the Eden as well as the lower entranceway to the Tree. Since the expulsion into Malkuth of man, the ten Sephiroth have an additional entranceway to Eden through the old doorway of Yesod, when Malkuth was not attached to the Tree. This is further shown by the Divine State of Innocence of the Child in Key 0, whose sphere of influence goes no lower than Yesod.

The topmost letter on the Wand of the Kerux is Shin, shown by the red colouring. This is related to Key 20 and stands for the

Supernal of the Tree. This is the point the serpents (as man) will not rise above the entranceway of Daath. Man is judged here, his worthiness to enter the exalted state, the impurities are removed through Fire and Water, both are shown in Key 20. The trial of Fire and Water separate the entwined serpents so that they are complete in themselves. The triangle in Key 20 shows the Supernal of the Ain Soph Aur from which the sevenfold nature arrives in the Tree through the Rainbow of Promise.

The Caduceus in Ritual

The magical imprint of the Caduceus on the Temple floor, when the Candidate is admitted into Yesod is a real energy formation. The god forms are placed on or near this energy symbol and regulate it. The placement of the diagram in the central portions of the Caduceus is not there by accident but by design. The Candidate is first brought to Yesod on this symbol, whose Astral presence is guarded by the God form of Nekhebet who allows the Candidate to enter the Caduceus through the birth state, one of the functions of this God form. The Path of the serpent is then followed up until Daath where Hormaku takes over the Guardian position as the point of a higher journey. The Candidate must return again to the base of the serpent's tail where the God form of Kephera greets him. This God form is the Resurrection symbol and it is no accident that Alchemical Sephiroth symbols are placed here. For these are the symbols of renewal. The journey finishes with the Candidate being taken to Nu at the top of the Caduceus. What we have here in the 2 9 grade is merely of a partial use of the power and symbology of the Caduceus using mainly the serpent whose tail is based on the lefthand side of the temple, in the West. The further circumambulation to the opposite serpent where Kephera stands guard is merely a start of another journey through the symbology of Transmutation (through alchemy).

Kundaline and the Caduceus

I have mentioned more than once that the Golden Dawn in the 1920's onwards worked more on the Chakras and subtle bodies than the kabbalistic soul in terms of explaining the actions of the

Adept in Magickal ritual. It was so in Whare Ra temple and it was so in the other Stella Matutina and A.O. temples. In the case of the latter we have the example of former British Golden Dawn (A.O.) Chief Langford Garstin, who wrote in his book *Secret Fire* in 1932:

> ...*the junction of the three principal Nadis (pipes or tubes) , Sushumna. Ida and Pingala, of which the first corresponds to the spinal cord, while other two are the left and right sympathetic chains respectively. These latter cross the pinal column from one side to the other, making with Sushumna and the two lobed Ajna (Brow Chakra) the figure of the Caduceus of Hermes, which is itself another form of the Tree of Life of the Qabalah, with which latter all we have said is in harmony... Now the object of Kundaline Yoga is to awaken the coiled and sleeping force by Pranayama (breathing exercises) and other Yogic postures, so that it shall be dynamic. She is thereupon immediately drawn upwards to that other static centre Sahasara (Crown Chakra) the thousand petalled lotus, which is, in fact Herself but in union with Shiva – consciousness, or the consciousness of ecstacy beyond the world of forms.When she sleeps, man is awake in the material world, but when she awakens the Yogic loses all consciousness of the world and enters his Causal Body, passing thus to formless consciousness...*

Wand of the Chief Adept and the Caduceus

The Caduceus is related to the Wand of the Chief Adept, used in the Inner Order. Each time the serpent's cross (in the astral form of it) it is symbolised by a colour. The supernal of the Tree relates to the Wings and Solar Disk, surmounted on the top of the Wand.

Black Portion - First crossing

The first crossing of the serpents is represented by the Black of Malkuth, for this is the 10th Path of Resplendeth Intelligence and is so called because it is exalted above every other head, and sits on the Throne of Binah, which represents the Planet saturn and Illuminates the Splendour of all Lights and causes the currents of influences to flow from Metatron. The reflection here is because Binah is the first point of separation, and the firm establishment of the feminine polarity, which in turn relates to the Mother concept of Gaea, the earth Element, the beginning of all things material in the plane of Assiah. For here you have the Material Base of the alchemists, also shown in Macrocosm by the revolution of the Aces around the pole (in the Convoluted Forces paper). Within the Black portion of the Wand there are four forces (the four colours of Malkuth in the Queen Scale) which in Macrocosm, are analgous to the four Kerubs in the 21st Key of the Tarot. We are told in the 'Convoluted Forces' paper that the colour Black represents more horizontal movement than vertical. This is the influence for the crossing of the serpents. Black is the colour of Malkuth in the Princess Scale, but the Golden Light that accompanies this colour, is the unrevealed nature of the Astral Light above. When the wand is held in its lowest portion (for this is a symbol of Tau) in the first point of the 5=6 ritual, where it represents a crossing over from matter, as the candidate is taken through the Dark Veil of Poroketh. The blackness is the Portal of the 5=6 where the earthy nature must be faced before one can enter the vault through the higher nature of Venus. It is the material being, aware of the higher nature. The Blackness represents the Night before the dawn. For each must be faced in its own time. The energy level here is the Etheric Body as this is the one stimulated from this position. It is stimulated from the lowest chakra which stimulates awareness of spirituality. The Etheric Body is the body next to the physical and it is the one that activates the energy that goes to and from the physical. It is the one that is first used during magical ceremonies as a type of 'kick start' and get the energy directed from the chakras and subtle bodies, mostly used in opening parts of the ceremony and initial invocations. For work within the vault the grip is never used here and it before an entrance or after an exit from it. On entry to the Vault the meridians are stimulated, along with the extra vessels which the energy is stimulated like the effect of qi gong in some internal Chinese exercises.

> *And he lighted upon a certain place, and tarried there all night: because the Sun was set; he took all the stones of that place, and put them for his pillows and lay down in that place to sleep. And he dreamed, behold a ladder set upon the earth, and the top of it reached the heaven; and behold the angels of God ascending and descending it.*
> Genesis 28-11,12.

Blue Portion – Second Crossing

The second crossing of the serpents relates to the Sephirah Yesod, shown by the colour a deep bluish purple in the Prince Scale – though within the blue spectrum of colours. The Yetziratic Text calls this Path *Pure Intelligence because it purifies emanations.* It proves and corrects the designing of their representations, and disposes of the unity with which they are designed without diminution or division. This relates to the energy flow from Tiphareth being refined from Kether, by Tiphareth, and in conjunction with the dual forces of Hod and Netzach, by producing Yesod – compatible vehicle for both polarities of the Tree. The purification of this colour reminds us of the 12th Key of the Tarot, the *Hanged Man.* The alchemists associate the following Biblical passage here:

> *Therefore God gave the Dew of heaven and the fatness of the earth, and plenty of corn and wine. And Isaac his father answered and said unto him, behold thy dwelling shall be the fatness of the earth, and the dew of heaven from Above*

The Blue grip position represent the second chakra and the Astral/ Emotional level which is directly applied to Yesod's Astral status – through her Luna associations. Firstly it is a power base and holds the focus of the Astral Energies and it slowly rises until some of the lower levels are cast off. It is a fine tuner for the higher energies. The Emotional content of the personality during the ritual stabilises the Adept from the tremendous input of energies as the potency of the rituals increases. It is used for entrance into the vault. The Chief Adept will be the point – man for all these energy currents. The stimulation is the lower grip with the lower chakra and the next grip with the next higher centre. These take the main input of power from the Brow and Crown (in the lowest grip) and the Throat. They transmute their power force through these lower centre equivalents.

Yellow Portion - Third Crossing

The third crossing of the serpents is in Tiphareth, which is shown by the golden solar colour – from the Queens Scale in Tiphareth. This relates to the 6th Sephirah and is called Mediating Intelligence because in it are multiplied the influxes or emanations; for it causes the influence to flow into all reservoirs of the blessings with which they themselves are united. This refers to the central position of Tiphareth on the Tree in balanced disposition, not only from the two polarities, but of the energy forces moving down and up the Tree. For the Chief Adept, this is the main point or grip position in the ritual when power is at its peak. A good example of this is in the Opening and first part of the first point, second and third point (there are some exceptions to this rule). It is the most obliging force to wield that will offer the least resistance. The alchemists say of this:

> 'And of Zebulun he said. Rejoice Zebulun, In Thy going out: and Issachar, in thy tents. Israel shall dwell in safety alone: the fountain of Jacob shall be a land of corn and wine; and his heavens shall drop down dew;'
>
> Deut. 33-18, 28.

The Lower Mental body is represented by this band and is stimulated (though not exclusive to) through the heart centre. The energy coming through is processed and clarified by this Subtle Body. It intensifies the focus for the desired purpose. The heart centre and its emotional stimulus firmly link the kavanah (intent) of the Adept to the Divine quality of purpose of the ceremony.

Red Portion - Fourth crossing

The fourth crossing of the serpents is in the shadow of the Sephirah –Daath. It is the point where the Tree and Knowledge of Good and Evil are joined equally. There is no real colour associated to Daath. In the Zohar, from the *Book of Lesser Holy Assembly* we are told 'The masculine Power is extended through Daath; and the assemblies and conclaves are filled'. This of course relates to the higher emanations filtering down. In this instance it relates to the Yod Force which some have associated to red.

The grip position here is one never used outside of the 8=3 ceremony where it is held for the whole of the ceremony. The Throat chakra is stimulated and its function is not through any subtle body directly, but through the alignment of all the subtle bodies acting in tandem with each other.

White Portion

The White upper portion is the bridging gap between worlds, since white is the colour that inlcudes all other colours, it is in a sense, an extension of Daath, for it is the separating cloud of the Supernal from the lower part of the Tree, or in this instance the wand. We are told in the explanation of the 'Garden of Eden after the Fall' that the heads of the Dragon rose into the seven lower Sephiroth and even unto the feet of Amia Elohim (equated with Binah). This portion of the wand is reserved for the 9=2 ritual and for contact with the third order within the Vault.

The Serpents

We are told in the Zohar, that at the point of Daath, the Serpent of Wisdom extended herself into two halves, to help balance the Tree and maintain the Abyss, or Gulf, between the Supernal and the Lower Tree. Each serpent has a conical crown of the South and North (shown by the red and white) of the Egyptian mystery Schools. This is symbolic, and shows the power of the wand is sanctified by those gods above – according to Egyptian tradition. The Uraeus symbols were related to divinity and the office of the High Priest as well, as the Priest King, and the Wand of the Chief Adept. On each serpent there are three double marks, making a total of six on each side. These are analogous to snake scales, and relate to the point of Balance of the Equinox, and show the changing nature of the earth's cycles around the Sun. This again, is analogous to the serpents around the central shaft of the Wand. The symbolism here is that both forces of Light and darkness are held in abeyance, neither one winning or losing.

Winged Disk

Above the symbol of the twin serpents is that of the winged Sphere or disk. Now each wing is a mirror image of the others. The key number of permutations is 120, the number of years Christian Rosenkruetz (and the number of Sephiroth multiplied by the Zodiac) said after which the vault would open. Directly above the central shaft are 15 black feathers, which when divided into 120 is 8 - the number of Hod and Thoth, the wielder of the wand who is associated to the Planet Mercury. There are a total of 17 feathers each side of the Disk (7+1 reduces to 8). If you place the circular disk over the 64 Square Kamea of Mercury, you in effect, square the circle. The diameter is ten units and the circumference is 32, when taken to the next whole number. Here is a blueprint for the ten Sephiroth and the 22 Paths is given in its seed form.

There are a total of 24 dots (eight red, blue and black) on each side of the wing, which in turn relates to the number of hours in the day and the thrones of the Elders of the Apocalypse. This is obtained by dividing 120 by 5 (the number of the four elements and spirit). The 120 is then divided by the ten Sephiroth (coming to 12), which stands for HUA, the symbol of the Higher Genius which the Chief Adept holds above the heads of the Adepti.

Other titles from Thoth Publications:

TALISMANS & EVOCATIONS OF THE GOLDEN DAWN
by Pat Zalewski

Practical Magic Techniques of the Golden Dawn Revealed! Founded in 1888 by legendary magicians Wynn Westcott and S.L.MacGregor Mathers, the Golden Dawn has been a major influence on the development of Western Magic. Although the material which inspired adepts such as Aleister Crowley and W.B.Yeats has been available, until now there has been little explanation as to how this group performed its rites of ritual magic.

Now at last Pat Zalewski, himself an adept within the Golden Dawn system, has revealed secrets that have never before been published or which were only communicated orally to a handful of select pupils.

For years people have known that the Golden Dawn adepts could summon spirits so that they could be seen, but no one could explain how they did it. Likewise their techniques of manufacturing and empowering talismans were a closely guarded secret until now.

Here readers will learn the secrets of evocation and how to make Talismans of Power. This book is a very valuable tool into understanding the practical considerations of Golden Dawn ritual magic at its best. It is a must for serious Golden Dawn students.

Mr.Zalewski's books are a gold mine for anyone interested in the Golden Dawn or practical magic.
- V.H. Fr.I.U.S.
Hermetic Order of the Golden Dawn

ISBN 978-1-870450-36-2

PYTHONESS - The Life & Work of Margaret Lumley Brown
By Gareth Knight

Margaret Lumley Brown was a leading member of Dion Fortune's Society of the Inner Light, taking over many of Dion Fortune's functions after the latter's death in 1946. She raised the arts of seership to an entirely new level and has been hailed with some justification as the finest medium and psychic of the 20th century. Although she generally sought anonymity in her lifetime her work was the source of much of the inner teachings of the Society from 1946 to 1961 and provided much of the material for Gareth Knight's *The Secret Tradition in Arthurian Legend* and *A Practical Guide to Qabalistic Symbolism.*

Gathered here is a four part record of the life and work of this remarkable woman. Part One presents the main biographical details largely as revealed by herself in an early work *Both Sides of the Door* an account of the frightening way in which her natural psychism developed as a consequence of experimenting with an ouija board in a haunted house. Part Two consists of articles written by her on such subjects as Dreams, Elementals, the Faery Kingdom, Healing and Atlantis, most of them commissioned for the legendary but short lived magazine *New Dimensions.* Part Three provides examples of her mediumship as Archpythoness of her occult fraternity with trance addresses on topics as diverse as Elemental Contacts, Angels and Archangels, Greek and Egyptian gods, and the Holy Grail. Part Four is devoted to the occult side of poetry, with some examples of her own work which was widely published in her day.

Gareth Knight was a colleague and friend of Margaret Lumley Brown in their days in the Society of the Inner Light together, to whom in later years she vouchsafed her literary remains, some esoteric memorabilia, and the privilege of being her literary executor.

ISBN 978-1-870450-75-1

PRINCIPLES OF ESOTERIC HEALING

By Dion Fortune. Edited and arranged by Gareth Knight

One of the early ambitions of Dion Fortune along with her husband Dr Thomas Penry Evans was to found a clinic devoted to esoteric medicine, along the lines that she had fictionally described in her series of short stories *The Secrets of Dr. Taverner*. The original Dr. Taverner was her first occult teacher Dr. Theodore Moriarty, about whom she later wrote: "if there had been no Dr. Taverner there would have been no Dion Fortune!"

Shortly after their marriage in 1927 she and Dr. Evans began to receive a series of inner communications from a contact whom they referred to as the Master of Medicine. Owing to the pressure of all their other work in founding an occult school the clinic never came to fruition as first intended, but a mass of material was gathered in the course of their little publicised healing work, which combined esoteric knowledge and practice with professional medical expertise.

Most of this material has since been recovered from scattered files and reveals a fascinating approach to esoteric healing, taking into account the whole human being. Health problems are examined in terms of their physical, etheric, astral, mental or spiritual origination, along with principles of esoteric diagnosis based upon the structure of the Qabalistic Tree of Life. The function and malfunction of the psychic centres are described along with principles for their treatment by conventional or alternative therapeutic methods, with particular attention paid to the aura and the etheric double. Apart from its application to the healing arts much of the material is of wider interest for it demonstrates techniques for general development of the psychic and intuitive faculties apart from their more specialised use in assisting diagnosis.

ISBN 978-1-870450-85-0

AN INTRODUCTION TO RITUAL MAGIC
By Dion Fortune & Gareth Knight

At the time this was something of a unique event in esoteric publishing - a new book by the legendary Dion Fortune. Especially with its teachings on the theory and practice of ritual or ceremonial magic, by one who, like the heroine of two of her other novels, was undoubtedly "a mistress of that art".

In this work Dion Fortune deals in successive chapters with Types of Mind Working; Mind Training; The Use of Ritual; Psychic Perception; Ritual Initiation; The Reality of the Subtle Planes; Focusing the Magic Mirror; Channelling the Forces; The Form of the Ceremony; and The Purpose of Magic - with appendices on Talisman Magic and Astral Forms.

Each chapter is supplemented and expanded by a companion chapter on the same subject by Gareth Knight. In Dion Fortune's day the conventions of occult secrecy prevented her from being too explicit on the practical details of magic, except in works of fiction. These veils of secrecy having now been drawn back, Gareth Knight has taken the opportunity to fill in much practical information that Dion Fortune might well have included had she been writing today.

In short, in this unique collaboration of two magical practitioners and teachers, we are presented with a valuable and up-to-date text on the practice of ritual or ceremonial magic "as it is". That is to say, as a practical, spiritual, and psychic discipline, far removed from the lurid superstition and speculation that are the hall mark of its treatment in sensational journalism and channels of popular entertainment.

Deluxe Hardback Limited edition
ISBN 978-1-870450-31-7
Soft cover edition
ISBN 978-870450-26-3

THE FOOL'S COAT
By Vi Marriott

The story of Father Bérenger Saunière, the poor parish priest of Rennes-le-Château, a remote village in Southern France, who at the turn of the 19th century spent mysterious millions on creating a fantastic estate and lavishly entertaining the rich and famous, is now as well known as "Cinderella" or "Eastenders". He would never divulge where the money came from, and popular belief is that in 1891 he discovered a priceless treasure; yet Saunière died penniless, and his legacy is a secret that has continued to puzzle and intrigue succeeding generations.

Since *The Holy Blood and the Holy Grail* hit literary headlines in the nineteen eighties, hundreds of solutions have been suggested. Did he find documents that proved Jesus married Mary Magdalene? Was he a member of The Priory of Sion, a sinister secret society that knew the Da Vinci Code? Did he own the equivalent of Harry Potter's Philosopher's Stone?

A ragbag of history, mystery, gossip and myth, THE FOOL'S COAT investigates Father Saunière's extraordinary life against the background of his times, and suggests that the simplest solution of his rise from penury to riches is probably the correct one.

Vi Marriott is a theatre administrator, writer and researcher. Her play *Ten Days A-Maze,* based on Count Jan Pococki's *Tales of the Saragossa Manuscript,* had seasons in London and Edinburgh; and she contributes regularly to three "house" magazines concerned with the mystery of Rennes-le-Château and other esoteric matters.

ISBN 978-1-870450-99-7

PRACTICAL MAGIC AND THE WESTERN MYSTERY TRADITION
Unpublished Essays and Articles by W. E. Butler.

W. E. Butler, a devoted friend and colleague of the celebrated occultist Dion Fortune, was among those who helped build the Society of the Inner Light into the foremost Mystery School of its day. He then went on to found his own school, the Servants of the Light, which still continues under the guidance of Dolores Ashcroft-Nowicki, herself an occultist and author of note and the editor and compiler of this volume.

PRACTICAL MAGIC AND THE WESTERN TRADITION is a collection of previously unpublished articles, training papers, and lectures covering many aspects of practical magic in the context of western occultism that show W. E. Butler not only as a leading figure in the magical tradition of the West, but also as one of its greatest teachers.

Subjects covered include:

What makes an Occultist
Ritual Training
Inner Plane Contacts and Rays
The Witch Cult
Keys in Practical Magic
Telesmatic Images
Words of Power
An Explanation of Some Psychic Phenomena

ISBN 978-1-870450-32-4

THE GRAIL SEEKER'S COMPANION
By John Matthews & Marian Green

There have been many books about the Grail, written from many differing standpoints. Some have been practical, some purely historical, others literary, but this is the first Grail book which sets out to help the esoterically inclined seeker through the maze of symbolism, character and myth which surrounds the central point of the Grail.

In today's frantic world when many people have their material needs met some still seek spiritual fulfilment. They are drawn to explore the old philosophies and traditions, particularly that of our Western Celtic Heritage. It is here they encounter the quest for the Holy Grail, that mysterious object which will bring hope and healing to all. Some have come to recognise that they dwell in a spiritual wasteland and now search that symbol of the grail which may be the only remedy. Here is the guide book for the modern seeker, explaining the history and pointing clearly towards the Aquarian grail of the future.

John Matthews and Marian Green have each been involved in the study of the mysteries of Britain and the Grail myth for over thirty-five years. In THE GRAIL SEEKER'S COMPANION they have provided a guidebook not just to places, but to people, stories and theories surrounding the Grail. A reference book of Grail-ology, including history, ritual, meditation, advice and instruction. In short, everything you are likely to need before you set out on the most important adventure of your life.

This is the only book that points the way to the Holy Grail Quest in the 21st. century.

ISBN 978-1-870450-49-2

LIVING MAGICAL ARTS

By R.J. Stewart

Living Magical Arts is founded upon the author's practical experience of the Western Magical Traditions, and contains specific teachings from within a living and long established initiatory line of British, French, and Russian esoteric tradition.

Living Magical Arts offers a new and clear approach to the philosophy and practice of magic for the 21st century, stripping away the accumulated nonsense found in many repetitive publications, and re-stating the art for contemporary use. This book offers a coherent illustrated set of magical techniques for individual or group use, leading to profound changes of consciousness and subtle energy. Magical arts are revealed as an enduring system of insight into human and universal consciousness, combining a practical spiritual psychology (long predating materialist psychology) with an effective method of relating to the physical world. Many of the obscure aspects of magical work are clarified, with insights into themes such as the origins of magical arts, working with subtle forces, partaking of esoteric traditions, liberating sexual energies, magical effects upon the world of nature, and the future potential and development of creative magic.

ISBN 978-1-870450-61-4